The Money Formula

The Money Formula

DODGY FINANCE, PSEUDO SCIENCE, AND HOW MATHEMATICIANS TOOK OVER THE MARKETS

Paul Wilmott
David Orrell

WILEY

This edition first published 2017
© 2017 Paul Wilmott and David Orrell

Registered office
John Wiley & Sons Ltd, The Atrium, Southern Gate, Chichester, West Sussex, PO19 8SQ,
United Kingdom

For details of our global editorial offices, for customer services and for information about
how to apply for permission to reuse the copyright material in this book please see our
website at www.wiley.com.

A catalogue record for this book is available from the Library of Congress.

A catalogue record for this book is available from the British Library.

ISBN 978-1-119-35861-9 (paperback) ISBN 978-1-119-35866-4 (ebk)
ISBN 978-1-119-35868-8 (ebk)   ISBN 978-1-119-35872-5 (ebk)

10 9 8 7 6 5 4 3 2 1

Cover design concept: Beatriz Leon

Set in 11/13pt NewBaskervilleStd by Aptara Inc., New Delhi, India
Printed in Great Britain by TJ International Ltd, Padstow, Cornwall, UK

To Oscar, Zachary, Genevieve, and Horatio
—Paul Wilmott

To Wendy and Katherine
—David Orrell

Contents

Acknowledgements

The authors would like to thank publisher Thomas Hyrkiel, project editor Jeremy Chia, production editor Samantha Hartley, and the rest of the Wiley team. Thanks also to Seth Ditchik, Ed Howker, Julia Kingsford, Robert Lecker, Beatriz Leon, Robert Matthews, Myles Thompson, and Andrea Wilmott.

About the Authors

Paul Wilmott is a mathematician and serial entrepreneur. His textbooks and educational programs provide the definitive training for quants; his website wilmott.com is the center of the quant community; his eponymous bi-monthly – and according to *Esquire* the world's most expensive – magazine is a quant must-have. As a practitioner he has been a consultant to leading financial institutions and managed his own hedge fund. As a commentator he has appeared on many TV and radio programs and written OpEds for the *New York Times*. Nassim Nicholas Taleb calls him the smartest quant in the world: "He's the only one who truly understands what's going on… the only quant who uses his own head and has any sense of ethics." Paul divides his time between London, the Cotswolds, and New York.

David Orrell is an applied mathematician and writer. Founder of the scientific consultancy Systems Forecasting, his scientific work has encompassed diverse areas such as particle accelerator design, weather prediction, cancer biology, and economics. His books on subjects including prediction, economics, and science have been national bestsellers and have been translated into over ten languages. A revised and expanded version of his book *Economyths: ~~10~~ 11 Ways That Economics Gets it Wrong* is also published this year. He lives in Toronto.

Introduction

"How about the scandalous stories of thousands of families with small and medium investments who have been ruined because of the greed of financial institutions in the United States and Europe. Look at the evictions, ruined families, and suicide attempts caused by the financial crisis of those who have failed to control the capital markets or the prices of raw materials. ¡Vaya mierda! "[1]
—Response to the survey question: "Do you have any outrageous or hilarious stories that you think ought to be in Paul and David's new book? Share some details, please!" at wilmott.com

"The truth about their motivation in writing."
—Response to the survey question: "What topics should definitely feature in the book?" at wilmott.com

The global financial crisis that peaked in late 2008, and whose aftershocks have yet to fully dissipate, was the culmination of many years of dubious financial practices. If carried out alone they might have caused only localized harm, but they became aligned in the way that only the most dramatic of astrologers can dream of: a quadrillion dollars in complex financial products that no one understands; risk-management techniques that hide risk rather than decrease it; moral hazard and dangerous incentives; lack of diversification; regulators that are oblivious; mathematicians acting as psychological enablers. It was a story where the naïve, the negligent, and the downright nasty all pulled together in seizing as much as possible for themselves while almost destroying the financial foundations of the planet.

---

[1] We're translating from the Spanish. We think that "*¡Vaya mierda!*" is slang for "Have a great day!" but we're not sure.

Of course, things have moved on since then. The banking system has become even more concentrated. Global debt – the engine fuel of finance – has grown to unprecedented levels. Markets, in which activity is increasingly dominated by high-frequency-trading robots, experience constant "flash" events where prices suddenly go wild before returning to more normal levels. The world financial system is once again rattling at its cage, ready to blow. And quantitative finance – the use of mathematical models to assist or dictate investment decisions – has become more powerful and influential than ever.

The story, in other words, isn't over – not by a long shot. Indeed, the stakes have never been higher, which is why previously arcane topics such as hedge funds, high-frequency trading, and too-big-to-fail banks have become a major topic of often-confusing debate for everyone from TV pundits to politicians. And why the confusion is often deliberate.

It has been estimated that in 2010 the notional value of all the financial derivatives in existence was $1.2 quadrillion.[2] That's $1,200,000,000,000,000. For comparison, it's about 17 times the market capitalization of all the world's stock markets, or 150 times the value of the above-ground gold supply, or $170,000 for every living human on the planet. Actually, it's larger than the entire global economy. We'll explain this number, and how it could be interpreted, later. For the moment, let's just say that whatever it means in terms of risk, it seems like a dangerously big number for what is, let's be honest, just a service industry.

This book is not about the fallout from the crisis – plenty of books and column inches have been written about that – but about helping to prevent the next one (which won't look like the last one). To do that, it is necessary to go into the engine room of this massive shadow economy and understand how quantitative analysis works. How do you create a quadrillion dollars out of nothing, blow it away,

---

[2] This was estimated by the economist Tim Harford and Paul for the BBC Radio 4 program *More or Less* based on data from the website of the Bank for International Settlements. This "headline" figure, which is open to interpretation, includes both the contracts traded through an exchange and the over-the-counter market in which two parties trade directly. It is also what is called the "notional" value. If a contract specifies that it will pay you 1% of $1 million in a year's time then that would be recorded as a notional of $1 million, whereas it's really just worth about $10,000. So it's tricky to say what amount really is at risk in that $1.2 quadrillion.

and leave a hole so large that even years of the deliberately misnamed "quantitative easing" can't fill it – and then go back to doing the same thing, only faster? Part of a quant's job, as we'll see, is science, and another part (the one where mathematics is used to obfuscate reality) is the opposite of science. We will discuss both, starting with the science.

The book is divided into two main parts. The first five chapters dip into the history of quantitative finance and explain its key principles, such as risk analysis, bond pricing, portfolio insurance – all those gold-standard techniques, in short, which completely failed during the crisis, but have yet to be properly reinvented. We explore the elegant equations used in financial mathematics, and show how the deadly allure of their ice-cold beauty has misled generations of economists and investors. We trace the development of financial derivatives from bonds to credit default swaps, and show how mathematical formulas helped not just to price them, but also to greatly expand their use to the point where they dwarfed the real economy. And we show how risk-management and insurance schemes have led to more risk and less insurance than arguably at any time in history.

The second part is about the quantitative finance industry today, and how it is evolving. We will show what quants do, the techniques they use, and how they continue to put the financial system at peril. Part of the problem, we'll see, is that quants treat the economy as if it obeys mechanistic Newtonian laws, and – by nature and by training – have no feel for the chaos, irrationality, and violent disequilibrium to which markets often seem prone. The same can also be said of the regulators watching the system. We'll lower ourselves into the hidden caves of finance, with their "dark pools" navigated by swarms of high-frequency traders, and show how new ideas from areas such as complexity science and machine learning are providing analytic tools for visualizing and understanding the turbulent eddies of financial flows. Along the way, we will grapple with some of the philosophical and practical difficulties in modeling the financial system – and show how models are often used less for predicting the future than for telling a story about the present.

The authors are both Oxford-trained applied mathematicians, who have worked in a variety of industries but otherwise come to this project from different angles. Paul is a quintessential insider – named "arguably the most influential quant today" by *Newsweek* – but he is also (as visitors to quant forum wilmott.com will know) a longstanding critic of standard practices. David works primarily in the areas of mathematical forecasting and computational biology (he invented a program called "Virtual Tumour," which gives you an idea). He has argued in a number of books that economics needs to take a similarly biological approach – and that our out-of-control financial sector is in serious need of a health check.

The Money Formula provides new insights into one of the largest, best-paid, but least-understood industries in the world – and the one with the most capacity to either help our future economic development or give it the financial equivalent of a cardiac arrest.

We begin by turning to the early 18th century, when France was seeking financial advice from a mathematician.

Early Models

"Nature, and Nature's Laws lay hid in Night.
God said, Let Newton be! And All was Light."
—Alexander Pope

"Beelzebub begat Law
Law begat the Mississippi
The Mississippi begat the System (etc.)"
—Het Groote Tafereel der Dwaasheid
(The Great Mirror of Folly)

The mathematical models used by quants are based on ideas and concepts developed by generations of economists. They in turn were heavily influenced by physics. But is it really possible to model the markets as a kind of physical system, or is quantitative finance more like a set of mathematical tricks for betting on markets? This chapter traces the development of economics; looks at the basic assumptions such as equilibrium and rationality that have shaped both economics and finance; and considers the dual nature of quantitative finance, as exemplified by two men – John Law and Isaac Newton.

In 1705, Scotland was contemplating union with its neighbor England. The English economy was riding high, and Scotland's leaders thought this might be an opportune moment for a merger. However, not everyone thought hooking up was a good idea. One person who argued against it was the banker, gambler, and social climber John Law. He went so far as to propose an entirely new monetary system for Scotland, which he claimed would go beyond the English system and in a stroke solve his country's monetary problems while boosting trade.

Part of England's success was due to its newly created central bank, the Bank of England, and efficiencies created by the introduction of bank notes. However, Law thought he could do better. According to him, the problem with this new English paper money was not that it was too radical, but that it was not radical enough, since it was still exchangeable for gold. Its supply was therefore determined not by the needs of the economy, but by the quantity of precious metal that happened to be in circulation at the time. In his text *Money and Trade Consider'd with a Proposal for Supplying the Nation with Money*, he argued that Scotland needed a central bank of its own, that issued its own paper currency, but one that was backed only by the state rather than by precious metal. After all, according to this son of an Edinburgh goldsmith, money was just a "Sign of Transmission," like a casino chip, and not a store of real wealth.

The stakes for Law were greater even than the questions of Scottish independence or the meaning of monetary value. Ten years earlier, he had been charged with murder following a duel in London. After being imprisoned, he soon escaped and fled to Amsterdam. For several years he had toured around Europe, supporting himself and his young family by gambling (a trained mathematician, he claimed to have a system), before returning to Scotland. But if that country joined with England, he would have to leave or find himself back in jail.

This time, the dice did not fall in Law's favor. His radical monetary proposal was rejected by parliament, the union with England went ahead, and Law was again on the run from the law.

He set himself up in Paris, playing cards at all the fashionable salons. His system was extremely successful – so much so that he drew the attention of the Chief of Police, M. d'Argenson, who expelled him from the city. Again he hit the road, touring through Germany and Italy in a coach, amassing considerable wealth from his winnings; his prowess at gambling becoming something of a legend. When the "Sun King" Louis XIV died, leaving his country with a massive debt (incurred from wars and the construction of his palace at Versailles) and a bankrupt treasury, Law saw an opportunity and returned to

France. There was a shortage of money, and he had the answer. He quickly won over the regent, Philippe d'Orléans, who took a chance on the Scotsman and appointed him as Controller General of Finances – perhaps with the hope that his "system" would work as well for the economy as it did at cards.

Monetary Alchemy

Law's plan for the country – and he did not lack ambition – consisted of two parts. The first was to set up a state bank financed initially by himself, the Banque Générale, that would issue paper money redeemable in gold or silver. The bank was hugely successful, and its notes soon attracted a premium just for their convenience over coins. The second, which followed two years later, was to establish a company called the Mississippi Company, that would be granted a royal monopoly on trade with Louisiana – a vast region that encompassed the entire Mississippi River Valley.

Neither idea was new. The Bank of England and the Bank of Amsterdam already issued paper receipts for gold that could be traded as money. The Mississippi Company was modeled on the East India Companies of Britain and Holland. Law's brilliant idea was to connect the two, and unleash the alchemical power of paper money. Paper shares in the company could be bought using the paper money produced by the bank, in what seemed like a kind of perpetual-motion machine. In 1718 the bank was nationalized, becoming the Banque Royale; with this royal approval obtained, it was then announced that its notes would no longer be redeemable for precious metal.

Money was finally untethered from metal, its value determined instead by the authority of the French crown. A positive consequence was that the state could print as much money as it needed to satisfy the ravenous public appetite for shares, as people flocked from all over the country and abroad to take part in the economic miracle of Law's system. With all this money circulating around at a ferocious rate, the economy boomed. The word "millionaire" came into use for the first time. In 1719 alone, the Company share price vaulted from 500 livres to over 10,000 livres. The dropping of the dead-weight connection to metal also released any restraints on Law's bounding ambitions. In no time he was arranging for the Company to buy the national debt, and have the right to collect taxes. This required issuing many more shares, and many more paper notes to buy them with. Which is when Law's system started to reveal its flaws.

While Law was certainly correct that money serves as a "Sign of Transmission," its value also depends on the confidence and trust of the community, and he had made the same mistake that he had made as a gambler in Paris, which was to fail to arrange buy-in from all the relevant players. Then it was the Chief of Police, d'Argenson, now it was the business and banking community (which included d'Argenson, who had become a prominent businessman). Rumors began to circulate that Louisiana was not quite the wealth generator it was cracked up to be, and Mississippi Company shareholders began to suspect they were being sold down the river.

The trip down was just as brief and thrilling as the way up. Suffice to say that, as the Company's share price drained away, and the value of the bank's paper notes approached zero, Law was again drummed out of Paris, and the country, and ended up near destitute in Venice. The story ought to serve as a cautionary tale for present-day central bankers. Oh, except that these days no bankers, central or otherwise, ever end up destitute.

Gold Standard

While Law was introducing the French to the benefits, perils, and general excitement of fiat currencies and financial innovation, Isaac Newton was serving as Warden of the Mint in England. Newton is of course best known for his famous contributions to physics, but he worked at the Mint from 1696 until his death in 1727. It is safe to say that his approach to finance was the opposite of Law's. At exactly the same time that Law was arranging to delink the livre from gold or silver, Newton was putting the pound on the gold standard, where it would remain for the next couple of hundred years.[1] While Law was issuing what some considered to be fake money, Newton was sending counterfeiters to their death. One wonders what he would have said about the situation in France, from his position at the Tower of London. Perhaps he felt some sympathy with Law's fall from grace; he did manage to lose £20,000 himself (over £2 million in today's money) on his investment in the South Sea Company, the British version of the Mississippi Company.

---

[1] By accident. He set the exchange rate for silver too high, so silver coins left the country.

The two certainly had completely different personalities. Here is a portrait of the young John Law by journalist John Flynn: "He got access to the smartest circles. He was a young man of education and culture, handsome, quick-witted, a good athlete excelling at tennis, a graceful dancer, and a redoubtable talker. He spent his mornings in the city, where he got a reputation for skill in speculating in government paper. He passed his afternoons in the parks, his evenings at the opera or theater, and the later hours at the routs, balls, masquerades, and gaming houses. He played for high stakes and won large sums. He was a man with a system. Had he lived in our time he would have been in Wall Street with an infallible formula for beating the market."[2] Perhaps he would have launched a hedge fund, or penned a bestseller about his "system."

Isaac Newton, in contrast, was a decidedly more solitary type. As a child, he showed great talent at making models, such as a working windmill. This skill later came in useful while constructing his own experimental apparatus, including a new design of telescope. He attended Cambridge University, but his most creative period came when the university was closed for two years because of the advancing plague, and Newton returned to his home in Lincolnshire to work alone. It was there that he claimed to have been prompted to discover the law of gravity after seeing an apple fall from a tree. Throughout his life he had a passion for alchemy and mysticism; in fact, most of his output consisted of religious writings, including a 300,000-word tract on the Book of Revelation.[3] He was famously anti-social and incommunicative; if no one showed up for his lectures, he just gave them to the empty room. There is no record of him being an expert dancer, or really fun at parties. As economist John Maynard Keynes wrote, he became instead the "Sage and Monarch of the Age of Reason."[4]

Researchers at Oxford and Cambridge have suggested that Isaac Newton may have had Asperger's Syndrome.[5] There is quite a business in such historical psych evaluations nowadays (see Box 1.1), but this one has a ring of truth about it. Often those with Asperger's Syndrome have a very narrow field of interest, with little curiosity in or appreciation of the bigger picture. They can exhibit intense concentration and understanding, and in many cases there is increased

---

[2] Flynn (1941).
[3] Manuel (1974).
[4] Keynes (1946).
[5] Muir (2003).

intelligence in areas such as mathematics. Which perhaps would explain why Newton was better with celestial mechanics than the financial sort.

These two contemporaries, Law and Newton, represent two aspects of the relationship between mathematics and finance. Mathematical finance is about using objective, rational, Newtonian models to simulate markets and make predictions about their future evolution. Quants are often described as modern-day wizards, hidden away in secret laboratories, who use mind-bending techniques inspired by areas such as quantum physics and string theory, coupled with the power of massive computers, to find hidden patterns in the markets. As Scott Patterson puts it in his book *The Quants*: "Think of white-coated scientists building ever more powerful devices to replicate conditions at the moment of the Big Bang to understand the forces at the root of creation."[6]

However, these scientists are trying to make money, not discover the next Higgs boson. (Juan Maldacena, Professor of Theoretical Physics at the Institute for Advanced Studies at Princeton and winner of many prizes for his work on such things as black holes, has said that finance is harder than physics. However, he has also given a public lecture in which he uses exchange rates as an analogy to explain the very same boson.) Mathematicians, like Law, are attracted to practical finance because they think they can use a system to beat the market, or even create an entirely new one. As seen later, their financial innovations often amount to creating new forms of credit, which like Law's scheme boost the money supply, at least for a while. In place of paper money, they invent credit default swaps or collateralized debt obligations. ("Make your very own 'credit default swap' and find out how to create money out of thin air!" as guides in a bus tour around the City of London now shout.[7]) They see the markets, with their rhythms and patterns, as a kind of music, which they can shape and control – and would agree with former CitiGroup CEO Chuck Prince who famously said, in the midst of the credit crunch, that "As long as the music is playing, you've got to get up and dance."

As we will see, it is the tension between these two aspects that drives mathematical finance, in both its inventiveness and creativity, and its tendency toward self-destruction.

---

[6] Patterson (2009, p. 8).
[7] Gitlin (2014).

The Systems of Nature

After his losses in the South Sea debacle, Newton famously said: "I can calculate the movement of the stars, but not the madness of men." While Newton may not have tried to calculate the markets, and preferred chemical alchemy to the financial kind, he probably did more to shape the world of mathematical finance than any other scientist. His law of gravity, coupled with his three laws of motion, provided an archetype for a successful mathematical model that would influence not just areas such as physics and chemistry, but also social sciences including economics, and serve as an inspiration for quants to the present day.

One person who appreciated the power of Newton's approach was Adam Smith. He is of course best known for his book *The Wealth of Nations*,[8] which was the first to present economics as an objective, rational science, separate from areas such as ethics and political science. Some insight into his motivations is provided, however, by an earlier work on astronomy, written around 1758 but not published until after his death, in which his examination of "all the different systems of nature" culminates in a celebration of "The superior genius and sagacity of Sir Isaac Newton." He was less impressed by John Law. As he wrote in *The Wealth of Nations*, "The idea of the possibility of multiplying paper to almost any extent was the real foundation of what is called the Mississippi scheme, the most extravagant project both of banking and stock-jobbing that, perhaps, the world ever saw." (Smith would no doubt have been surprised to learn that we now organize our economies around Law's idea of a fiat currency, which was ahead of its time, rather than Newton's gold standard.)

Smith saw philosophy as a kind of calming device for making sense of the world, with its random events and its John Laws, its "chaos of jarring and discordant appearances." The beauty of Newton's method was the way in which it took a simple idea, such as gravity, and showed how "all the appearances, which he joins together by it, necessarily follow."

In the same book, Smith makes his first mention of the invisible hand. However, the passage was about the tendency for polytheistic religions to interpret events as being caused by gods: "the invisible hand of Jupiter." It was only later that he attributed this miraculous

---

[8] Smith (1776).

power to the markets. In *The Theory of Moral Sentiments*, he used the term in the context of wealth distribution: the rich "divide with the poor the produce of all their improvements. They are led by an invisible hand to make nearly the same distribution of the necessaries of life, which would have been made, had the earth been divided into equal portions among all its inhabitants, and thus without intending it, without knowing it, advance the interest of the society." (We wonder if he asked the poor.) Finally, and most famously, the phrase pops up again in *The Wealth of Nations*, in which – in a section on trade policy – an individual is again "led by an invisible hand to promote an end which was no part of his intention."

No one paid any attention to the metaphor until 1948, when Chicago School economist Paul Samuelson published his textbook *Economics*, which would go on to become the best-selling economics textbook of all time, translated into over 40 languages.[9] As he paraphrased: "Every individual, in pursuing only his own selfish good, was led, as if by an invisible hand, to achieve the best good for all, so that any interference with free competition by government was almost certain to be injurious." Which is when widespread use of the term, both in academic papers and general use, suddenly took off.[10]

Box 1.1   On the Couch

As mentioned above, it's unreliable to psychoanalyze people who aren't around to lie down on the couch, and sometimes it's annoying – as in the 2014 film *The Imitation Game*, in which Benedict Cumberbatch, the actor playing mathematician Alan Turing, might as well have worn a button saying "Hi, I have Asperger's!" Also, we're not psychologists and have no idea what we're talking about. But Adam Smith does seem worth a look.

From our case notes, it seems that tales abound of Smith's bizarre character. Friendly and good-tempered, he was also, according to one friend, "the most absent man in Company that I ever saw, Moving his Lips and talking to himself, and Smiling."[11] He did things like absentmindedly walk into a tanning pit, from which he needed to be rescued, or go for a stroll in his nightgown and end up 15 miles outside town. He was frequently ill and his doctors diagnosed him as a

---

[9] Samuelson (1973).
[10] Kennedy (2005).
[11] Alexander Carlyle, quoted in Özler (2012).

hypochondriac. He had no known serious romantic relationships, and lived with his mother (his father died two months after he was born) until she died at the age of 90, just six years before his own death in 1790. As his biographer Dugald Stewart noted, Smith was "certainly not fitted for the general commerce of the world, or for the business of active life."[12]

Usually these quirks are presented as the harmless foibles of a genius – but there does seem to be a connection with this invisible hand business.

As UCLA's Şule Özler wrote in the journal *Psychoanalytic Review*, Smith was financially dependent first on family income, and then on "rich businessmen, gentry, intellectuals, and aristocrats for teaching positions and his pension."[13] And there is a striking contrast between his life and his economic theories. "Denying his reality of lifelong dependence on his mother and benefactors, Smith appears to have idealized independence," according to Özler. The invisible hand, after all, only works if everyone acts independently to further their own interests, without collusion. There is no room for things like money, power, or the fact that we can be financially dependent on one another.

Smith found solace and refuge in Newtonian laws, which treated people as independent atoms, and he turned the market into a kind of parental figure that always knows what is right. Rather like a lot of modern economics then (whose practitioners often have about as much experience as Smith of "the general commerce of the world").

Rational Mechanics

Smith's work was influential on the USA at the time of its formation – the Founders were early readers of his work – and remains so today. Economist George Akerlof describes the "central ideology" of the United States as conforming to "the fundamental view of Adam Smith," which even today "drives huge amounts of policy" (he should know, being married to Federal Reserve Chair Janet Yellen).[14] According to this picture, the market is made up of firms and individuals acting to further their self-interest by buying and selling. If a good or service is too expensive, then more suppliers enter the market, supply increases, and competition drives the price down to its

---

[12]Hamilton (1858, p. 77).

[13]Özler (2012).

[14]Fleischacker (2002), Kiladze (2015).

"natural" level, which serves as a "center of repose." If instead the price is too low, then suppliers go broke or leave the market, and the price goes up: "The natural price, therefore, is, as it were, the central price, to which the prices of all commodities are continually gravitating." The invisible hand is the market version of gravity.

This view of society as a collection of atomistic individuals, each pursuing their economic self-interest, was modeled directly after Newton's view of nature as a mechanistic, law-bound system.[15] Just as Newton had showed that a wide range of phenomena were all explained by the law of gravity, Smith had shown that market behavior could be explained by what was later known as the law of supply and demand. However, there was an important difference, for the theory lacked what Smith had so admired in Newton's work, namely the ability to make accurate predictions. It was qualitative rather than quantitative; descriptive rather than predictive. This problem would be addressed by a new generation of "neoclassical" economists in the late 19th century, including William Stanley Jevons in England and Léon Walras in France, who aimed to put the field on a solid mathematical footing, and turn it into a kind of "rational mechanics" for society. Their work would pave the way for the development of quantitative finance.

Any model is a simplification of reality, and the neoclassical economists had to make some rather sweeping assumptions in order to make progress. The most basic of these was that people act to optimize their own utility – defined rather hazily as whatever makes them happy – but not that of other people. As Francis Edgeworth put it in 1881, "the first principle of Economics is that every agent is actuated only by self-interest."[16] People also had a fixed set of preferences. So if they liked cereal for breakfast, they didn't suddenly swap over to eating toast. And people always acted in a completely rational fashion.

Thus was born the notion of *homo economicus*, or rational economic man. While these assumptions had obvious flaws – surely we do change our minds? – they did allow economists to construct elegant mathematical models of the economy.

---

[15]Greene (1961, p. 88).
[16]Edgeworth (1881, p. 16).

Finding Equilibrium

An obvious difference between economics and physics was that physical quantities could be measured in well-defined units, while "utility" was rather vague and no one knew what its units were ("utils" was suggested). However, Jevons argued that in reality we can never directly measure a force like gravity, only its effects. Even if utility could not be directly measured, or even defined, we could infer it from market prices. Today, it is fair to say that quants do not suffer from lack of data – we have more information about markets than we have about other things that we wish to predict, such as the weather.

Another problem was that, while the atoms of physics are believed to have the same properties everywhere in the universe, people – who are the atoms of the economy – show a high degree of variability. According to Jevons, though, what counted was the behavior of "the single average individual, the unit of which population is made up."[17] This meant that the agents in the economy – i.e., individuals and firms – could be treated as if they were all the same. The idea was inspired by the "social physics" of the 19th-century Belgian scientist Adolphe Quetelet, who wrote of *l'homme moyen*, or the average man.[18] He claimed that "the greater the number of people observed, the more do peculiarities, whether physical or moral, become effaced, and allow the general facts to predominate, by which society exists and is preserved."[19]

Here we have a social science version of the probabilist's Law of Large Numbers. This mathematical law states that the average of a large number of trials will converge to the expected value of a single trial. A die has 21 spots and six sides, giving an expected throw of $21/6 = 3.5$. As you roll the dice more frequently, the average will converge to this expected value. The idea that the expected behavior of humans, as with dice, is all that matters in the long run could be an explanation behind Isaac Asimov's fictional character Hari Seldon in the *Foundation* series of novels. Professor Seldon is one of the creators of "psychohistory," a science that makes predictions about the future based on the statistics of large groups of people. When asked

---

[17]Jevons (1957).
[18]Quetelet (1842).
[19]Quoted in Bernstein (1998, p. 160).

"Can you prove that this mathematics is valid?" he replies, "Only to another mathematician." Nobel Laureate Paul Krugman says that he became interested in economics thanks to Hari Seldon and his ability to predict mankind's actions.[20] Of course, it's all poppycock, but entertaining reading nonetheless.

Whatever the equations governing man's economic behavior, the neoclassical economists faced a rather daunting computational problem. One way to make it tractable was to assume that prices were at equilibrium. Jevons compared the price mechanism to the motion of a pendulum, which came to rest at the ideal balance between supply and demand. Even if one could not compute the daily permutations of the markets, it should be possible to compute the average equilibrium position to which the invisible hand was pushing them. Furthermore, it made sense that markets should be at or near equilibrium; since if prices were too low or too high, then this would imply that market participants were not making rational decisions. The assumption of equilibrium was therefore also tied up with the idea of rationality.

Intrinsic Value

As economics developed in the 20th century, concepts such as rationality and equilibrium remained at the heart of the theory. In the 1960s, economists Kenneth Arrow and Gérard Debreu created a model of an idealized market economy, and famously showed that it would reach a kind of optimal equilibrium (a result that did not displease their sponsors at the US Department of Defense, at a time when the country was embroiled in an ideological conflict with its communist foes[21]). But to prove its results, its authors had to assume that market participants act rationally to maximize their utility, not just now but also in the future. Since the future is unknown, this means they have to know what is the best course of action for every possible future state of the world – something which implied infinite computational capacity. The Arrow–Debreu model of the economy

---

[20]We find this a bit disturbing. But not as disturbing as Alan Greenspan's extreme fondness for Ayn Rand. As he wrote in *The Age of Turbulence*, "Ayn Rand became a stabilizing force in my life... I was intellectually limited until I met her" (Greenspan, 2007).
[21]Bockman (2013, p. 47).

served as the theoretical foundation for general equilibrium models, versions of which are used today to determine the effects of policy changes on the economy.

Unfortunately, these models – despite being "aesthetically beautiful" to theoreticians[22] – turned out to be little better at predicting the economy than random guessing (which is why they are not used by quants). Psychohistory they weren't. However, the University of Chicago's Eugene Fama came forward with a convenient excuse for why economists were doing such a poor job of predicting the future, at least for markets. His efficient market hypothesis portrayed the market as a swarm of "rational profit maximizers" who drive the price of any security to its "intrinsic value." It was therefore impossible to beat or out-predict the market, because any information would already be priced in. The invisible hand of the market was the epitome of rationality. This leads to the weird situation where individuals are assumed to be able to make perfect predictions (Arrow–Debreu), but this in turn means that no one can predict the markets (Fama).

This would normally be the point at which most investors turned their backs on too much theorizing – as ex-Fidelity fund manager Peter Lynch told *Fortune* magazine, "Efficient markets? That's a bunch of junk, crazy stuff" – but it is precisely the elegance of this "result" that excites the academic economists.[23] As discussed further below, the efficient market idea formed the backbone of academic models used in risk analysis, and much of quantitative finance in general. As with Adam Smith and the neoclassical economists, the central idea was of the market at equilibrium, with the invisible hand constantly restoring it to what Smith called a "tone of tranquillity and composure."

Quants in general have a somewhat conflicted attitude toward the efficient market hypothesis. If it were really true, then they would be out of a job. On the contrary, many quants came out of the Chicago School of Economics, or were otherwise influenced by Fama and his academic accolades, so at least pay lip service to the idea.[24] From a quant survey we performed at wilmott.com, some 43% of

---

[22]Haldane (2014).
[23]Para (1995).
[24]E.g., Cliff Asness (co-founder of AQR Capital Management) (Patterson, 2009, p. 265).

respondents described it as true. One way to square the circle is for quants to see themselves as enforcers of efficiency, whose job it is to drive prices to their correct level – even if that means driving them off a cliff. (We'll give our own verdict on the theory in the next chapter, but basically, Lynch is right.)

The assumptions of neoclassical economists therefore had a dual nature. On the one hand, they were designed to make the economy mathematically tractable. It is obviously easier to model people who are selfish, have fixed preferences, and are completely rational than it is to model people who are influenced by the opinions of others, change their minds for no reason, and make puzzling and bizarre life choices. On the other hand, they shaped the way that we see and model the economy – as a beautifully rational, stable, and efficient system – which as we'll see, shaped the economy itself.

Of course, no one – even business school lecturers – thinks that people are perfectly rational, or that markets are perfectly stable or uniform, or that models are perfect. Much work has been done exploring deviations from these assumptions. As we will see, though, the models used in finance continue to treat the world as a very rational, stable, and symmetric place – and this has as much to do with aesthetics, mathematical ego, and the desire to impress and intimidate as it does with making money. In the next chapter, we look at how these elegant but unrealistic assumptions and formulas were made to seem compatible with markets that often appear to be driven more by chaos than by reason – more Law than Newton.

2

Going Random

"We are floating in a medium of vast extent, always drifting uncertainly, blown to and fro; whenever we think we have a fixed point to which we can cling and make fast, it shifts and leaves us behind; if we follow it, it eludes our grasp, slips away, and flees eternally before us. Nothing stands still for us. This is our natural state and yet the state most contrary to our inclinations. We burn with desire to find a firm footing, an ultimate, lasting base on which to build a tower rising up to infinity, but our whole foundation cracks and the earth opens into the depth of the abyss."

—Blaise Pascal, *Pensées*

"Random; a dark field where dark cats are chased with laser guns; better than sex; like gambling; a little bit of math, some finance, lot of hypotheses, a lot of assumptions, more art than science; an attempt to predict or explain financial markets using mathematical theory; the art of collecting rent from the real economy; mathematical rationalisation for the injustices of capitalism; much like math, physics, and statistics helped meteorologists in building technology to predict weather, we quants do the same for markets; well, I could tell you but you don't have the necessary brain power to understand it * Stands up and leaves*."

—Responses to the survey question:
"How would you describe quantitative finance at a dinner party?" at wilmott.com

Quantitative finance is about using mathematics to understand the evolution of markets. One approach to prediction is to build deterministic Newtonian models of the system. Alternatively, one can make probabilistic models based on statistics. In practice, scientists usually use a combination of these approaches. For example, weather predictions are made using deterministic models, but because the predictions are prone to error, meteorologists use statistical techniques to make probabilistic forecasts (e.g., a 20% chance of rain). Quants do the same for the markets, but then bet large amounts of money on the outcome. This chapter looks at how probability theory is applied to forecast the financial weather.

In 1724, after the collapse of his French monetary experiment, John Law supported himself in Venice by gambling. He would sit at a table at the Ridotto casino with 10,000 gold pistole coins arranged in stacks like casino chips, and offer any challenger the chance to make a wager of a single pistole. If they rolled six dice and got all sixes, then they could keep the lot. Law knew the odds of this happening were only 1 in 46,656 (6 multiplied by itself 6 times). So people always lost, but would go away happy at having gambled with the notorious John Law.

A key concept from probability theory is the idea of expected value, which equals the payout multiplied by the probability. For Law's gamble, this was 10,000 multiplied by 1/46,656, or 0.21 gold pistoles. Since the stake was 1 pistole, Law had an edge (a fair payout would have been 46,656 coins instead of 10,000). It was his money, after all, so he wanted to make a profit. We'll see later that he could still have made money even if he had offered the punters better odds, odds giving them the positive expectation. The solution to this apparent paradox is that he would have to do his gambling via a financial vehicle, a hedge fund, and he'd have to be betting with *other people's money*.

The connection between basic probability theory and something like the stock market becomes clear when we consider the result of a sequence of coin tosses, as in Figure 2.1. Here the paths start at the left and branch out to the right with time. If the coin comes up heads, you win one point, but if it is tails, you lose a point. The heavy line shows one particular trajectory, known as a random walk, against the background of all possible trajectories. At each time step,

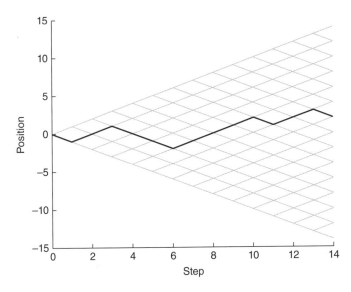

Figure 2.1 Coin toss results

The black line shows one possible random walk, with a vertical step of plus 1 (up) or minus 1 (down) at each iteration. The light gray lines are an overlay of all possible paths through 14 iterations. The plot shows how the future becomes more uncertain as the possible paths multiply.

the path takes a random step up or down. Most paths remain near the center. Figure 2.2 shows how the final distribution looks after 14 time steps. The mean or average displacement is zero, and over 20% of the paths end with no displacement. If this were a plot of price changes for a stock, and the horizontal axis represented time in days, we would say that the expected value of the stock after 14 days would be unchanged from its initial value.

After n iterations, the maximum deviation from 0 is equal to n – so after 14 steps, the range is from –14 to 14. But most paths stay near the center, so the average displacement is much smaller.[1] A longer random walk, of 100 steps, is shown by the solid line in Figure 2.3. The light-gray lines are the bounds for possible paths: the upper bound is the path with an increase of 1 at every step, while the lower bound

---

[1] Since displacements to the right are positive and displacements to the left are negative, the average is always zero, so it is more convenient to use the root mean square (RMS) – defined as the square root, of the average, of the squares. Measured this way, the deviation of the hypothetical stock from its starting point grows with the square root of time.

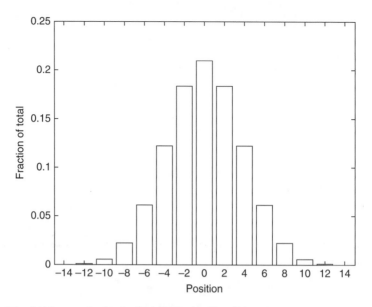

Figure 2.2   A histogram showing the final distribution after 14 iterations

The range is −14 to 14, but over 20% of paths end with no change in position (center bar). The shape approximates the bell curve or normal distribution from classical statistics.

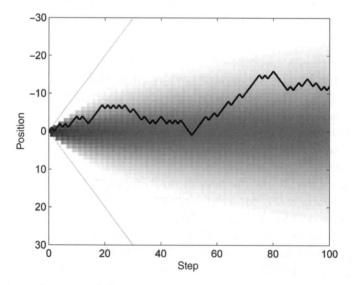

Figure 2.3   100-Step random walk

The solid line is a random walk of 100 steps, starting at 0, with a displacement of plus or minus 1 at each step. The light-gray lines show the upper and lower bounds, corresponding to the paths in which the displacement at every step is plus or minus 1, respectively. The density of the grayscale at any point corresponds to the probability of a random walk going through that point. This is highest for paths with small displacement. The probability of a path entering the white area is very low, or zero outside the light-gray lines.

is the path with a decrease of 1 at every step (the probability of these paths is extremely low, since they are the same as tossing a coin and getting heads 100 times in a row). In the background, the density of the grayscale at any point corresponds to the probability of a random walk going through that point. Note how this probability density spreads out with time, rather like an idealized, turbulence-free version of a plume of smoke emitted from a chimney. Random walks sound wild, but on average they are very well-behaved.

Such computations become unwieldy when there are a very large number of games or iterations; however, in 1738 the mathematician Abraham de Moivre showed that after an infinitely large number of iterations, the results would converge on the so-called normal distribution, or bell curve. This is specified by two numbers: the mean or average and the standard deviation, which is a measure of the curve's width.[2] About 68% of the data fall within one standard deviation of the mean, and about 95% are within two standard deviations. The *homme moyen* of statistics, this formula got its name because of its ubiquity in the physical and social sciences. The distinguishing feature of the normal distribution is that, according to the central limit theorem, which was partially proven by de Moivre, it can be used to model the sum of any random processes, provided that a number of conditions are met. In particular, the separate processes have to be independent of one another, and identically distributed. So, for example, if 18th-century astronomers made many measurements of the position of Saturn in the night sky, then each measurement would be subject to errors, but they could hope that a plot of the measurements would look like a bell curve, with the correct answer close to the middle.

The normal distribution is perhaps the closest the field of statistics comes to a Newtonian formula. The equation is simple and elegant, there are only two parameters that need to be measured (the mean and the standard deviation), and it can be applied to a wide range of phenomena. The "Law of Unreason," as its Victorian popularizer Francis Galton called it, would find perhaps its greatest application in mastering, or appearing to master, the chaos of the markets.[3]

---

[2] The standard deviation is just the RMS again, see note above, but with all distances measured from the mean rather than from zero.

[3] Galton (1889).

Theory of Speculation

The desire to bring order out of chaos, and to see the hidden pattern in the noise, is basic to human nature. In mathematics, even chaos theory is not so much about chaos as about showing that what appears to be wild and unruly behavior can actually be explained by a simple equation. As the field's founder, French mathematician Henri Poincaré, told one of his PhD students: "what is chance for the ignorant is not chance for the scientists. Chance is only the measure of our ignorance."[4]

The student who earned this rebuke was called Louis Bachelier. His mistake, perhaps, was choosing a thesis subject that was a little too chaotic – the buying and selling of securities that took place within the mock-Greek temple building of the Paris Exchange, or Bourse. He was awarded a good but undistinguished grade on his 1900 dissertation, entitled *Théorie de la Spéculation,* and his work failed to unite the academic community in a frenzy of excitement (it took him 27 years to find a permanent job).[5]

Bachelier began his thesis as follows (imaginary editorial remarks in italics):

> The influences which determine the movements of the Stock Exchange are innumerable. Events past, present or even anticipated, often showing no apparent connection with its fluctuations, yet have repercussions on its course. (*I had a dog like that once*)

> Beside fluctuations from, as it were, natural causes, artificial causes are also involved. The Stock Exchange acts upon itself and its current movement is a function not only of earlier fluctuations, but also of the present market position. (*Chased its own tail*)

> The determination of these fluctuations is subject to an infinite number of factors: it is therefore impossible to expect a mathematically exact forecast. Contradictory opinions in regard to these fluctuations are so divided that at the same instant buyers

---

[4] Quoted in Bernstein (1998, p. 200).
[5] Bachelier (1900).

believe the market is rising and sellers that it is falling. (*Sounds like we're wasting our time, people*)

Undoubtedly, the Theory of Probability will never be applicable to the movements of quoted prices and the dynamics of the Stock Exchange will never be an exact science. (*Thought this was a science exam?*)

However, it is possible to study mathematically the static state of the market at a given instant, that is to say, to establish the probability law for the price fluctuations that the market admits at this instant. Indeed, while the market does not foresee fluctuations, it considers which of them are more or less probable, and this probability can be evaluated mathematically. (*Too much on finance!* – this was a real comment on Bachelier's thesis by France's leading probability theorist, Paul Lévy)

Bachelier's starting assumption, which he called his "Principle of Mathematical Expectation," was that the mathematical expectation of a speculator is zero. As in the random walks of Figure 2.1, some bets will win, and others will lose, but these cancel out in the long run. Note that we are referring here to the mathematical chances of success – a speculator's psychological expectations may be very different. He then assumed that prices move in a random walk, with price changes following a normal distribution, and referred to what he called the "Law of Radiation (or Diffusion) of Probability," which described how the future price became more uncertain as you went further into the future. The results are very similar to Figure 2.3 (the displacements at each iteration were there set to plus or minus a fixed amount, in this case 1, rather than being normally distributed, but the effects are almost identical over large enough times). From this, he derived a method for pricing options, which grant the purchaser the right to buy or sell an asset at a fixed price at some time in the future. As discussed further later, the technique he developed is essentially a special case of the ones commonly used today.

To reach his conclusions, Bachelier assumed the existence of a "static state of the market." This did not mean that prices themselves were static, but that price fluctuations could be modeled as random perturbations to a steady state. The price movements of a stock therefore resembled the so-called Brownian motion of a tiny dust particle, as it is buffeted around by collisions with individual atoms. In 1905, Albert Einstein used techniques similar to those employed by Bachelier to model Brownian motion, and estimate the size of an atom.

Bachelier's thesis eventually became famous in the 1960s, for three separate reasons. The first was empirical, the second was cultural, and the third had to do with a subtle piece of rebranding. The empirical evidence was that price movements did indeed seem to be random, in the sense that no one could accurately predict them. In 1933, a wealthy investor called Alfred Cowles III analyzed the investment decisions of the top 20 insurance companies in the United States and came to the unfortunate conclusion that they showed "no evidence of skill."[6] In 1953, Maurice Kendall found that stock and commodity prices behaved like an "economic Brownian motion," with random changes outweighing any systematic effects, but was pleased to note that a "symmetrical distribution reared its graceful head undisturbed amid the uproar."[7] And in 1958, the physicist M.F.M. Osborne showed that the proportional changes in a stock's price could be simulated reasonably well by a random walk, as Bachelier had claimed.

The cultural reason for Bachelier's thesis suddenly becoming trendy was that his idea of random walks and probability diffusions fit the post-war scientific zeitgeist. Following the development of quantum theory in the early 20th century, the Newtonian mechanistic model had been replaced with quantum mechanics. In a way this was equally mechanistic (hence the name), but it was now probability waves that were being described mechanistically. According to Heisenberg's uncertainty principle, you could never measure both the exact position and momentum of an object – only the probability that it was in a certain state. Quantum mechanics therefore used probabilistic wave functions to describe the state of matter at the level of the atom. The probability plot of Figure 2.3 above is similar in spirit to the probability plots used to illustrate the behavior of a subatomic particle.

The difference between Newtonian mechanics and quantum mechanics probably seemed rather subtle and abstract to most people, right up until the summer of 1945, when the test detonation of

---

[6] Cowles (1933).
[7] Kendall and Hill (1953).

the first atomic bomb in the desert of New Mexico, and the subsequent deployment of the bomb in Hiroshima and Nagasaki, demonstrated both the power, and horror, of the new physics. Research funding poured into weapons laboratories and universities around the world to develop new techniques for analyzing probabilistic systems, and some of this effort spilled over into economics and finance. One example of this research was the Monte Carlo method, which we discuss later. The Black–Scholes equation for option pricing, discussed in Chapter 4, can be rephrased as a probabilistic wave function using the formalism of quantum mechanics.[8] Random walk theory was used by physicists to compute the motion of neutrons in fissile material, and therefore the critical mass needed for a nuclear device. Warren Buffett later quipped that "derivatives are financial weapons of mass destruction" (which didn't stop him from being a champion user of them), but their intellectual genesis was largely forged by a real weapon of mass destruction.

Finally, one factor which must have displeased the highly rational examination committee was the fact that Bachelier treated the stock market as being fundamentally irrational. Price changes, he believed, are caused in part by external events, but also represent an internal response, with the market reacting to itself. No one ever has a clear idea what is going on, and opinions about the market "are so divided that at the same instant buyers believe the market is rising and sellers that it is falling." This jarred with the traditional, mainstream economics view of markets as being inherently rational and self-correcting. Bachelier's theory of speculation therefore became acceptable only when the unpredictability was reframed as being caused not by the market's irrationality, but by its very opposite: incredible efficiency.

All models tell a kind of story about a system. But this was the point where the story became bigger than the model.

Efficient Markets

In another doctoral thesis, published this time by the University of Chicago in 1970, Eugene Fama defined his efficient market as a place where "there are large numbers of rational profit maximizers actively

---

[8] Baaquie (1997).

competing, with each trying to predict future market values of individual securities, and where important current information is almost freely available to all participants."[9] In such a market, "competition among the many intelligent participants leads to a situation where, at any point in time, actual prices of individual securities already reflect the effects of information based both on events that have already occurred and on events which as of now the market expects to take place in the future. In other words, in an efficient market at any point in time the actual price of a security will be a good estimate of its intrinsic value."

Of course, Fama noted, there will always be some disagreement between market participants, but this just causes a small amount of random noise, so prices will wander randomly around their intrinsic values. As soon as prices get too far out of line, the "many intelligent traders" will quickly restore prices to their correct setting.

Fama's view of the market therefore differed from that of Bachelier. The Frenchman had implied that not only was news random, but so was the reaction of investors, with "events, current or expected, often bearing no apparent relation to price variation." According to Fama, though, an efficient market always reacts in the appropriate way to external shocks; since if this were not the case, then a rational investor would be able to see that the market was over or underreacting, and profit from the situation. The market's collective wisdom emerged automatically from the actions of rational investors.

Fama's efficient market hypothesis (EMH), which led after 40-odd years to the 2013 economics Nobel, was essentially a more scientific-sounding version of Adam Smith's invisible hand, applied to the stock market. The traditional test of deterministic, scientific models is their ability to use a mechanistic explanation to make accurate predictions. The EMH proposed a specific mechanism – the actions of "rational profit maximizers" interacting in a market – and made a kind of prediction, namely that markets are unpredictable, so no one can consistently beat the market. As Fama argued, this meant that techniques discussed in the next chapter such as chart analysis (looking for recurrent patterns) or fundamental analysis (looking, e.g., for companies that are undervalued relative to earnings or future prospects) can never work, because all the information

---

[9] Fama (1965).

is immediately priced in by the market. Other forms of quantitative analysis would presumably be equally pointless.

Indeed, empirical evidence does show that markets are hard to predict (different versions of the EMH assume varying amounts of efficiency, and take into account factors such as insider trading, where traders profit from information which is not widely available). The fact that, for example, managed funds find it hard to beat index funds is often deployed as a defense of the EMH.[10] As economist John Cochrane wrote, "The surprising result is that, when examined scientifically, trading rules, technical systems, market newsletters, and so on have essentially no power beyond that of luck to forecast stock prices. This is not a theorem, an axiom, a philosophy, or a religion: it is an empirical prediction that could easily have come out the other way, and sometimes does... The main prediction of efficient markets is exactly that price movements should be unpredictable!"[11]

While the EMH "predicts" that markets are unpredictable, however, one needs to be careful about predictions that only give an explanation for something that is already known. In physics, for example, proponents of string theory have argued that it can predict gravity, but it would be more accurate to say that it offers a possible explanation for something that is already well understood.[12] Far more convincing are predictions of things that are not yet known – for example, James Clerk Maxwell's prediction in the 19th century that light is an electromagnetic wave. While the EMH is consistent with markets being unpredictable, you cannot conclude from the unpredictability of markets that they are efficient. In most areas, the fact that something is unpredictable is not interpreted as evidence that it is efficient or hyper-rational. Snow storms are unpredictable, but no one thinks they are efficient. A simpler explanation is that the system is driven by complex dynamics that resist numerical prediction. Many such systems exist – for example, people, clouds, fashions, turbulent flow, the climate, and so on.

Instead, then, it could be that the EMH is right for the wrong reasons. The key assumptions of the theory are that market participants

---

[10] E.g., Moffatt (2012).
[11] Cochrane (2013).
[12] According to string theorist Edward Witten, "String theory has the remarkable property of predicting gravity" (Witten, 1996).

have access to the same information and act in a rational manner to drive prices to an equilibrium. But are these really a sound description of markets?

Irrational Markets

Consider, for example, the idea that investors are rational at least on average. The Greeks said that man was a rational animal, but maybe they were erring on the side of generosity. At the same time that Fama was writing his thesis, the psychologists Daniel Kahneman and Amos Tversky, together with the economist Richard Thaler, were performing psychological experiments that led to the creation of the field known as behavioral economics.[13] These experiments demonstrated, rather convincingly, that investment decisions are based on many factors which have little to do with rationality. For example, they showed that we have an asymmetric attitude toward loss and gain: we fear the former more than we value the latter, and bias our decisions toward loss avoidance rather than potential gains. Some of our other various foibles and predilections include the following:

- *Status quo bias.* We prefer to hold onto things rather than switch to a better alternative – even if it is better. For example, if you inherit $10,000 in Blackberry shares you would be inclined to hold onto them. However, if you were to inherit the same amount in cash you wouldn't put it all into Blackberry.

- *The illusion of validity (i.e., denial).* We maintain beliefs even if they are at odds with the evidence.

- *Loss aversion.* We avoid selling poorly performing stocks.

- *Power of suggestion.* We are influenced by the opinions of others. (We're really enjoying this book so far!) An extreme example is the way traders sometimes egg each other on to take more and more risk.

- *Trend following.* When the market is going up or down, we think it will continue.

---

[13]Kahneman and Tversky (1979).

- *Illusory correlations.* We look for patterns in things like stock prices where they don't exist (they're talking about you, chartists!).

- *Immediacy effect.* One study showed that we will pay on average 50% more for a dessert at a restaurant when we see it on a dessert cart, rather than when we choose it from a menu.

Many of these behavioral patterns have been confirmed by the experiments of neuroscientists, who put people in scanners and see which parts of their brains light up when offered the choice between a fully funded pension on retirement or an ice-cream that they can have right there! (These profound insights no doubt came as a complete shock to advertisers and retailers, who overnight realized, for the first time in history, that they could continue selling things using sexy images, just like always.)

Of course, one could argue with the neoclassical economists that these peculiarities come out in the wash for a large number of investors. But in a situation like the markets, where investors are influencing and reacting to one another, the opposite is probably true. As Kahneman explains, "when everybody in a group is susceptible to similar biases, groups are inferior to individuals, because groups tend to be more extreme."[14] Indeed, a common phenomenon in markets is herd behavior, where investors rush into, or out of, the same investments together, greatly amplifying risk instead of reducing it. The idea that "many intelligent traders" drive prices to their intrinsic value, so that fluctuations can be considered as random perturbations around an equilibrium state, therefore seems a bit of a stretch. This problem was captured by author James Buchan in his 1997 book *Frozen Desire,* when he wrote (before the Internet bubble burst): "You buy or sell a security, say the common stock of Netscape Inc., not because you *know* it will go up or come down or stay the same, but because you *want* it to do one of those things. What is condensed in a price is the residue not of knowledge but of embattled desire, which may respond to new information and may not. At the time of writing, Netscape is priced in the stock market

---

[14]Schrage (2003).

at 270 years' profits… such a price belongs outside the realms of knowledge. The efficient-markets doctrine is merely another attempt to apply rational laws to an arena that is self-evidently irrational."[15] Or, as Claude Bébéar, founder of the French insurer AXA, put it, mathematical models "are intrinsically incapable of taking major market factors into account, such as psychology, sensitivity, passion, enthusiasm, collective fears, panic, etc. One must understand that finance is not logic."[16]

Not Normal

A separate but related question is that of equilibrium. According to Fama, "Tests of market efficiency are tests of some model of market equilibrium and vice versa. The two are joined at the hip."[17] But from the standpoint of complexity science, it makes more sense to view the markets as being, not at some kind of rationally determined equilibrium, but in a state that is *far* from equilibrium. An early critic of the EMH was Fama's thesis adviser, Benoit Mandelbrot, who pointed out that price changes do not follow a normal distribution, as in the random walk model, but are better modeled by an equally ubiquitous formula known as a power-law distribution, which applies to everything from earthquakes to the size of craters on the moon. For example, the probability of an earthquake varies inversely with size to the power 2, so if you double the size it becomes about 4 times rarer (a number raised to the power 2 is the number squared; a number raised to the power 3 is the number cubed; and so on). In the same way, the distribution of price changes for major international indices have been shown to approximately follow a power-law distribution with a power of about 3.[18]

The normal distribution is symmetric and has a precise average, which defines a sense of scale. A power-law distribution, in contrast, is asymmetric and scale-free, in the sense that there is no typical or normal representative: there is only the rule that the larger an event is, the less likely it becomes. However, it still allows for extreme events,

---

[15]Buchan (1997, p. 240).
[16]*Paris Tech Review* (2010).
[17]Clement (2007).
[18]Gopikrishnan *et al.* (1998).

such as massive earthquakes, or Mississippi Company-style financial meltdowns, which have vanishingly small probability in a normal distribution. The power-law distribution is a signature of systems that are operating at a state that is far from equilibrium, in the sense that a small perturbation can set off a cascade of events (the classic example from complexity research is a finely poised pile of sand, where dropping a single grain might do nothing, or might trigger an avalanche). The normal distribution was derived for cases where processes are random and independent from one another, but markets are made up of highly connected people all reacting to one another. The idea that markets are inherently stable is therefore highly misleading, and as seen in later chapters has led to many problems in quantitative finance.

As a kind of preview, Figure 2.4 is a version of the density plot of Figure 2.3, except that it is based on actual data from the Dow Jones Industrial Index. This index has tracked the performance of 30 large publicly owned companies in the United States since 1928

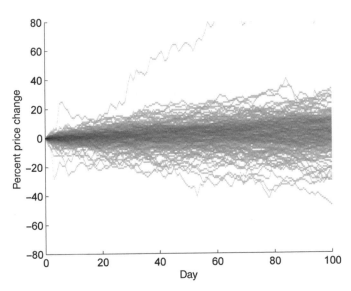

Figure 2.4   Density plot for the Dow Jones Industrial Index, which dates back to Oct 1, 1928

The data was chopped up into segments of 100 days. The growth over each 100-day segment was then plotted, and the results used to calculate a probability density for comparison with previous figures. You can easily distinguish some of the more wild trajectories, which appear as isolated lines.

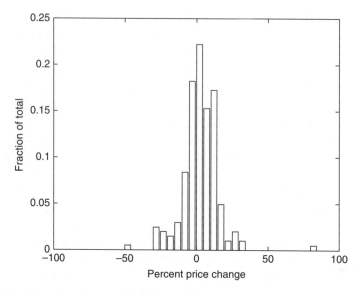

Figure 2.5   Histogram of the price changes after 100 days for each segment of the Dow Jones data
Unlike Figure 2.2, the data does not approximate a bell curve, and there are a significant number of outliers which would be effectively impossible under a normal distribution.

(earlier versions of the index go back to 1896). The historical time series was divided into sequential segments of 100 days, and we looked at the growth of the index over each 100-day segment.[19] If price changes for the companies within the index are "normal," one would expect the index itself to be too; however, the data swings shown in the plot seem considerably wilder than those of the normal distribution.

Figure 2.5 is a histogram of the price changes after 100 days for each segment. Unlike Figure 2.2, the plot is quite asymmetrical and does not seem to approximate a bell curve. The largest increase over a period of 100 days, which occurred during the rebound following the Great Depression, was 79%. Given that the standard deviation of the results is 14.4, the probability of that event, according to the normal distribution, is such that it shouldn't happen once in the age of the universe, let alone the age of the Dow Jones. The reason, of course, is that the data does not follow a normal distribution; if

---

[19]Data starts at 1928.

you don't believe in symmetry or efficiency, there is no reason why it should.[20]

Mental Virus

Given the fact that these flaws in the EMH have been known since the time it was invented, it therefore seems strange that, as noted by *The Economist*, and explored further in the next chapter, the theory "has been hugely influential in the world of finance, becoming a building block for other theories on subjects from portfolio selection to option pricing."[21]

One reason is simply that it enabled both economists and quants to continue using the standard statistical tools they were comfortable with. Power laws may be ubiquitous in nature and finance, but they lack the symmetry, ease of calibration, and mathematical usefulness of the normal distribution. The financial economist Paul Cootner, for example, included a paper by Mandelbrot in his 1964 book *The Random Character of Stock Market Prices*, but panned him in the introduction by writing that "Mandelbrot, like Prime Minister Churchill before him, promises us not utopia but blood, sweat, toil and tears. If he is right, almost all of our statistical tools are obsolete… Surely, before consigning centuries of work to the ash pile, we should like to have some assurance that all our work is truly useless."[22] (Which is a strange use of Churchill's words, when you think about it – like hearing Churchill say that fighting the Nazis would involve a lot of hard work, so better just to have a good nap.) Mandelbrot's work in finance only became popular in 2007, after more people had become personally acquainted with the idea of a financial earthquake.

Another reason, though, is that as economist Myron Scholes put it, "To say something has failed, you have to have something to replace it, and so far we don't have a new paradigm to replace efficient markets."[23] The traditional test of scientific theories, as mentioned above, is their ability to make predictions. In this case, the main prediction of the theory is that the system is unpredictable. The only way to displace it, by the traditional standard, is to come up

---

[20]Some economists appear to be blissfully unaware of this. See Orrell (2017).
[21]Anonymous (2006).
[22]Cootner (1964, p. 337).
[23]Anonymous (2009).

with another theory that can make accurate predictions, but that isn't possible. There is no equation, for example, for irrationality (though people have tried). As seen later, hedge funds don't try to predict the global economy, they look for small pockets of predictability in market prices that can be exploited while they last. No one has a perfect model of the economy, and so the theory remains in place. Like some kind of mental virus, it has found a way to disable the usual processes that would get rid of it.

Following the financial crisis, the EMH came under increased scrutiny. To most people, it seemed implausible that markets with such a demonstrated ability to blow themselves up should be described as efficient. In testimony to Congress in 2008, as discussed later, Alan Greenspan did admit that conventional risk theory had failed.[24] However, he blamed the problem on only calibrating the models with recent data, and not including periods of historic stress. When asked by *The New Yorker* in 2010 how the efficient market theory had performed, Fama replied: "I think it did quite well in this episode."[25] The economist Robert Lucas made the usual defense that the reason the crisis was not predicted was because economic theory predicts that such events cannot be predicted.[26]

This failure to let go of the idea that markets are near-perfect machines is perhaps best explained by behavioral economists – after all, it is typical human behavior to deny there is a problem, cling to the illusion of validity, maintain the status quo, and thus avoid loss. As money manager Jeremy Grantham wrote to his clients in 2009: "In their desire for mathematical order and elegant models, the economic establishment played down the inconveniently large role of bad behavior, career risk management, and flat-out bursts of irrationality… Never underestimate the power of a dominant academic idea to choke off competing ideas, and never underestimate the unwillingness of academics to change their views in the face of evidence. They have decades of their research and their academic standing to defend."[27]

---

[24]Greenspan (2008).
[25]Cassidy (2010).
[26]Lucas (2009).
[27]Grantham (2009).

Getting academic economists to think identically is like herding sheep. They all go in the same direction, although there's no one with any obvious leadership skills. We will discuss this phenomenon further in Chapter 9. In the next chapters, though, we show how all this theory plays out in the real world (if you consider finance to be the real world). As we'll see, efficiency is a con, and the markets can be gamed. You just need to know the flaws in the system.

CHAPTER 3

Risk Management

Applying — theory to / Put numbers on concepts

> *"ANTONIO:*
> *... I thank my fortune for it,*
> *My ventures are not in one bottom trusted,*
> *Nor to one place; nor is my whole estate*
> *Upon the fortune of this present year:*
> *Therefore my merchandise makes me not sad."*
> —Shakespeare, *The Merchant of Venice*, Act 1, Scene 1

> *"Risk–reward."*
> —Response to the survey question: "How would you describe quantitative finance at a dinner party?"
> at wilmott.com

Investment advice used to be simplistic. Don't put all your eggs in one basket, or, as Mark Twain said, "Put all your eggs in one basket, and then watch that basket." There was little in the way of quantification. In the 1950s, economists began to apply probability theory to the problem of asset allocation, and showed how to put numbers on concepts such as risk and reward. Asset managers now had a way of quantifying their strategies. The seeds were being sown for a dramatic shift from finance as art to finance as science – or at least, something that looked a lot like science. But can risk and reward be reduced to hard numbers?

It's a feeling in the pit of your stomach, or a light-headedness. Perhaps a sudden chill, or worst of all the three-o'clock-in-the-morning cold-sweats panic attack. The risk in your portfolio has just been realized and it's much worse than you feared.

Human beings are very poor at estimating probabilities. We tend to be optimistic about our investments, and even the most pessimistic of us is usually pessimistic about the wrong things. So shocks often seem to come out of nowhere. In contrast, investors put their money at risk because they want to earn a reward. And these two aspects – risk and reward – are somehow related, but not in an obvious way. Putting all your cash under the mattress is probably safe, unless your house burns down.

Financial risk management – the craft of balancing risk with reward – is a subject that has had a relatively recent quantitative makeover. One of its great advantages is that it takes the emotions out of estimating risks, and perhaps prepares you when it hits the fan. But that advantage is only as good as the quant methods. If the methods are no good, then risk management is at best a trick for temporarily soothing the psyche. To understand whether it is a useful tool for navigating the choppy waters of finance, we need to step back into asset management history and look at the development of investment techniques.

If we go back to before the 1950s, an optimal investment was considered to be the one that had the best perceived prospects. Of course, people had an innate sense of risk, at a gut level. More cautious investors could mitigate danger by diversifying, in the same way that Antonio in Shakespeare's *The Merchant of Venice* split his shipments between a number of boats (or "bottoms"), so that if one sunk all his goods were not lost. But risk wasn't something that you could easily quantify, unlike profit which you could. So people usually went for the profit. This approach did have one advantage, that of simplicity. In deciding which investment to concentrate on, you only needed to analyze each one in isolation.

There are several ways in which to analyze stocks, the three most important being fundamental analysis, technical analysis, and what one might call quantitative analysis. We'll look first at each in turn, and then describe the revolution in the 1950s that changed the face of investing.

I see thru this piece of paper – stock as pefe too or circuit

Fundamentals

Fundamental analysis means studying the business of the company itself, reading balance sheets, income statements, and so on. It's easy to understand why it might be important to know about a company's sales, the quality of its management, whether it is involved in any legal battles over intellectual property, how its competitors are doing, demographics, and so on. However, while it's obvious that such matters are important to the wellbeing and future of the company, it's quite tricky to turn that into a share valuation. We don't know how many of you reading this book are accountants and understand balance sheets and income statements. We are both self-employed, running our own businesses, and we struggle. No, it's not easy to go into all the details of the business of a company, and to interpret them correctly.

To simplify the analysis you will find that people commonly use "multiples" to turn basic accounting concepts into a share price. One such multiple that you'll see in the share pages of the newspapers is the price-to-earnings (P/E) ratio. This quantity is simply the current share price divided by the recent (last 12 months, say) or future forecast earnings per share. For example, if the current share price is $100, and the earnings per share over the last four quarters was $10, then the P/E ratio is 10.

We can try to use the P/E ratio to estimate a company's correct share price. Companies within the same sector may have broadly similar P/E ratios, but ratios vary from sector to sector. If you want to get a ballpark share price for a company you just need to google to find its earnings, number of shares, and what the typical P/E ratio is for that sector. Or conversely, you can see how a company's P/E ratio compares with others in the sector to figure out whether the company is perhaps undervalued by having a low P/E ratio, or overvalued if the P/E ratio is uncharacteristically high. The P/E ratio thus levels the playing field: the size of a company (its earnings), its share price, and how many shares there are, are all scaled out.

If only it were so simple! Unfortunately, for anyone wanting to get a hold on a company's share price there are a multitude of reasons why the P/E ratio doesn't quite fit the bill. Perhaps the last year's earnings don't reflect how well the company is going to do next year, and if you are buying the stock now it's the future you are concerned with, rather obviously. Perhaps the earnings that the

Industry	P/E
Consumer Goods	14.97
Financial	18.75
Utilities	23.21
Industrial Goods	25.29
Healthcare	25.82
Conglomerates	28.20
Services	31.18
Technology	40.33
Basic Materials	51.10

Sector	P/E
Foreign	12.00
Water	15.20
Diversified	19.90
Gas Utilities	23.10
Electric	38.90

Figure 3.1   P/E ratios by industry

company are quoting aren't quite as, ahem, accurate as they would like you to believe. In the UK the supermarket Tesco immediately springs to mind, it having overstated its profits by £263m in 2014. Or perhaps it's just that even within a sector there is an enormous range of P/E ratios (see Figure 3.1).[1]

Other numbers can also be calculated for valuation purposes. A company's earnings before interest, taxes, depreciation, and amortization (EBITDA) is a common measure of profitability. It takes the earnings and subtracts off costs that really have nothing to do with the actual running or success of the business (the I, T, D, and A). And instead of the stock price you can use the company's enterprise value (EV). This is the theoretical price you would have to pay to buy the company, so it accounts for things like debt. The EV/EBITDA ratio is in some ways a better metric than P/E, because it strips out any dependence on the capital structure of a company. Whether a company has a lot or not much debt is irrelevant, since interest payments are subtracted from the earnings. It's another playing-field leveler.

Even here, though, we don't get the whole story. Consider, for example, a small drug company with a handful of cancer drugs in its pipeline. Investors are attracted to such companies because, for the price of a small investment, they might just get rich, while simultaneously helping to cure cancer. But how do you value a company where the success will only be known after the drug has succeeded

---

[1] Go to biz.yahoo.com/p/s_peeu.html and drill down to see what we mean.

in a plethora of animal and human trials, been approved by drug regulatory agencies, and beaten its competitors in the marketplace? Getting a drug to market is a bit like selling a screenplay in Hollywood: the potential payoff is huge, but for a newbie your chances of receiving it are miniscule. Analyzing metrics such as EBITDA is not much use, because the company will consistently lose money until it has a hit. It is like looking at the screenwriter's dingy low-rent basement apartment and his depleted bank account and concluding that the screenplay has no chance, when it might be the next *Citizen Kane*.

These multiples also don't tell you anything about risk. They may give you a rough estimate of where the share price of a particular company theoretically *ought* to be, perhaps relative to its peers, at one point in time, but they don't give you much information about the probabilities of the value being higher or lower in the future, and so how your investment might turn out. Risk is about variation around an expected share price, and particularly how much it might fall. In practice, as an investor you might not be too bothered about whether that variation is due to changes in a company's profit, whether it's a sector thing, or even if it's just an irrational whim of the market. You just want to know how much your downside might be and what is its probability – and that will affect the price you are willing to pay.

Beauty Contest

But there is also a deeper problem with fundamental analysis, relating to the whole idea of value. You may be the greatest analyst of all time, able to calculate EV and EBITDA to the nth decimal place, but that ability might not amount to a hill of beans. The reason, unfortunately, is that *there is no* exact fundamental value. The price of a company in the market is determined by what other investors will pay for it. So the task of a stock investor is not to figure out the true worth of a company, no, he should be figuring out what *other* investors think. In his *General Theory of Employment Interest and Money* (1936), the economist John Maynard Keynes compared the stock market to a beauty contest: "It is not a case of choosing those that, to the best of one's judgment, are really the prettiest, nor even those that average opinion genuinely thinks the prettiest. We have reached the third degree where we devote our intelligences to anticipating what average opinion expects the average opinion to be. And there are some, I believe, who practice the fourth, fifth and higher degrees."[2]

Of course, you might believe that you have unique insight into the future, which means that the share price should converge over time to the calculated value, once everyone has come to their senses. But as Keynes pointed out, "The market can stay irrational longer than you can stay solvent." In fact, it can stay irrational forever. Furthermore, future prospects are even harder to divine than the actions of investors. Keynes again: "If we speak frankly, we have to admit that our basis of knowledge for estimating the yield 10 years hence of a railway, a copper mine, a textile factory, the goodwill of a patent medicine, an Atlantic liner, a building in the City of London amounts to little and sometimes to nothing."

The price of a stock therefore depends less on hard numbers than on inherently fuzzy and unquantifiable factors such as investor sentiment and ideas about where the company, and the rest of the world, is headed. It all rather makes a mockery of deep fundamental analysis. However, if you are really convinced that a company is seriously undervalued you could always just buy the whole thing, which takes the opinion of other investors out of the equation. But that's beyond the resources of most of us. (We do hope Warren Buffett is reading this book though.) The approach can also be applied to things such as houses, see Box 3.1. *open door*

quant note Sandberg

Also, some people manage to get rich using a value approach – such as Keynes himself, who parlayed fairly modest savings into what would amount to about £10 million in today's money.[3] His technique evolved over time, but after a couple of mishaps in which he was nearly wiped out, he settled on the quaint but effective notion of investing in good companies. In a 1934 letter to a business associate, Keynes wrote: "As time goes on, I get more and more convinced that the right method in investment is to put fairly large sums into enterprises which one thinks one knows something about and in the management of which one thoroughly believes. It is a mistake to think that one limits one's risk by spreading too much between enterprises about which one knows little and has no reason for special confidence… One's knowledge and experience are definitely limited and there are seldom more than two or three enterprises at

---

[2] Keynes (1936, p. 156).
[3] Wasik (2014).

any given time in which I personally feel myself entitled to put full confidence."[4] We will now stop quoting Keynes.

Box 3.1 Rent or Buy?

When it comes to the housing market, the nearest thing to a P/E ratio is the ratio of house prices to rent. For example, if a house costing a million dollars can be rented out for $4000 per month, then the price/rent ratio is 250. This measure, along with others such as price to income, is used by organizations such as the International Monetary Fund (IMF) and the Organisation for Economic Co-operation and Development (OECD) to determine the health of a country's housing market. It can also be used by an individual to decide whether it is better to rent or buy.

One way to get a handle on an appropriate ratio is to consider two different scenarios. In one, the person buys a house by making a downpayment of say 10% and taking out a mortgage on the rest. At the end of the mortgage period they own a house, which has appreciated in value. However, they have also paid out a considerable sum in annual maintenance and property taxes.

In the second scenario, the person rents the house, invests the downpayment, and also invests any monthly savings. So in either case we assume the same initial and monthly payments, but in the first scenario the purchase is a house, while in the second it is an investment portfolio (plus a rented home for the duration).

Which of these ends up ahead in financial terms will depend on the details, but if you conduct the accounting exercise with reasonable values for mortgage rates, house price inflation, investment returns, maintenance charges, and so on, then it turns out that the house/rent ratio which balances the two out is somewhere in the area of 200 to 220.[5] Below that and buying looks like a better deal. Much above that and you should probably rent.

Of course, as with other such estimates, this is only a rough guide, and many people are willing to pay a premium for owning. However, like the P/E ratio, it is a playing-field leveler that can also give a warning when things are out of whack. So according to this calculation, the entire city of Vancouver should rent.

Another way to approach the question is to look at historical norms. According to Moody's Analytics, the average ratio for metro areas in the USA was near its long-term average of about 180 in 2000, soared to nearly 300 in 2006 with the housing bubble, and was back to 180 in 2010 – mean reversion in action.[6]

---

[4] In a letter of August 15, 1934 to F.C. Scott.

[5] Try it out for yourself using the RentOrBuyer web app: systemsforecasting.com/web-apps/.

[6] See Zandi *et al.* (2009), Leonhardt (2010).

Technical Analysis

Good companies are hard to find, and not everyone has the same access to information as a Keynes or a Buffett. If fundamental analysis is difficult to do, and unreliable thanks to Keynes's clever observations, then we've got something much simpler for you. But sadly it's equally unreliable. Technical analysis (or "chartism") means looking for patterns in stock prices in an effort to predict their future values. Figure 3.2 is a simple example.

The figure shows the General Motors share price over a period of more than 3 years. Notice how we've superimposed a couple of straight lines on this. They are meant to represent the trend over an 18-month period. The chartist would look at this and conclude that General Motors is following a trend that will continue into the future. He would advise buying the stock and reaping the rewards. No need to stress about those boring accounting details.

This trendline is only one of the many patterns that chartists look for. Other patterns have names like "saucer bottoms" (a shallow U-shape), "head and shoulders" (a small hump, followed by a big hump, followed by another small hump), "flags" or "triangles" (a stock price that bounces up and down with decreasing amplitude so it looks like a child has badly colored in a flag with a crayon),

Figure 3.2   General Motors

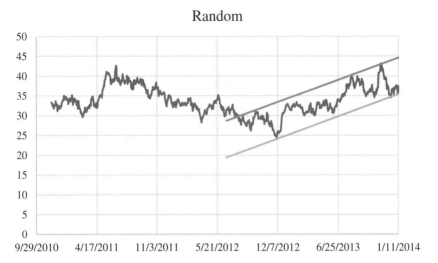

Figure 3.3   Random

and more. They also measure quantities such as moving averages, and plot these on top of the stock price graph. When two moving averages collide, it means something apparently. Elliott waves, Bollinger (cheers!) bands, candlestick charts, and more are all supposedly important.

Sadly the evidence is very strong that there is little predictive power in such patterns.[7] However, there is also very strong evidence that humans do tend to see patterns where there aren't any. To emphasize this point we have plotted a similar graph and associated trendlines in Figure 3.3. However this share price is a fake, it was generated using random numbers in Excel – there is no trend here. Technical analysis often amounts to reading patterns into events that probably have no pattern. In his efficient markets paper, Fama made a similar point: "If the random walk model is a valid description of reality, the work of the chartist, like that of the astrologer, is of no real value in stock market analysis."[8] We would agree, with the difference that we don't think markets follow a random walk either, even if they sometimes look like it.

---

[7] For a discussion of the track record of technical trading, with references, see Malkiel (1999, p. 160).
[8] Fama (1965).

For our present discussion, like fundamental analysis, technical analysis also says nothing about risk. The chartist is trying to tell us where the share price will be in the future (with a large supply of excuses in preparation for when the prediction goes wrong), not about the probabilities, the variation, and the risks. The main risk to the technical analysis believer is that it is all rubbish.

Now, as an aside, we do have some sympathy with technical analysts. And we believe that there could be a grain of truth in their ideas. There is a simple mechanism which they could exploit to make their predictions do much better. But this requires them to change their current thinking, in two ways.

At the moment, the technical analysts present their predictions with the sort of conviction used in UK weather forecasts: There won't be a hurricane tomorrow. Period. But when there is a hurricane, as famously happened in the UK in October 1987, then people tend to remember, and not trust future predictions. The exact quote by weatherman Michael Fish in 1987 was "Earlier on today, apparently, a woman rang the BBC and said she heard there was a hurricane on the way... well, if you're watching, don't worry, there isn't!" The following day was the worst storm to hit the UK for hundreds of years. In the USA the weather forecasters are more sophisticated, presenting their predictions with a probability, which is also useful as a get-out clause. Technical analysts are as emphatic as UK weather forecasters, perhaps because they rarely have the quants' training in probability theory. Instead, what technical analysts do when they are wrong is to blame it on the pattern, it wasn't a "head and shoulders," it was a "Mount Rushmore" (we made that one up!). So, Step 1: give percentages. After all, you only need to be a few percentage points above 50% accuracy to make a fortune.

This still doesn't make technical analysis work, it just makes it harder to disprove. The second step is to get together and decide on a single indicator that they are all going to use for prediction. Ideally nothing too simple, since they don't want everyone to be able to do it themselves. Once they are all using the same single indicator, and all making the same prediction, then a BUY alert from them would result in people buying the stock, followed by the stock, as a consequence, rising. Thus making their prediction come true. This is a simple feedback effect – the power of suggestion and herding – of which psychologists are aware, but it has only recently been studied with respect to share prices. While chartists are all making different predictions their buys and sells will cancel out, and there is no feedback. We will discuss the good and bad sides of feedback later, and will have more to say on more modern versions of market prediction.

Again we have mentioned probabilities. And this is key to the modern methodology for risk measurement and management.

Quant Analysis

In the 1950s some pretty straightforward ideas in probability were applied to this problem, and asset allocation suddenly became something that you could write about in respected journals. Fundamental analysis and technical analysis both concentrate on the possible rewards, while neglecting risk, and up until the 1950s risk didn't really get a look in as far as asset management was concerned. This changed with the work of University of Chicago's Harry Markowitz, published in 1952, which was known as modern portfolio theory (MPT). His great insight was to quantify share price behavior in a probabilistic sense, and relate it to the idea of risk. Even today, if you have a robo-advisor running your investments, or for that matter a human one, the strategy is probably based on a version of MPT.

There is always an implicit trade-off between risk and price. Consider a simple game where you toss a coin, and get $10 if you call it correctly and nothing if you lose. Since you have a 50/50 chance of winning, the expected gain (i.e., the average over a large number of tosses) is $5. Therefore, the fair value for an option to play the game is also $5. But who would want to play that game? Contrary to Bachelier's assumption of zero expected profit, most people would say that they'd play only if they had an edge, in mathematical language they'd want a positive expectation. Maybe we could tempt you to play if the upfront premium was only $4. With an expected payoff of $5 that gives you an expected, but not guaranteed, profit of $1.

In this situation most people would be "risk averse." In financial terms, this means that you want a positive expectation. More subtly, you might link your expectation to the degree of risk you are taking. If you are "risk neutral" then you don't need an expected profit. And if you are "risk seeking" then you are comfortable with negative expectations. This is lottery territory, where you expect to lose but the potential enormous payoff outweighs losing a few dollars now and then. It can be totally rational to play games with negative expectations. If winning the lottery is your only way of getting a life-saving operation, then you will play.

Markowitz expressed this trade-off by representing the behavior of an individual share over a set time horizon in terms of two parameters: the expected return and the standard deviation. The first measured reward, the second measured a kind of risk. A stock whose price tended to experience wild fluctuations was considered riskier than one which was more stable. Knowing these two parameters amounted to knowing the probabilities for stock price behavior in the future. One could answer questions such as what is the probability of the stock doubling in value over the next year? Or how long before we can expect the stock to hit a key level?

The means and standard deviations for stocks were estimated using historical time series. As an example, let's say you have the daily closing prices for the stock going back 10 years. From this you can calculate daily returns. This is just the percentage change from one day to the next. So, if the stock was at $50 one day and the day after it is at $51, then that's a 2% return. If it was at $49 then that's a −2% return. You now have a time series of returns. You can calculate the expected return by averaging all the returns, and the standard deviation gives you the risk.[9]

Of course, we can't guarantee that the future parameters will be the same as the historical ones. Using past data to estimate future returns looks suspiciously like a chartist using a trendline to predict the future. And there is no reason why volatility, as measured by the standard deviation, should be stable either. But this problem will crop up over and over in our book.

Markowitz would then plot individual shares on a risk/return chart. The horizontal axis representing risk, the standard deviation, the volatility, and the vertical axis representing the expected return. Figure 3.4 shows an example.

---

[9] There's a bit of multiplying by 252 and the square root of 252 to turn these into annualized numbers. Why 252? Because we've mentioned daily data and 252 is the typical number of business days in a year. A recently joined member of wilmott.com said that the reason for his joining was "Have a mancrush on Paul and googled what he had to say about annualising volatility by taking the sqrt(252), and what discrepancies would come about." Volatility can do that to a chap.

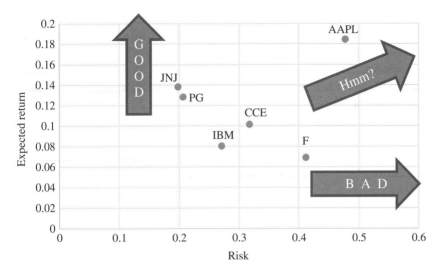

Figure 3.4   Example risk/return chart

In the figure we see six US stocks: Apple, Coca Cola, Ford, IBM, Johnson & Johnson, and Procter & Gamble. Take IBM for example. It has a horizontal coordinate of 0.27, meaning that its standard deviation, volatility, or risk is 27%. And it has an expected return, measured on the vertical axis, of 8%. These are both annualized numbers.

From plots like this we can immediately see which stocks are appealing and which are no-hopers. Ford (F) is clearly useless. It has quite a large risk, almost as much as Apple (AAPL), but without Apple's impressive return. Johnson & Johnson (JNJ) and Procter & Gamble (PG) are pretty similar, it's not worth distinguishing between them based on this data alone. Actually, all of Ford, Coca Cola (CCE), and IBM are worse than JNJ/PG on the grounds of having higher risk yet lower expected return. If we were to invest in a single stock then we'd have to rule out all of those three. That leaves JNJ/PG and AAPL as possibles. However, we can't decide between AAPL and JNJ/PG. Why not?

All things being equal (i.e., the same risk or volatility), then the higher up (vertically) this plot the better. See the large arrows in the plot. And then it's better to have lower risk than higher risk, again all things (now expected return) being equal. So you want a stock further to the left. But if you have a choice between bottom left and top right, it's not necessarily easy to make a choice. In our example here AAPL has a great expected return but that comes at a cost, high risk. Even with simple pictures like this, Markowitz is giving us an easy way of quantifying our investments, helping us to compare individual investments while taking both the two dimensions of risk and reward into account. However, there's more to come, because Markowitz had another trick up his sleeve.

Right at the start of this chapter we talked about analyzing stocks in isolation, and so far that is all we've done. In his MPT, Markowitz also looked at how two stocks behave together, and then how entire portfolios of stocks behave. The key to this analysis is the concept of correlation.

Correlation

In statistics, a correlation is a number which measures how two quantities tend to vary together. For example, the purchase of umbrellas is highly correlated with rain storms; ice-cream sales with heat waves. Some correlations are spurious, nothing more than statistical flukes. As just one example, US spending on science, space, and technology in the period 1999–2009 had an uncannily exact (0.99) correlation with the number of suicides by hanging, strangulation, and suffocation, which is not very useful information.[10] There are many ways to measure correlation, but the one most commonly used in quantitative finance is that developed by Karl Pearson in the 1880s. To measure the Pearson correlation between two stocks you need two time series of their returns, measured at the same times. The calculation gives you a correlation coefficient that is between plus and minus 1. Loosely speaking, a positive number means that ups and downs are more or less in sync. If it's negative then an up in one stock tends to be associated with a down in the other, and vice versa. If the correlation is zero then we say that the stocks are uncorrelated.

To see why correlation could be important, suppose you have a portfolio of two stocks which have the same expected return and are highly correlated. Then the prices of the individual stocks will tend to move up and down in unison, and the portfolio which includes both will therefore bounce along in time as well. However, if the stocks are uncorrelated, the volatility will be lower; and if the two stocks have

---

[10] See Vigen (2015).

negative correlation, it will be lower still, because when one stock zigs the other zags, and the fluctuations cancel each other out. The same idea can be extended to a larger portfolio of many stocks. By selecting stocks with the right mix of correlations, it is possible to reduce overall risk while retaining expected rewards.

For example, in Figure 3.4 we can ask what would happen if we buy 1000 shares of AAPL and 1000 shares of JNJ. While we won't go into the sums, it's an obvious concept that this portfolio too will have an expected return and a risk. It's then a small step to asking, why buy 1000 of each stock? Why not different amounts for each? And that will give us more dots, more potential portfolios to invest in. And why just AAPL and JNJ? Why not throw the other stocks into the pot? And why just buy? Can we perhaps sell stocks short? We could also broaden the mix with other securities such as bonds (the price of bonds is usually supposed to be inversely correlated with stocks, although that relationship broke down after the recent financial crisis when assets of all types were pumped up by quantitative easing).

The end result is that we can get a much wider range of risks and expected returns if we allow our portfolio to have any possible combination of assets. See the dot in Figure 3.5 labeled "A portfolio." Varying the constituents of the portfolio and their quantities we can move that dot up, down, and sideways.

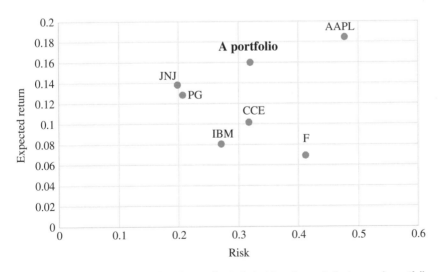

Figure 3.5   A selection of stocks plotted according to their risk and expected return, and a portfolio

Given that we can generate all these different portfolios with varying risk/reward characteristics, the next question Markowitz tackled was: how can we choose a portfolio such that for a given amount of risk we maximize the expected return? That is, move the dot up as high as possible. It might even be that poor old F finds a role, either as a stock to sell short or because its correlation with other stocks decreases risk sufficiently to make it appealing.

This is a nice optimization problem. Markowitz answered it by applying a mathematical technique known as linear programming, which is a method to optimize some quantity subject to certain constraints (represented by linear equations). It was first invented in 1937 by the mathematician Leonid Kantorovich who, while working for the Soviet government, used it to optimize the production of plywood. It was kept secret during World War II, when the Russians used it to optimize the war effort, but afterwards began to be adopted more widely in business. Markowitz had the good idea of adapting the technique to the problem of risk and reward. The result was a chart like in Figure 3.6.

There's a lot going on here, so bear with us. The first thing to notice is the curve marked "Efficient Frontier." We get this by doing the above optimization, choosing a number for risk, and optimizing the expected return. We then move onto a different level of risk. All of the points on this curve can be attained by different portfolios. MPT says that there's no point in investing in any portfolio that is

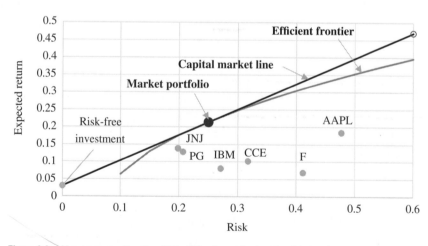

Figure 3.6   Lines representing the efficient frontier and, when the risk-free investment is included, the capital market line and market portfolio

below this curve, since you can do better by optimizing your portfolio, increasing the expected return for a given amount of risk.

Of course, no portfolio analysis would be complete without including a risk-free asset, such as cash held in a bank account, in the mix. Because risk is zero, this is a point on the vertical axis. It's marked "Risk-free investment" in the figure. The bold line which joins this point to the tangent of the efficient frontier is called the capital market line, and the tangent point itself is the tangency portfolio. You can get to any point between the risk-free dot and the tangent point by holding a mix of cash and the tangency portfolio. The higher-risk portion of the line to the right can also be reached by employing leverage (i.e., borrowing cash to buy the shares in the tangency portfolio). Choices anywhere on this line therefore give the maximum reward for a given risk. All you need is the right mix of cash (or debt) and the tangency portfolio. It is an efficient frontier with bells on. We'll come back to this tangency portfolio shortly.

Markowitz now has no more to say. Where you personally want to be on the straight line is entirely a matter for you. Markowitz cannot help. Feeling nervous? Hold 50% cash and 50% stocks. Want to take a flutter? Borrow cash and double up on the market.

This is clever stuff. We've got some statistics, some mathematics (nothing too complicated, but more than most people are comfortable with), and some great concepts including an optimization, and it's always nice when you can optimize something. We have mentioned the word "efficient" many times, which makes us sound like engineers. And it still leaves a little bit of room for personal preference in choosing your portfolio. Best of all is the way it reduces the task of choosing from an enormous array of securities, with their complex and intractable mix of risks and rewards, to a simple, straight, elegant line. No wonder Harry Markowitz was awarded an economics Nobel gong in 1990. What could go wrong?

Well...

Quite a lot, as it turns out. The problem with MPT, and with all of quantitative methods in finance, is that it is only as good as the underlying assumptions. Some of these concern the basic properties of markets. Like the efficient market hypothesis, MPT assumes that investors act rationally to further their self-interest, make decisions independently, have access to similar levels of information, etc. As a result, stock prices follow a random walk, with an upward bias that corresponds to the average growth rate and daily changes that follow a normal distribution.

So far, nothing new. But in addition, MPT assumes that we can measure meaningful correlations between different securities. If we have N stocks then we have N expected returns to calculate and N volatilities. But how many correlation parameters are there? If you ever did combinations and permutations at school you may have a vague memory of how to work this out. Each correlation is between two stocks. So the question is, how many combinations of two stocks are there if there are N stocks to choose from? First choose one of the stocks, there are N ways to do this. Now choose one of the remaining stocks, there are $N-1$ of these. Choosing the two together gives $N(N-1)$ ways. But we don't care whether we choose stock A first and then B, or vice versa, so divide this number by 2. This leaves the number of combinations and thus the number of correlation parameters as $N(N-1)/2$.

Now that's a lot of parameters to measure! For example, if we had 500 stocks to choose from (say, from the SPX Index) then that would be 500 return parameters, 500 volatilities, and $500 \times 499/2$ correlations, a total of 125,750 parameters to estimate!

The problem is not so much the number of parameters that need to be measured, because the method is relatively simple. No, it's more a question of the stability of the parameters. Some correlations will be completely spurious and go away, others just fluctuate with time. This can particularly be a problem during a market crash, when asset price changes tend to be highly correlated because they are all falling together.

But perhaps the most important assumptions, whose problems go to the core of the theory, are that we can compute expected risk and reward for each stock in the first place. Astute, or skeptical, readers may have noticed that MPT asks us to input expected growth rates for individual stocks; but as seen above, it is not possible to accurately predict expected returns using either fundamental or technical analysis. This empirical fact was one of the main justifications for efficient market theory.

Just as concerning is the idea that we can measure risk using the standard deviation of past price changes. When we estimate returns, we are making a prediction about the future; but when we estimate risk, we are predicting the uncertainty in our forecast – a prediction about our prediction – which is even more difficult. The standard deviation tells us something about past fluctuations, but there is no reason why it should remain constant (there are ways around this, as discussed in Chapter 7, but none of them are very appealing). It also seems to be a slightly strange way of measuring risk, because it assumes that sudden price increases are as bad as sudden decreases, while in fact we only worry about the latter. You probably don't lose sleep or go into a blind panic if your portfolio suddenly surges overnight. Then there is the fact that risks might not express themselves through volatility. Consider the previous example of a drug company. Its share price might be quite stable, or not, but that says nothing about the probability of its drugs being successful. There is also a more subtle point, which is whether the standard deviation is even a meaningful concept for financial data in the first place. We return to that below.

Efficiency Squared

Some of these concerns were addressed by William Sharpe, who later shared the 1990 economics Nobel with his mentor Markowitz. When asked in a 1998 interview what had appealed to him about Markowitz's work, he replied: "I liked the parsimony, the beauty, of it... I loved the mathematics. It was simple but elegant. It had all of the aesthetic qualities that a model builder likes."[11] Searching for a way to simplify MPT even further, and make it even more beautiful, he asked what would happen if everyone in the market optimized their portfolio according to Markowitz's calculations. The answer was that the "market portfolio" – defined as a portfolio whose holdings of each security are proportional to that security's market capitalization – would be an efficient portfolio. In other words, the market itself would adjust prices to an equilibrium level that optimally balanced risk and reward.

Here at last we had a kind of synergy between efficient markets and efficient portfolios. Some economists and analysts took this a little too seriously. In their minds, they had found the unique, perfect, beautiful portfolio, and it was called the market. Blah, blah,

---

[11]Burton (1998).

gibberish, gibberish. Wild flights of fancy ensue. To the efficient frontier and beyond! As everyone followed MPT, and behaved perfectly rationally, so the market portfolio and the tangency portfolio would move toward each other, eventually becoming one. Everyone would own the one portfolio, and it would be perfectly efficient. No more annoying uncertainty, or risk, or irrationality. All would be well with the world.

If anyone can flog an already sick horse to death, it is an economist.

This unquestioning enthusiasm for elegant theory was dented somewhat on October 19, 1987, otherwise known as Black Monday, when stock prices mysteriously became completely correlated as they plunged by 22% in the USA and by similar amounts around the world. In surprise terms it was the economic equivalent of the UK hurricane, which had hit just the week before. As discussed further below, the crash was later partly blamed on portfolio management – the very thing which was supposed to protect against such crashes – because, with beautifully choreographed synchronization, institutions using the same models were all managing their portfolios in the same direction by selling assets at the same time. Whenever a model becomes too popular, it influences the market and therefore tends to undermine the assumptions on which it was built.

Despite economists getting a bit carried away with unrealistic theories, a number of good and useful ideas came out of MPT, such as the Sharpe ratio. This is the ratio of a stock's, or a portfolio's, expected return in excess of the risk-free rate to the volatility. In our MPT plots you just take the line that joins the risk-free dot to the dot representing a specific investment and measure its slope. This can also be called the "market price of risk" (for the stock in question), because the greater the slope, the greater the compensation you get in terms of expected return above the risk-free rate for each unit of risk taken. Each financial instrument has its own market price of risk. This is another one of those nice quantities that level the playing field; in words it is just the risk-adjusted return, where volatility is a proxy for risk. Investments with higher Sharpe ratio are essentially better than those with lower Sharpe ratio. And the capital market line is clearly the highest and therefore best you can achieve. The Sharpe ratio is also measured for hedge funds, and if you read the prospectus of a hedge fund they will invariably quote theirs, trying to entice new investors.

Another useful invention was that of the index fund. If markets represent the optimal portfolio, then just buy the market index. Of course, this raises the question of which index. But cue the invention in the mid-1970s of funds such as the highly successful Vanguard 500 Index Fund. This does nothing more complicated than track the Standard & Poor's 500 Index, but still handily beats most fund managers once expenses are taken into account. Sharpe told the *Wall Street Journal*: "When I taught Investments at the M.B.A. level at Stanford, I started the first class by writing a phone number on the board. I then told the students that it was the most valuable information they would get from me. You probably guessed that it was the number for Vanguard."[12] Note that the index fund approach represents the exact opposite of Keynes's advice, which was to focus on a handful of companies.

The success of index funds is routinely supplied as evidence that markets are efficient. But a better way to look at it is that index funds are a very good business model that acts as a kind of parasite on the financial system. The market is made up of scores of funds and individual investors, who are making judgments about the value of companies. An index fund represents a kind of average of their decisions, a way of replicating their strategies, so by definition it should give average performance. However it can achieve this without any research or thought at all, so of course its expenses are minimal. That gives it an advantage over other funds. It also has the positive effect of keeping industry management fees in check. But if every fund adopted an index approach, the system would fall apart, since all a company would have to do to succeed is get in whatever index is the most popular. Indeed, index funds have grown so large that the heaviest trading of the year often occurs on the day when the Russell indices – a favorite among US fund managers – are updated.

Value at Risk

Perhaps the main contribution to come out of portfolio theory, though, was that asset managers were now quantifying their strategies, they were measuring expected returns and risk, and balancing them off as two sides of the same coin. Following Black Monday, the investment community started to take risk measurement and risk

---

[12]Zweig *et al.* (2014).

management even more seriously. A methodology called "value at risk" (VaR) began to gain traction. This was based on the portfolio risk measurement used in MPT and gave senior management a single number designed to give a sense of how much a bank might be expected to lose. In its basic form VaR has two key elements. The first is a degree of confidence: 95%, say. The second is a time horizon: 1 day, say. The risk manager might then say that the VaR is $2 million.

This is interpreted as meaning that 95 days out of 100, losses on the portfolio will be less than $2 million. If instead the degree of confidence is 97%, then this statement would change to 97 days out of 100. If the time horizon is 1 year then it would be adjusted to so many years out of 100. And so on. The manager would then decide whether the $2 million VaR was acceptable or not. If not then action would be taken to reduce the number by changing the portfolio or hedging.

VaR has come under a great deal of criticism. In fact, since 2008 it is impossible to find anyone in the field who hasn't criticized it. Before 2008 it was a different story. The main criticisms are as follows.

- It focuses on typical market movements, the frequent events. This is fine, but understand that it's not the frequent events that usually cause institutions to collapse.

- It can lead to a false sense of security.

- It usually assumes normal distributions. However, share price returns are not normally distributed.

- It doesn't tell you how much you might lose on those days when the VaR number is exceeded.

- It uses highly unstable parameters. During typical market movements there may be some correlation between assets, but come the big crash then all assets tend to be extremely highly correlated, and this totally destroys the VaR numbers.

- It creates dangerous incentives.

- It is easily abused.

All of these are fairly obvious criticisms, and mostly can be improved by different mathematics. The last two, however, are more subtle.

First, incentives. Let's modify the casino game of roulette to make it on average profitable (i.e., give it a positive expectation). We'll work with the European wheel which has 37 numbers, 1 to 36 plus a single zero. We'll play the game where a $100 bet will get you an extra $3 if any nonzero number comes up. But if it's zero then you lose the $100. You expect to make a profit of $36/37 \times 3 - 1/37 \times 100 = 21.6$ cents. This is positive, so you expect to make money. (If only real roulette were like this.) However one time in 37, that is about 3% of the time, you expect to lose everything you've bet. If you look at VaR at the level of 95% with a time horizon of one spin of the wheel, then it will look like there is no risk. This is because the 3% chance of losing is within the $100\% - 95\% = 5\%$, and not seen. If you are senior management with little clue about the subtleties of this "investment," then you might be rather pleased with the trader who has found it. And since there seems to be no chance of a loss at the 95% level, you might be tempted to gamble rather a lot. If you do, then it won't be that long before you are wiped out.

Second, abuse. There follows a true story told to Paul by a risk manager. We shall tell it in the risk manager's own words. "I'm a quant on a trading desk. One of my jobs is to measure the risk in our traders' portfolios. Last week one of them gave me a breakdown of his portfolio and asked me to tell him his VaR so he could report the number back to his boss. I went away and did the numbers. I gave the trader my report, essentially just a single number as the conclusion, his VaR. The trader looked at this and then looked at me. He said to me 'No, it's not. Go away and come back with the right answer.' He said it in a way that made it clear what I had to do. I had to do something with the model, or the parameters, or anything that would produce a significantly lower number. If I couldn't then the trader would have to scale back his positions. He didn't want to do that. He could make my life very difficult."

If the model is based on unreliable assumptions, and if the parameters are unstable, then it is easy to choose the model or the parameters to make the reported risk as low as possible. (Hey, there's another optimization problem here... albeit an evil one. We'll see this again in Chapter 9.) And this is all that the traders want. The lower the reported risk the greater the volume they can trade, and if all goes well the bigger their profit and bonus.

In the early 1990s the investment bank J.P. Morgan released its RiskMetrics™ methodology for measuring VaR. It involved a special way of measuring volatility, and some software. There was nothing particularly earth shattering about what they were doing, but it did throw another spanner into the works... systemic risk. Once everyone is using the same (wrong) techniques, then the risk to the system increases. On a personal note, Paul had a meeting with the RiskMetrics™ team in the late 1990s with the goal of explaining to them the importance of extreme stock movements in the risk of portfolios. He and a student of his, Philip Hua, had recently developed a model for analyzing portfolios in anticipation of crashes – and cheekily called it CrashMetrics.® J.P. Morgan didn't seem to care. CrashMetrics didn't involve measuring any correlations or volatilities, so was obviously not going to be of interest to them.

The Edge of Chaos

One of the main advantages of using hard numbers to measure risk is that it is supposed to make decisions scientific and objective. But clearly, if a trader can adjust his VaR calculation in order to please his boss, something strange is going on with the mathematics itself. The process looks objective, but is actually subjective.

The reason for this flexibility can be traced back to the above-mentioned fact that portfolio theory is based on the idea that price changes follow a normal distribution, with a stable and easily measured standard deviation. Real price data tend to follow something closer to a power-law distribution, and are characterized by extreme events and bursts of intense volatility, which as discussed earlier are typical of complex systems that are operating at a state known as self-organized criticality. This is also sometimes called the "edge of chaos," because such systems aren't fully random, or perfectly ordered, but instead operate in the interesting space between those extremes. In the case of financial data, one technical implication is that the measured volatility depends on the particular time period over which it is measured. Leave out those awkward moments like Black Monday and you get a very different result. Which can be convenient, if the aim is to tell a story.

Now, we have nothing against a degree of chaos, in moderation. A plot of the human heartbeat, for example, has chaotic qualities, though an overly rough or erratic pulse is a symptom of a heart condition known as atrial fibrillation. However, these properties are a powerful reminder that we are dealing with a complex, living system, rather than a deterministic, mechanical one. They also undercut the picture of calm rationality projected by MPT. Instead of operating on the efficient frontier, we are operating at the edge of chaos, which somehow doesn't have quite the same reassuring ring to it.

Theories such as MPT or VaR fail just when you need them most, in the moments when apparent stability breaks down to reveal the powerful forces beneath. The reason is that they model the financial system in terms of random perturbations to an underlying equilibrium, and can't handle the inherent wildness of markets, where storms can come out of nowhere. In particular, as discussed later, they ignore the nonlinear dynamics of money, contagion between institutions due to network effects, and the bad things that happen when credit suddenly dries up. "No investment strategy based on mainstream finance theory can… protect investors from market-wide crashes," according to a recent study by the CFA Institute.[13] In other words, for risk-management techniques, they aren't much good at managing risk – and in fact can create risks of their own. But that doesn't stop them from being taught in every business school. In the next chapter, we'll look at how probability theory was used to not just try and manage risk, but eliminate it altogether – and how risk responded by mutating into new, and even more virulent, forms.

---

[13]Skypala (2014).

CHAPTER 4

Market Makers

"There is a theory which states that if ever anybody discovers exactly what the Universe is for and why it is here, it will instantly disappear and be replaced by something even more bizarre and inexplicable. There is another theory which states that this has already happened."

—Douglas Adams, *The Original Hitchhiker Radio Scripts*

"Money is, to most people, a serious thing. They expect financial architecture to reflect this quality – to be somber and serious, never light or frivolous. The same, it may be added, is true of bankers. Doctors, though life itself is in their hand, may be amusing. In Decline and Fall *Evelyn Waugh even has one who is deeply inebriated. A funny banker is inconceivable. Not even Waugh could make plausible a drunken banker."*

—John Kenneth Galbraith, *Money: Whence It Came, Where It Went*

One of the most basic of financial instruments is the option. This is a contract or agreement which gives you the option (but not the obligation) to buy or sell something in the future at a certain price. Even a coin can be considered as an option to purchase government services, or pay taxes – if we don't want to keep the option, then we can melt the coin down, which people sometimes do when the cost of the metal exceeds the value of the option. Despite the fact that options have been around for millennia, it was only in the 1970s that traders began to use mathematical models to price them. In this chapter, we show how mathematicians developed formulas for valuing options – and in doing so completely changed the market for them.

"And in the financial markets today the Dow Jones rose by 123 points, a positive note on which to end an otherwise disappointing week. Yields on government bonds fell... Meanwhile, thanks to instability in the Middle East, the price of a barrel of crude oil rose to..." or something similar, is commonly heard on the TV news reports. However, it's only news of the simplest financial instruments that gets the publicity. You don't hear so much about the more complex financial products, the ones that only the mathematicians understand, the ones that add up to quadrillions of dollars. (A quadrillion, again, is a one followed by fifteen zeros. It's a thousand times a trillion, which is itself a thousand times a billion, which in turn is a thousand million.) These are amounts, in other words, that would put John Law to shame. After all, in a world of quadrillions, who wants to be a millionaire?

The simplest instruments are the shares, the indices, bonds, and futures. You can buy shares in individual companies. The indices, such as the Dow Jones, are the values of baskets of representative or important assets. Bonds are just loans, to governments or companies, giving you a fixed amount at a set date in the future. Yields are the interest rates that these bonds are effectively paying. And then there are the commodity futures, such as oil, whereby you promise to pay a set amount to receive the oil at a set date in the future.

And that's all you need to know, in one snappy paragraph, if you want to build your own portfolio using the basic asset classes. You don't need much mathematics, just a gut feel for what's going up and what's going down, or a dart and a copy of the *Wall Street Journal*. We could have expanded on the details, given you lots of examples, but there are enough such books around already. No, we are going to shift gear and introduce you to the more complicated financial contracts. These are the ones that stay under the radar, and that's not easy for a quadrillion dollars. Did we say that they're the ones that only the mathematicians understand? Well, maybe we were being a bit optimistic, even they have problems, as we'll be seeing.

Options

We quite fancy an electric car. A really swish one, not a Prius, no, something a lot more glam. There's a company starting up that reckons it has new battery technology and a great design team (Italian, of course). But they haven't got the cash for development. To raise the cash, they have this deal going in which you give them $10,000 now, and they promise that when (if?) they produce the car you will be able to buy it at a cost of $40,000. This deal is just an option, an option to buy the car in the future.

In essence, buying the option is equivalent to making a bet on the future value of this electric car. Your downside is limited to the upfront premium, the $10k. If the car doesn't get made then you've lost the premium. You've also lost the premium if, when the car is finally unveiled, it turns out to cost only $39,995. After all, why pay the $40k when its showroom cost is less? But if the car is priced at $95,000 then you are laughing. It's only costing you $40,000, plus the $10,000 premium, meaning that if you decide to buy and then immediately sell the car there's a $45,000 profit, assuming you don't crash it on the way out of the lot. In fact, if the car costs more than $50,000 ($10k + $40k) you've made a profit, anything less and you've made a loss.

Financial options work in a similar way. A call option is a contract that allows you to buy, at some date in the future, a specific share for a price set now. This is the same as the electric-car example above, except for some details. First, the call option has a set date on which you must make the decision whether or not to buy the share. Second, the person who sells you the financial option may have nothing to do with the company whose shares the call option is based on.

Before proceeding further, let's get some jargon out of the way. The strike or exercise price is the amount you are allowed to buy the option for (the $40,000 in the example). The expiration is the date on which you have to exercise the option, if you so wish. The premium is the amount you pay upfront for the right to buy the share (the $10,000), and the underlying asset is the share on which the option is based.

There's another type of option that is very popular, known as the put option. This contract allows you to sell (rather than buy) a share for a specified price. To understand this contract you really need to understand how these option contracts are used and by whom.

What are Options for?

Call options are easy to understand. You would buy one if you think that the asset is going to rise by the expiration date, but you didn't want to buy the asset itself just in case you are catastrophically wrong. The underlying share will cost you a lot more to buy than the call option's premium, so there's a lot less downside with the call option. This also means that there's more leverage. If the asset does rise significantly then your return, in percentage terms, will be that much greater with the call. The downside to the option is that if the asset doesn't move up much then you will have lost out.

Put options are a bit trickier. It's probably easiest if you imagine holding shares in XYZ, but are worried that there might be a fall in their value. You could sell the shares, but if you turn out to be wrong and instead the shares rise then you will have missed all that upside. Regret is a terrible thing. So you buy a put option which gives you the right to sell the shares for a set price. If the stock does fall then your downside is limited; if the stock falls from $50 to $10, but you have a put with a strike of $40, then you can sell the stock for $40 rather than for the $10 you'd get in the market. And who do you sell the shares to? Why, the person who sold you the put option, known as the writer.

With put options you don't even need to own the shares in the first place to buy this protection. In which case "protection" is totally the wrong word to use. Buying a put option without owning the underlying asset is then a way of betting on the share price falling, something which is otherwise not so simple.

Options can therefore be used either for speculating on share prices, if you have a view on the direction, or for insurance, if your aim is to protect a portfolio.

Options have been around for a while. In *Politics*, Aristotle describes how the Greek philosopher Thales predicted, on the basis of astrology, that the coming olive harvest would be much larger than usual, so arranged an option with local olive pressers to guarantee the use of their presses at the usual rate. "Then the time of the olive-harvest came, and as there was a sudden and simultaneous demand for oil-presses he hired them out at any price he liked to ask. He made a lot of money, and so demonstrated that it is easy for philosophers to become rich, if they want to; but that is not their object in life."[1]

In the 17th century, options were being sold at stock exchanges in financial centers including Amsterdam and London. However, they were generally viewed as a disreputable way of gambling on stock price movements, and regulators attempted to ban them from time to time. In the United States, they came close to being outlawed after the crash of 1929, and even in the 1960s were only traded on an ad hoc basis in a small New York market.[2] But their unpopularity was due not just to their lack of respectability, but also to the fact that no one prior to 1973 knew how to price them. What is the correct premium to sell these options for?

Before explaining further, we ought to point out that such niceties didn't completely stop people trading options. Oh no. The traders didn't say "Sorry, we can't sell you that option because we don't yet have a sound theoretical foundation for our valuation. I know you really want to buy it, we really want to sell it to you, and we are both over twenty one. But until we get the green light from the boffins…" For example, an ad hoc approach option would be to just sketch out the probability of a few different scenarios, and base the price on the average payoff over the different scenarios. If you're unsure of your estimates you can always add a hefty profit margin before you sell the thing. Or you can look at what other people are charging. Or you can trade in small quantities, so a big mispricing doesn't lead to a big disaster. Or you can diversify perhaps, by trading in options on many different stocks. But as we'll see, it was only when a model was discovered (or rediscovered) that options hit the big time.

Bachelier's Return

Faith in the abductive
physics in economics

As discussed in the previous chapter, the first to apply formal mathematical theory to options pricing, at the very start of the 20th century, was the French mathematician Louis Bachelier. His random

on are too !

---

[1] Aristotle (1943).
[2] Mackenzie (2006, p. 120).

who is it Reflectuy
of

Social Efficiency
physical Efficiency

walk model described the behavior of a stock's price based only on its initial price, and the amount of randomness or standard deviation (Bachelier referred to it as the "nervousness" of the stock).[3] From these assumptions, Bachelier derived the correct or fair price for an option, which accurately reflected the odds of it paying off. Problem (almost) solved! Unfortunately his thesis remained filed away for the next 60 years, until the economist Paul Samuelson found a copy "rotting in the library of the University of Paris" while chasing a reference for a friend. He found it so interesting that he arranged for a translation, which was published in Paul Cootner's 1964 book of finance papers (the one which included a paper by Mandelbrot, see Chapter 2).

As Samuelson later told the BBC: "After the discovery of Bachelier's work there suddenly came to the mind of all the eager workers the notion of what the Holy Grail was. There was the next step needed. It was to get the perfect formula to evaluate and to price options."[4] There were a couple of problems with Bachelier's model. For example, it allowed an asset's price to go negative – it didn't matter where it started, it could still random walk all the way down to zero and just keep going. This was corrected when Samuelson and the physicist M.F.M. Osborne suggested that it would make more sense to work with logarithms of prices. Logarithmic charts are often used in finance because they give a more realistic picture of price changes. For example, if a share price grows exponentially by 6% on average each year, then after 20 years it will have more than tripled from its initial value, and recent fluctuations will seem disproportionately large. A logarithmic plot, in contrast, will show growth as a straight line, so recent fluctuations will have the same scale as those from earlier in the series.

The plot therefore conveys how large a change is relative to the current state, which is what we usually care about. Osborne quoted as support the Weber–Fechner law from psychology: "equal ratios of physical stimulus, for example, of sound frequency in vibrations/second, or of light or sound intensity in watts per unit area, correspond to equal intervals of *subjective* sensation, such as pitch, brightness, or noise." A similar point was made by the mathematician Daniel Bernoulli in the 18th century when discussing the

---

[3] Schachermayer and Teichmann (2008).
[4] BBC (1999).

psychological effect of different rewards. Our reaction to stimuli such as noise depends not on the absolute change, in terms of decibels, but on relative change, and the same is true of stocks.

Economists therefore tweaked Bachelier's model by simply adapting it for logarithms of asset prices. In this model the asset prices themselves could never become negative, because negative logarithms still correspond to positive prices. This so-called lognormal random walk had the daily stock price return determined by a sophisticated version of dice rolling. The standard deviation could be estimated from the past variability of the stock.

This still left open the question of how to balance the risk and reward involved in purchasing the option, for those involved in just purchasing the stock, or for that matter holding the money risk free in cash. These parameters in the model seemed impossible to estimate from empirical data. Bachelier had avoided the issue by assuming that expected profits were always zero, but that didn't seem very realistic. Probably the first person to crack this problem, and get within a gnat's whisker of a fully fledged option valuation theory, was the mathematician Ed Thorp.

The Ultimate Machine

Today, wearable technology is all the rage. In 1960, though, it was rather less common. So when a woman looked across a crowded room at an MIT professor called Ed Thorp, and noticed a wire dangling from his ear, she registered astonishment. It didn't help that they were in a Las Vegas casino, and Thorp was trying to beat the casino at roulette.

Thorp's partner was Claude Shannon, who is better known today as the father of information theory (he invented the word "bit" for the 0s and 1s that make up computer language). Thorp had initially approached Shannon for advice on his research into blackjack. Shannon loved inventing machines, and his house was full of odd devices, such as automatons that could juggle, or toss coins. He didn't have a perpetual-motion machine, but he had something called the "ultimate machine," which was in some sense the opposite. This consisted of a box with a lid and a single switch. When the switch was turned on, the lid would open and a hand would emerge and turn it off again. The science fiction writer Arthur C. Clarke saw it on Shannon's desk at Bell Labs and wrote: "There is something unspeakably sinister about a machine that does nothing – absolutely nothing – except switch itself off."[5] (This is somehow reminiscent of the efficient market theory, whose only prediction is that it cannot predict.)

The 17th-century French mathematician – and one of the founders of probability theory – Blaise Pascal may have invented both the mechanical calculator and an early version of the roulette wheel, but Shannon and Thorp were certainly the first to develop a toe-operated wearable computer that could predict the trajectory of a ball as it rolled around a roulette wheel. One person, whose shoes housed the computer, would give a toe tap when the wheel's zero passed a fixed point, another tap when it passed again. Wheel position and speed calibrated. Then, as the ball was sent in the opposite direction, two more taps to calibrate the ball position and speed. The computer would do its calculations and then transmit a tone to the earpiece of the person who was placing the bet (usually Thorp), telling him which octant of the wheel to bet on.

The project was plagued with technical difficulties, and was risky since being caught cheating at a casino, at a time when such venues were often run by organized crime, was likely to lead to a beating or worse. (It seems strange to think of two professors, one of whom was the father of information theory, involved in this kind of ruse – a bit like hearing that Newton and Law had joined forces to play a shell game on the streets of Paris.)

Blackjack was a somewhat safer bet.

Thorp's idea was that the odds favored the player at some times, and the dealer at others, depending on the composition of cards that were left in the deck. So by keeping track of which cards had already been dealt, the player would know when the odds were in his favor – so when to bet small, and when to go all in. The exact fraction of the bankroll to bet, as a function of the odds, was determined using a formula – known as the Kelly criterion – developed by one of Shannon's former colleagues, John Kelly Jr. from Bell Labs.[6]

---

[5] Clarke (1958).

[6] Toss a biased coin having probability of heads. What fraction of your bankroll would you bet, at evens, on this good but not guaranteed opportunity? The Kelly criterion says you should bet a fraction. Thorp actually found the Kelly amount too volatile, so reduced the stake by about half. This is equivalent to holding back half of the bankroll as a reserve. The Kelly fraction can be derived on a napkin. Later, Nobel Laureate Robert Merton did a continuous-time version, using advanced stochastic calculus, and many pages of mathematics… and got exactly the same result.

In 1961, Kelly was the first to synthesize speech, using an IBM computer to sing the song *Daisy Bell*. Arthur C. Clarke, on another of his visits to Bell Labs, witnessed the demonstration, and made it the swan song for the HAL computer in his novel and screenplay *2001: A Space Odyssey*.

Thorp first published his research in an academic journal, but it was soon picked up by journalists. He was then contacted by a couple of high-rolling businessmen with an interest in gambling, who agreed to fund him to the tune of $10,000 to try out his method in Reno. The method worked, and Thorp managed to double his money after a few days. Even more successful, though, was his 1962 book *Beat the Dealer*, which sold several hundred thousand copies and disseminated his ideas to a wide audience. Also there was no need to travel to Las Vegas in person to play cards while wearing a disguise and dodging security (in one incident he was offered a free, but spiked, cup of coffee which nearly knocked him out).

The English humorist Douglas Adams joked about a theory "which states that if ever anybody discovers exactly what the Universe is for and why it is here, it will instantly disappear and be replaced by something even more bizarre and inexplicable." Of course, when Newton discovered the laws of gravity, the universe didn't suddenly change its rules just to annoy him. Casinos, however, do. After the publication of Thorp's book, they modified their procedures to make life much harder for card counters, for example by increasing the number of decks or the frequency of shuffles.

Thorp soon shifted his attention to a much larger casino. According to Fama, markets were efficient so could not be gamed. But as Thorp wrote, he "arrived on this scene with a unique perspective." He had already demonstrated that "the blackjack 'market' was 'inefficient'" and his work with Shannon showed that "the casino gambling 'market' had yet another 'inefficiency.'" So, "by 1964 I began to consider the greatest gambling game of all time, the stock market. Whereas I thought of card counting in blackjack as a million dollar idea, my stock market explorations would lead to a hundred million dollar idea."[7] And just as card counting would change casinos, the mathematical ideas of Thorp and others would change the markets.

---

[7] Thorp (2002).

Beat the Market

Thorp attacked the problem by looking for empirical relationships between the current stock price and the price of a call option at a specified strike price. When the two are plotted against one another as in Figure 4.1, a basic feature of the curves is that the option price should never exceed the stock price, because otherwise it would make more sense just to buy the stock instead of the option. This defined an upper bound on the maximum option price, shown by the upper dotted line. Similarly, the option price should never fall below the difference between the stock price and the strike price; because if it did, then anyone could buy the option and exchange it for stock at a profit. (For example, if the stock price was $110, the strike price was $100, and the option price was $5, it would make sense to just buy the option, use it to purchase the stock at $100, and sell it at $110 for a quick profit of $5.) This minimum bound on price, shown by the lower dotted line, would be the actual value of the option at the expiry date.

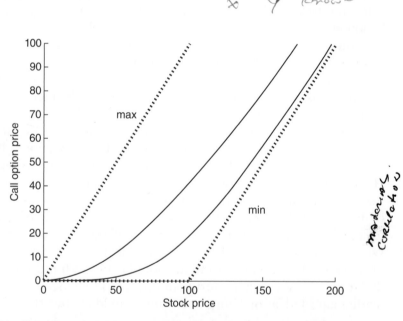

Figure 4.1   Plot of theoretical option vs. stock price curves, for a call price of $100

The upper and lower bounds are shown by dotted lines, and the empirical curves developed by Thorp and Kassouf are the solid lines between these extremes.

In practice, plots of option prices versus stock prices were somewhere between these two extremes. As the date moved closer to the expiration of the option, the price curve moved down toward the lower bound. Thorp used an equation first developed empirically by his collaborator, the economist Sheen Kassouf at Columbia, to define "normal price curves" that could then be used to identify pricing anomalies. If an option, when plotted in this way, appeared to be underpriced, they could buy the option and hedge the position by shorting the stock. More typically, they found the option was overpriced – investors were bullishly overestimating the probability that a stock would go up in price – so they would do the opposite: short the option and buy the stock. They didn't care much about the likely prospects for the underlying share, since they could profit if it went up, down, or sideways.

Either way the key idea was to hedge one contract, the option, with another, the stock. Since the option is a derivative of the stock (i.e., its value is derived from the stock), its value depends on the stock and the two are, at least theoretically, correlated with each other. See the example in Box 4.1.

Just as Thorp had used card counting to guide his betting at blackjack, so the discrepancy between theoretical and actual prices told them how much to bet in their hedging strategy. Thorp and Kassouf published their system in their 1967 book, *Beat the Market*. This method, which came to be known as convertible bond arbitrage, later spawned a number of copycat hedge funds.

Box 4.1   An Option on a Coin Toss

To get an idea of where the curves in Figure 4.1 are coming from, consider a simple gambling problem. You toss a coin four times: each time you get heads you win $1, and each time you get tails you lose $1. Sounds fair, except that you can't stand losing – so instead you decide to buy an option contract which pays as normal if you win. And you pay nothing if you lose. This contract only has upside, so you'll have to pay for it. What is the price of this option? It turns out that the answer can be found by sequentially averaging back from the possible values at the final time.

Figure 4.2 shows the possible scores (i.e. wins minus losses) on the vertical axis at each time. Also shown by the numbers on the plot are the fair option prices after each toss. The final score at time 4 can be −4, −2, 0, 2, or 4. The corresponding payouts from the option are 0, 0, 0, 2, and 4. We can solve for the other times by counting back from these "boundary conditions." At time 3, if the current score is 3, then you would pay $3 for the option, because that equals the expected payout at time 4, which is the average of $2 and $4. Continuing in this fashion, and taking the average at each step, we find that at time 0 the fair price of the option is $0.75.

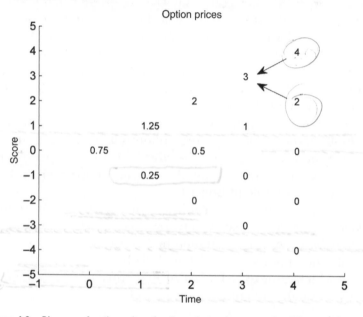

Figure 4.2   Diagram of option prices for the coin-tossing game, for different times and scores

Horizontal axis is time, which has values from 0 to 4. Vertical axis is score, which starts at 0, can be −1 or 1 at time 1, and finishes in the range −4 to 4. The numbers at each point are the option prices as a function of time and score. The option price at time 4 is equal to the payout, so is the same as the score if that is positive, and zero otherwise. The option prices at time 3 are found by averaging (indicated by arrows) the adjacent values at time 4, and so on.

Figure 4.3 compares plots of the option value as a function of the current score at time 2 and at the final time 4. At each time step, the option price curve converges to the final value. The shape of the curves is similar to those of real options, which makes sense given that price movements are usually modeled as a random walk, which is like a coin toss.

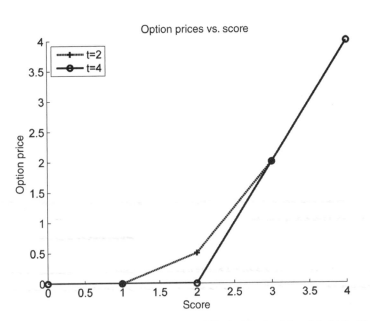

Figure 4.3   Plot of option price vs. score at time 2 (dashed line) and time 4 (solid line) for the coin-tossing game

At time 4, which is the final time, the option price is the same as the payout. The curves for other times converge to this final curve.

While this example is illustrative, it misses a couple of key attributes. One is that it does not account for things like lognormal price movements. Another is that we've already said that no one would play such a game unless they had an edge, a positive expectation. So zero expectation as a valuation method can't be right. We saw this in MPT with its theoretical link between expected return and risk. The higher the latter, the higher should be the former.

Hedging your Bets

Thorp continued to puzzle over the relationship between options and stock prices, and improving the hedging strategy, and developed an equation that seemed to capture all of the relevant details. He later said: "I just happened to guess the right formula and put it to use some years before it was published. I was convinced it was right because all the tests that I applied to it worked. It did all the right things; it gave all the right values, and had all the right properties."[8]

Thorp was using the formula for his hedge fund, making average 20%+ gains a year, and didn't want to make too much of a song and dance about it. But it would later go on to be rather well known: according to one author, it might be "the most widely used formula, with embedded probabilities, in human history."[9] The reason that it is called the Black–Scholes equation, rather than the Thorp equation, is because the University of Chicago's Fischer Black and Myron Scholes, working with MIT's Robert C. Merton, came up with – and of course published – a convincing mathematical proof, based on the accepted economic principles of equilibrium, rationality, and efficiency.

The trick was a process known as "dynamic hedging," which sounds like an advanced, and exhausting, gardening technique, but in finance actually refers to the practice of reducing or even removing risk by making trades whose risks cancel each other out as much as possible. It seems reasonable that the higher a share price is, the more valuable a call option will be. After all, the share is more likely to end up "in the money" so there's a positive profit. As the share rises in value, so does the call. As the share falls in value, so does the call. Here's a cunning idea: Why not buy a call option and simultaneously sell some stock, in such a ratio that as the stock moves about and the call moves about, this portfolio doesn't change in value?

In portfolio theory, the result of dynamic hedging is that option and stock portfolios collapse to that single point on the risk/reward diagram, the risk-free investment. But we are getting ahead of ourselves. Although Ed had found the right formula, and he knew a lot about hedging, he hadn't quite put two and two together to get 1.2 quadrillion.

Let's see an example of how hedging works. Suppose that our stock is priced at $100 and we do two things: buy a call option with a strike price of $100 and sell half a unit of stock (i.e., $50 worth) at the same time (even if we don't own the stock, we can still short it as discussed later). If the stock goes up to $101, the option pays $1, but we also lost out on $0.50 because we sold that stock before it appreciated. So the net outcome from our action is $0.50. In contrast, if

[8] Tudball (2003).
[9] Rubinstein (1994).

the stock goes down to $99, the option pays zero, but here selling the depreciating stock *saved* $0.50. So the net outcome is the same, $0.50. In other words, buying the option allows us to make $0.50 with no risk. That means the price of the option has to be $0.50 as well, because if it weren't then it would open up an arbitrage opportunity (which in theory is not allowed). Note here that we haven't used the probability of a price change anywhere in the discussion. The price is still $0.50, whether we think the stock is going up in price or falling, and such independence is the point of hedging. The value does, however, depend on our assumption that the stock moves up or down $1. If instead it was up or down $2 we'd get a different answer. And that's why option values still do depend on a stock's range, its volatility, even if not its direction.

Ed Thorp knew about the idea of hedging the option with a short position in the stock, but he hadn't considered doing this dynamically. By "dynamically" we mean that every day, and at every stock move, we have to rebalance this portfolio by more buying or selling of the underlying asset to maintain the perfect hedge ratio. Technically, every day isn't fast enough. Hourly? Minute by minute? Still not often enough. Technically we really do mean continuously. In the jargon this perfect hedge ratio is called the "Delta." In the example above, we sold half a unit of stock so Delta was 0.5.

It was Black, Scholes, and Merton who showed in an absolutely watertight mathematical framework that by maintaining this dynamic Delta hedge one could construct a portfolio that was entirely risk free. Its return should therefore be the same as a risk-free asset such as a bank account. In mathematical terms, this acted as a constraint on the equations and made it possible to solve for the option price. Dynamic hedging also pointed to a way for banks to construct any kind of option and make money from it. They could sell an option to a client with a built-in profit margin, and perform dynamic hedging so they carried no risk themselves.

The model was again based on a lognormal random walk model, with constant standard deviation, and assumed the other tenets of efficient market theory – for example, the hedging argument assumed that stocks were correctly priced, and that "speculators would try to profit by borrowing large amounts of money" to exploit any small anomaly that might appear. The solutions to the equation again look a lot like the curves in Figure 4.1, and can be solved numerically in a manner similar to that outlined in Box 4.1, by working backwards from the option's value at expiry. In the early 1970s Black and Scholes had difficulty getting their paper published, but the formula, or rather its rigorous derivation, later won Scholes and Merton a "Nobel Prize" (Black died before the award was made). See Box 4.2 for further details.

Box 4.2   Emission Control

At the risk of alienating our core audience of math-phobes, here is what the Black–Scholes equation looks like:

$$\frac{\partial V}{\partial k} + \frac{1}{2}\sigma^2 S^2 \frac{\partial V}{\partial S^2} + rS\frac{\partial V}{\partial S} - rV = 0$$

Here, S is the price of the underlying stock, which changes with time according to a random walk. V is the price of the derivative, which will depend on both time and stock price, and is what we are trying to solve. The fixed parameters are the stock's volatility σ, and the risk-free rate r. This is a differential equation because it includes rates of change – the first term for example measures how quickly V is changing with time. The equation is solved by including so-called boundary conditions, in this case the initial value of the stock and the strike price. Depending on context, the solution can be expressed as an equation, or there are many online calculators available. Plotting the price of a call option V as a function of initial stock price S gives a curve like one of the solid lines in Figure 4.1.

Many pages have been written, and much ink spilled, on the awesome beauty, elegance, and power of this equation. We should emphasize that when it was found in the 1970s, nothing like it had ever been seen before in the world of finance. The god Apollo himself would have marveled at the far-reaching nature of its mathematical… Hang on. This just in. Apparently the equation is the same as a… reaction–diffusion–convection equation? Has anyone heard of that? Used all the time in fluid dynamics. I see. Dispersion of pollutants. Vehicle emissions controls, that kind of thing. New then is it? More of a 19th-century thing. *Early* 19th century. Pretty much 200 years old. Did its inventors win a Nobel? No, I suppose it was before… Just doing their job. Right.

Well there we have it, an equation which can be used for finance or vehicle emissions controls. Who would have thought there could be a connection between those two areas?

Mathematical Dynamite

At this point we should acknowledge that certain writers and critics have pointed out that the economics version of the Nobel Prize is properly called the "Sveriges Riksbank Prize in Economic Sciences in Memory of Alfred Nobel."[10] The award was created in 1969, seven decades after Nobel's death, by the Bank of Sweden, so some consider it to be a glorified version of a bank prize. Peter Nobel said in 2004 that the bank had "infringed on the trademarked name of Nobel. Two thirds of the Bank's prizes in economics have gone to US economists of the Chicago School who create mathematical models to speculate in stock markets and options – the very opposite of the purposes of Alfred Nobel to improve the human condition."

On the contrary, as the inventor of dynamite, Alfred Nobel was clearly into *blowing stuff up*. And given that derivatives such as options would later help to blow up much of the world financial system, we think that the Nobel association is appropriate (he may even have felt kudos were due). So, in the context of this book, "Nobel" it is!

As discussed above, aesthetic principles such as elegance and symmetry play an important role in science and in finance; and in aesthetic terms at least the great appeal of Black–Scholes (sometimes called Black–Scholes–Merton or BSM in recognition of Merton's contribution) was that, unlike earlier versions of option-pricing models, it needed – in true Newtonian fashion – only a single parameter to describe the stock, namely its volatility. The growth rate of the stock had just dropped out somewhere in their derivation. What this means in practice is that the value of a call option, or indeed any option, depends only on the volatility of the underlying asset, and not on how fast the stock is growing. Even though a stock that is growing rapidly is more likely to end up in the money, is more likely to end up a long way in the money, is more likely to make a profit, and that profit is more likely to be huge… this doesn't affect the theoretical value of an option. The option value would be the same if the underlying share price was falling off a cliff. Only the volatility mattered. Counterintuitive or what? But the reason again is that Black–Scholes showed how to hedge the option with the stock. As they wrote in their paper, "in equilibrium, the return on such a hedged position must be equal to the return on a riskless asset." If you hold

---

[10] See, e.g., Henderson (2004).

this hedged portfolio you just don't care whether the stock is rising or falling.

Note that, while the Black–Scholes formula might not be able to directly incorporate *your* view of the growth rate as a tunable parameter, the market view does appear indirectly through the current stock price. If you are buying a stock, then the price you are willing to pay will depend on your perception of its expected future value, balanced against a risk premium. Two people with different views of these factors will therefore arrive at different prices, and the market price will reflect a kind of consensus view. When pricing an option with Black–Scholes, the formula takes the stock price as a given, and assumes that the option is priced "correctly" in the sense that it reflects the risk–reward balance baked into the market stock price. It does this by shifting to a risk-neutral setting, which takes the risk premium out of the picture. When this is done, the only parameter left over is volatility – and again, using different values will give different results. For this reason, option prices are often interpreted as reflecting views on volatility, while stock prices are seen as reflecting views on growth, but in fact both represent a similar trade-off between risk and reward. And if you disagree with the market's assessment of a stock's growth potential, then yes you will disagree with the option price produced by Black–Scholes, but you will also disagree with the current stock price produced by the market.

No Risk

Traders now had a rigorous framework for valuing options. It was a framework based on a model for the underlying asset, with some important concepts such as dynamic hedging. Valuation even got reinterpreted abstractly in terms of imaginary worlds where imaginary people valued imaginary options with imaginary behavior. Valuation had shrunk down to that single point on Markowitz's risk–return diagram, the market price of risk for hedged options was zero, economists had no reason to worry about inconvenient human characteristics such as risk aversion… never ever.

Now, at this stage in the book the average reader may be thinking, yay, so now I know how to calculate the price of an option – what's the point of that? Unless you're a quant – in which case you will already have been exposed to this information, albeit without the interesting historical background and pithy asides. However, our aim is to demystify the topic, show the assumptions that are being made, and also give a sense of how some fairly basic mathematics could dramatically affect the world of finance.

For this simple formula did much more than simulate option prices – it changed them, by putting option trading on what appeared to be a sound mathematical basis. Recall that in the early 1970s, option trading was very small scale, in part because of its association with gambling. This all changed after Black–Scholes caught on. With the encouragement of University of Chicago economics professors including Milton Friedman, the Chicago Board Options Exchange opened for business in April 1973. As its counsel explained: "Black–Scholes was really what enabled the exchange to thrive… [I]t gave a lot of legitimacy to the whole notions of hedging and efficient pricing, whereas we were faced, in the late 60s–early 70s with the issue of gambling. That issue fell away, and I think Black–Scholes made it fall away. It wasn't speculation or gambling, it was efficient pricing. I think the SEC [Securities and Exchange Commission] very quickly thought of options as a useful mechanism in the securities markets and it's probably – that's my judgement – the effects of Black–Scholes. [Soon] I never heard the word 'gambling' again in relation to options."[11] It also helped that Texas Instruments and Hewlett Packard came out with handheld calculators that could easily handle the Black–Scholes formula.

The formula also contained within it the promise of a perfect, automated system for making money. By dynamically hedging their bets, those who understood the Black–Scholes formula could exploit anomalies in bond and stock markets to make what appeared to be risk-free profits, without needing to worry about the messy realities of the underlying company. Finance now existed on a higher mathematical plane, serenely detached from the rest of the world. As the derivatives trader Stan Jonas puts it: "The basic dynamic of the Black–Scholes model is the idea that through dynamic hedging we can eliminate risk, so we have a mathematical argument for trading a lot. What a wonderful thing for exchanges to hear. The more we trade, the better off the society is because the less risk there is. So we have to have more contracts, more futures exchanges, we have to be able to trade the Nikkei futures in Japan, we have to be able to trade options in Germany. Basically in order to reduce risk we have

---

[11] Quoted in MacKenzie (2006, p. 158).

to trade everywhere and all the time."[12] In 2000, Alan Greenspan testified to Congress that this ability to hedge risk had made the financial system more robust: "I believe that the general growth in large institutions has occurred in the context of an underlying structure in markets in which many of the larger risks are dramatically – I should say fully – hedged."[13]

Positive Feedback

So, did the formula make the markets more efficient? It certainly seemed that way. As traders began to adopt the formula, prices converged so that it was more difficult to arbitrage between stock and option prices. A rule of finance, known as the "law of one price," says that the price of a security, commodity, or asset will be the same anywhere once things like exchange rates and expenses are taken into consideration, since otherwise an arbitrageur can buy cheap in one place and sell in another. However, as seen in the next chapter, the fact that markets agree on one price does not necessarily mean they have converged to the right price (whatever that is) or that the price will be stable. The Black–Scholes model is an elegant equation which is useful so long as its limitations are understood; but any formula which is based on the perfect, symmetrical, stable, rational, and normal world of abstract economics, where investors can effectively make predictions about the future of a stock based on nothing more than past volatility, will never be a realistic model.[14]

The disassociation from gambling was also not entirely positive. Gamblers are aware that they are dealing with risk and can lose their stake. The idea that in finance you could even come close to eliminating risk through the use of hedging strategies, in contrast, led some firms (not Thorp's) to a dangerous hubris.

As an example: in 1976, the three founders of the firm Leland, O'Brien, and Rubinstein (LOR) had a brilliant idea, which was to use the Black–Scholes option valuation model to protect stock portfolios against crashes. If you are worried about the possibility of a stock-market crash then there are several things you can do. You could

---

[12]BBC (1999).
[13]This was in response to a question from Bernie Sanders. See US House of Representatives, Committee on Banking and Financial Services (2000).
[14]See Haug and Taleb (2009).

sell some, or even all, of your portfolio. But then what if the market rises? Or you could buy put options to protect the downside. But put options are overpriced (most insurance is overpriced), and you'd be forever rolling over your options as they expire, and buying and selling as your portfolio changes. But Black and Scholes had shown how you can make options synthetically. We've explained that the Black–Scholes model shows how to hedge an option by dynamically buying and selling the underlying shares. Well, what if you go about the motions of buying and selling but without actually owning any options? If you do that then you've replicated a short position in the same contract. Change the signs, by buying when you would have sold and vice versa, and you've made a synthetic long position.

The result was a new form of portfolio insurance. On behalf of their clients, LOR would buy and sell index futures so as to replicate a put option, only more cheaply (again, futures are a contract which *obliges* you to buy or sell at a fixed price in the future, while puts give you the choice but at a price). And you could specify how much was the maximum loss you could sustain, a bit like the strike price of an option.

The technique amounted to something like the following. As the market fell, they'd start selling futures. As it rose, they'd buy them back. As the market fell further, the short position would grow so that beyond a certain point you'd stop caring anymore. As the market rose higher and higher, they'd buy back the futures so that you wouldn't lose out on the upside.

Can you see the fatal flaw in the business model? Or perhaps it's not a flaw (we'll return to this later in Box 10.1).

As the market rises so the model, the Black–Scholes model, says buy more of the futures. And what happens when people buy *en masse*? And when the market falls, the same formula tells them to sell. And when a lot of people sell, what happens to the price? Yes, it's positive feedback. And we don't mean positive in a good way.

Positive feedback accentuates small perturbations, the famous (but rather misleading[15]) example being the butterfly effect. Mainstream economics, being all about stability, has little to say on the

---

[15]The idea that the weather is a system so amazingly sensitive that even a butterfly's wings can disturb it (see Gleick, 1987, p. 18) is matched only by the efficient market hypothesis as a charming but fundamentally daft excuse for forecast error (see Orrell *et al.*, 2001; Orrell, 2002; Wolfram, 2002, p. 998).

topic of positive feedback; it prefers to concentrate on negative feedback, which reduces fluctuations. An example is the invisible hand, where if prices depart too much from their "natural" level, suppliers enter or leave the markets and equilibrium is restored. But both types of feedback play a role in finance.

In the period leading up to Black Monday in 1987 there was about $60 billion worth of assets protected by portfolio insurance. That's $60 billion following, religiously, the same formula. It's the mathematical equivalent of everyone on one side of the world jumping in the air at the same time. Which is why, ironically, portfolio insurance has been cited as one of the factors behind the crash.

Another firm to experience the risky and fragile nature of risk management was Long-Term Capital Management (LTCM), whose partners included both Scholes and Merton. It used its expertise in option pricing to construct complicated and highly leveraged financial bets. As their October 1993 prospectus said, "The reduction in the Portfolio Company's volatility through hedging could permit the leveraging up of the resulting position to the same expected level of volatility as an unhedged position, but with a larger expected return."[16] The strategy was highly profitable right up until August 1998, when the Russian government decided to default on its bonds. Dynamical hedging doesn't work so well in a crisis, when no one wants to execute your orders. The company had to be rescued at a cost of $3.6 billion in order to avoid an even greater crisis.

LTCM had miscalculated the real risk levels because they didn't take model error into account. Of course, this did not stop people from using the same models to trade/gamble on derivatives, or prevent the market/casino from growing in size. The next chapter looks at how derivatives allowed the world money supply to blossom in a way that John Law could only have dreamt of; and how this came to an abrupt end only in September 2008, when the lid of the box creaked open, the invisible hand reached slowly out, and the financial system turned itself off.

---

[16]Taylor (2004, p. 257).

CHAPTER 5

Deriving Derivatives

"The underpinning of quantitative finance is arbitrage pricing theory. The fundamental assumption is that markets are efficient."
—Response to the survey question:
"How would you describe quantitative finance
at a dinner party?" at wilmott.com

"We shape our tools, and afterwards our tools shape us."
—Marshall McLuhan, *Understanding Media:*
The Extensions of Man

Once the markets had a model for valuing derivatives there was no longer any excuse for not trading them. The market in options exploded. New financial instruments were created using the same kinds of mathematical model... new and increasingly complicated instruments. As the instruments got more complicated, so did the mathematical models. Where once there were traders in Savile Row suits drinking far too much at lunchtime, now there were geeks with badly fitting suits and PhDs. If you had a degree in mathematics or physics, then a job as one of those geeky quants became your goal.

A framework for valuing derivatives was all that was needed to ignite the fuse that led to the explosion in new and increasingly complex derivative contracts. The gullible might say that having a decent theoretical foundation for valuation and risk management allowed quants to create new instruments with known characteristics and whose risks could be understood, measured, and controlled. The cynical might say that having a foundation, any foundation, even the shakiest and dodgiest on sandy soil, over a defunct mine, at the edge of a cliff, in an earthquake zone, was perfect if all you needed was, in the language coined by the CIA, "plausible deniability" when the trade goes wrong. In this chapter we are going to look at some of the contracts that came into existence after the great derivatives-valuation breakthrough, as well as the new models that were created to value them. And we'll see how the brilliant idea of hedging was stretched to breaking point and beyond.

In the early 1970s, when the option-pricing work of Black, Scholes, and Merton was gaining recognition, the financial world was still reeling from the so-called Nixon Shock. In August 1971, Richard Nixon took the US dollar off the gold standard and ushered in a new era of floating currencies. As stock and commodity options began to be traded in force on the new Chicago Board Options Exchange (CBOE), they were soon joined by an even larger market: currency options. Chicago's International Money Market was initially set up in 1972 to sell currency futures, which are agreements to exchange set amounts of currencies at future dates, but it soon diversified into broader types of currency option. For the first time in the history of derivatives, theory and practice were in perfect alignment. Everything from yen/dollar swaps to pork bellies was up for the Black–Scholes treatment.

Standardization of contracts and trading on an exchange are important if participants are to trust the market, allowing large quantities to be traded with no risk of confusion about contract terms or risk of default. And a mathematical formula that everyone could agree on removed much of the mystery about these new derivatives. A trader only needed to tap some numbers into their Texas Instruments calculator to get a price on an option, courtesy of Black–Scholes. (This particular feature was announced by a half-page ad in the *Wall Street Journal.* Scholes, being an economist, approached the company for royalties, but was told the formula was in the public domain.[1])

Traders became so accustomed to using the Black–Scholes model that its parameters took on a life of their own. For example,

---

[1] See European Finance Association (2008).

suppose a call option on a stock was selling for a particular price. The model price for that option depends on the stock's volatility, whose value as discussed above is not completely certain or stable. But if you run the model, knowing already what the market price is, then you can infer what level of volatility is consistent with that price. Traders often found it convenient to quote this "implied volatility" along with the actual cost, because it acted as another playing-field leveler that could be compared for different contracts. In theory, the implied volatility should be the same for every option. In practice, Black Monday had taught traders that the Black–Scholes formula underpriced protection against extreme events, because of its baked-in assumption of "normal" behavior where such events are effectively impossible. Traders continued to use the formula, but tailored the volatility parameter according to the details of the contract. The implied volatility of an underlying therefore varied with things like strike price and exercise time. This was a warning sign that all was not well with this system, but at least it was convenient.

All of this convergence did not mean, though, that the derivative world became simpler. Instead, the scene was set for parallel stories of increasing complexity of products and their models. As soon as traders were comfortable with pricing the basic derivatives, they moved on to more sophisticated and exciting products.

Time to Exercise

One of the more straightforward, at least conceptually if not mathematically, variations to the terms of the basic call and put options is to change when you are allowed to exercise them. The options described here so far are what are known as "European." They allow exercise only at expiration. "American" options allow exercise at any time prior to expiration. (The designations are centuries old and have nothing whatsoever to do with location.) It's clear that American options can't have a value less than an equivalent, *ceteris paribus*, European contract, since if you hold an American option you could just decide not to exercise it early. The freedom to exercise any time you like clearly adds value: the question is, how much?

Although this seems a simple enough question, mathematically it's not so straightforward. Even the great Fischer Black had problems solving it. Ed Thorp tells of a meeting with Black at a Chicago securities conference in May 1975: "I brought along my solution to the

American put problem and had placed a folder of graphs on the table to show him. Then he said no one had solved the problem... I realized I had a fiduciary duty to my investors to keep our secrets, and quietly put my folder with the world's first American put curves back in my briefcase."[2] Thorp put his obligations to his investors above mathematical glory – which shows another difference between physics and finance, and is a good example of how the best ideas in finance are often in no rush to surface.

To understand why the American option is difficult to value theoretically you should put yourself in the shoes of the person selling the option, the writer. We've seen that options are risky investments because of the unknown behavior of the underlying asset, which we model mathematically as a random walk. And we've seen how to hedge exposure to this behavior by continuously buying or selling the underlying asset in a clever way as it moves around in price. However, with American options there's another risk for the writer that is harder to model mathematically, and that's the risk inherent in the timing of the option's exercise. If the American option cannot be worth less than a European option, then that potential extra value must be linked to when the American option is exercised. And there's the rub: We don't know when the option will be exercised because that's in the control of the owner of the option. And therefore we don't know how much extra value to add. Somehow we have to model the behavior of the option holder. Three methods spring to mind.

The first is to assume that the option holder exercises at a random time. After all, in finance we like to model everything we can as random. Before we start postulating distributions for this exercise (do we toss a coin, roll a die, consult the I Ching?), there is a big snag. If we value the American option this way and word gets around, then buyers might find a strategy that gives the option greater value than this "average value." We'll find people queuing up to buy American options from us, all exercising at the same time, and we'd lose a fortune.

An alternative, then, is to assume that the buyer acts in a rational way. He will exercise at a time that maximizes his expected utility. Or something. We've mentioned such ideas before. And as always with utility theories you have to figure out what the "utility function" of the holder is, assuming such a thing exists. If we were the holder then we

---

[2] Thorp (2003).

could conceivably model our own utility function. However, we are in the position of the option writer, and it's not as if we could ask the buyer to complete a psychometric-evaluation questionnaire. So, we've no idea about his utility function. Then there's method three.

Assume that the option holder exercises at the time that maximizes the option's theoretical value. This is subtle. We don't believe that the option holder will exercise at this time, but the point is that he *could* do, which is the worst-case scenario that we need to protect against. And this is the recognized correct method.

To understand how this works, let's break it down into manageable pieces. The first piece is that we, the option seller, are going to be delta hedging to remove market risk, leaving us with only exercise-time risk. We don't know the option holder's plans, he might even change his mind, but to guarantee we don't lose any money on this deal we have to assume that the holder exercises in whatever way is worst for us. (Even though we hope he won't. It's not as if it's personal, is it?) And that is like saying that the option holder will exercise whenever it maximizes the theoretical value of the option. So, whatever that theoretical maximum is, that's what we sell the option for (plus our profit margin). If we were to sell for less than this highest value then the holder himself would start delta hedging to get rid of market risk, and then exercise at the optimal time. He'd have the opposite position to us but with the benefit of having bought the option cheap, from us, and would therefore make a risk-free profit at our expense.[3]

As well as a theoretical option value, this method results in information about early exercise, which can be represented as a plot with time and asset price as the axes and regions, which can be called "hold" and "exercise." When the asset price moves into an area labeled "exercise," that's when our model assumes that the holder will exercise the option.

Part of the subtlety in this idea is that the option holder will almost certainly exercise at some time other than that we have modeled. Maybe he decides to exercise to lock in a profit or cut his losses, or isn't paying attention. Chances are he just isn't going to exercise at exactly the time we have modeled.

---

[3] It does happen that if a contract is mispriced by one bank then other banks start trading with them, taking advantage of the mispricing to make a profit. Word gets around, and the arbitrage tends not to last that long.

Now here's a question for you, intelligent reader: How do we feel about him exercising at a time different from that we have modeled?

If you think we are disappointed, because this then means that our model is wrong, then go back and reread the above. Go to the bottom of the class.

If you think we are pleased then you are correct. After all, exercise at any time different from the optimal exercise time means that the exercise was suboptimal, and means that we are going to make a profit (above even the markup). Go to the top of the class, you are smarter than the *Journal of Finance*.[4] Complexity usually works in favor of the person selling something, because it puts the onus on the buyer to figure out how to get maximum value from it (see mobile phone contracts).

It's worth mentioning at this point that we've now seen the three main ways that quants eliminate, or at least reduce, risks. To recap, we have the following techniques:

- *Diversify.* Used in MPT – exploiting correlations between assets to reduce risk.

- *Delta hedge.* An extreme form of correlation exploitation, if you like. Assuming that the option pricing model perfectly captures the option's dependence on the price of its underlying asset (it won't), then the correlation between an option and the underlying is also perfect, and thus you can theoretically eliminate risk entirely.

- *Worst case.* Some things are out of your control, but could be controlled and exploited by others, and they aren't simply random. Here you assume that the worst happens to give the worst possible outcome. The good news is that the worst is unlikely to happen, and so there is extra profit to be made. Which is one reason why exciting new financial products are often designed to be as complicated as possible.

---

[4] A paper on this topic was rejected by the *Journal of Finance*. Remember that optimality in the valuation of an American option is only meaningful to a writer who is delta hedging. Optimality to the option holder is a completely different (mathematical or not) problem, and he can exercise whenever he likes. Many businesses are like this. If you produce phone software you should add any features that are cheap to implement even if they aren't going to be used. If they are used and result in more calls then you will make more money. We don't think that the editors of the *Journal of Finance* have ever run a business.

Decision Cost

Early exercise is a simple example of a feature that you see in lots of sophisticated financial instruments. It's called a "decision" feature for obvious reasons. It's not always the option holder who gets to make the decision though, it can also be the writer, as in the case of a callable bond in which the issuer can call back the bond for a pre-specified amount. Or it could be a third party who makes the decision affecting the contract's value. Whoever makes the decision, the same valuation principle applies – value the contract by assuming that the worst happens (if it's not you making the decision) or the best (if you can make it).

As financial derivatives got more and more complex, so you would also see decision features cropping up in some of them. And they added a lot of mathematical interest to quant finance. Classical derivatives theory, as presented by Black and Scholes in 1973, was very similar to the physical problems of heat transfer and diffusion. Heat transfer is about how temperature changes through a medium, how the radiators in your living room will warm up the surroundings, for example. Diffusion is about how particles move through a medium, such as contaminants in a river. With derivatives, the probability distribution of asset prices is diffusing in time, and becoming less concentrated or certain as we go further into the future. But in all these cases, the geometry of the problem remains stable. A radiator heats your room by distributing heat, but – unless you have some really serious plumbing issues – doesn't itself move or change shape. Similarly, the buyer of a European option only cares about the price at the exercise time, so that restriction imposes a kind of fixed boundary on the problem.

In contrast, the mathematics one finds in American options is much trickier, because now the exercise time can move around. An analogous problem from the physical sciences would be something like the melting of an iceberg. Heat flows through the ice and the surrounding water. As ice melts, or as water freezes, the boundary between the ice and water moves. This boundary can be represented by physical coordinates as a function of time. Think of the ice/water boundary being like the exercise/hold boundary in the American option. It's not immediately obvious how that boundary changes, and in fact finding that boundary is part of the problem. In mathematical language it's called a "free boundary." In the American option the boundary to be found is the line between where it is optimal to exercise the option, and where it is optimal not to exercise.

This simple change to the contract specification, from European to American exercise, adds a great deal of interest for mathematicians. In most situations the equations cannot be solved directly, so approximate solutions must be obtained using computer simulations. Many PhDs have been written just on this one topic. And it's typical of how mathematically interesting quantitative finance was becoming, even in the early years after the Black–Scholes model was published.

New Flavors

In its early years, quantitative finance was mainly practiced in the halls of academe, or through the occasional consulting gig. In 1983, Fischer Black became one of the first full-time quants, when he left the University of Chicago to set up a Quantitative Strategies Group at Goldman Sachs. Recruiting newly minted math and physics PhDs to join the group was easy. The Cold War had led to a bubble in science education, as Americans tried to out-science their Soviet rivals; but there weren't enough actual jobs developing space laser systems or whatever to employ the graduates, with the result that many were happy to make the switch to finance – especially since the pay was much better.

European and American options are called in the jargon "vanilla" options, because of their simplicity and ubiquity, and they are usually traded on an exchange such as the CBOE. As quantitative finance developed into a profession, quants turned their collective genius to inventing contracts with more and more complex behavior. These contracts are typically not traded on an exchange, but might be designed for a particular client. They are called "over the counter" (OTC).[5] We'll describe a few to help you understand how traders and quants think:

- *Barrier option.* Suppose you think that a stock is going to rise, but only a little bit. You'd consider buying a call option for

---

[5] We don't know why they aren't called made to measure, or bespoke. Over the counter seems the opposite of what they are. Perhaps it's because quants buy their suits at Marks & Spencer or local equivalent?

its leverage. However, the price you pay for the call represents the potential for the stock to rise enormously, and you don't think this will happen. So you could buy an up-and-out call option. This contract pays off like a call option if the stock rises, but if the stock rises so far as to hit some pre-set trigger level any time before expiration, then it "knocks out" and becomes worthless. This is perfect for you, you just choose a trigger level above where you think the stock might rise. And this contract can cost far less than a vanilla call.

- *Lookback option.* Imagine you were the world's greatest investor. Your timing is perfect, such that you always buy at the lowest stock price and sell at the highest, during some timeframe. Dream on? No, there exists a contract that pays off exactly that amount, the difference between the highest and lowest price over some period. It's called a lookback option. It makes you the perfect trader. Oh, but it's very expensive.

As mentioned above, options don't have to be based on shares. They can have anything as an underlying. Commodity prices, exchange rates, etc. Let's look at an option that might be perfect for you if you run a business that sells stuff to a foreign country:

- *Asian option.* You manufacture widgets. You sell them abroad at a fixed price in the foreign currency. Your sales are fairly regular. Your skills are in manufacturing, not in forecasting exchange rates, so you really don't want to be exposed to exchange-rate risk. Quite frankly you'd like to focus on manufacturing and outsource any currency hedging. Well, you can. All you need is an Asian option. (Again, the name has nothing to do with Asia, except that in 1987 its American inventors happened to be working in Tokyo.) This contract has a payoff that depends on the average exchange rate over some period. And since your sales are regular, it's the average exchange rate that you are exposed to.

All of the above contracts require only fairly minor extensions to the Black–Scholes model, and all are still based on the idea of delta hedging to construct a risk-free portfolio. Such contracts are called "exotics" or "structured products" (the latter tends to be when the instruments have interest-rate exposure, of which more shortly). There are countless new products. Here's one that introduces us to new modeling challenges:[6]

- *Multi-asset options.* So far the derivatives we've seen have had a single underlying. This means that the payoff only depends on the behavior of a single financial quantity, such as a share or an exchange rate. It's not difficult to imagine a contract that pays off something to do with several assets. For example, the payoff is the best performing out of ten shares. Or with underlyings in several asset classes, such as a contract that pays off in dollars on a share that is quoted in sterling. When there are multiple underlyings, you have the same problem that you have with MPT, how to model the relationships between assets. Do you rely on correlation, given that it is so unstable?

You can't Always Delta Hedge

And then there is the bond market. Bonds represent loans, and so their value as investments fluctuates depending on interest rates. A bond which pays 8% might seem like a reasonable investment if the base interest rate is only 6%, but it loses some of its attractiveness if base rates suddenly go to 12%. Bond prices therefore tend to be inversely correlated with base rates. In the 1980s the Federal Reserve's benchmark rate was bouncing in the range of 6–19% as its central bankers struggled with the effects of stagflation. This made bonds an exciting area to work in, and it was only a matter of time before option theory was being adapted to model bonds as a kind of derivative, with interest rates as the underlying. The aim of the modeling was actually not so much to price the bonds themselves, whose prices are what they are in the market, but to value the more complex, non-traded exotics, the structured products.

Now, while option theory could be applied to bonds by assuming that interest rates follow a random walk, there is an important difference between things like stocks, currencies, and commodities on the

---

[6] Exotics have all sorts of strange names and features. Foodie quants might be interested to know that sadly a google of "Madagascan vanilla option" currently yields nothing. This might be a good opportunity to create a new derivative, one that's slightly more sophisticated than the usual. And it should be reassuringly expensive.

one hand, and things like interest rates and credit on the other. You can find derivatives with all of these, and more, as underlyings, but the first group are easier to model than the second. This is because the basic quantity that one models in the first group is traded.

Stocks and shares are traded, and so it's easy to hedge options based on them. The same is true for options on currencies and commodities.

However sometimes, in fact extremely often, we have options on things that aren't traded. And that presents valuation problems. If you can't construct a risk-free portfolio with options and its underlying then you're back in Markowitz's world, no longer at that single risk-free dot but out in the wide-open spaces of non-zero risk, hard-to-measure expected returns, and market prices of risk.

The most important such options are surprisingly those based on interest rates. And that's because interest rates aren't traded. No, seriously. Bonds are traded, so are swaps, but these aren't the same as the rate that you are getting from your bank right now. That 0.5% isn't traded. If it helps, think of bonds as like the above Asian options, the bond's value depends on the average of a fluctuating instantaneous interest rate until maturity.

This presents a modeling problem, because even the simplest zero-coupon government bond becomes like a derivative of an interest rate. We can go through the whole Black–Scholes dynamic hedging argument, but to eliminate interest-rate risk we have to do something clever like hedging a one-year bond with, say, a one-month bond.

Delta hedging, that most fundamental and crucial idea from the early days of quantitative finance, is much harder in some markets than in others. But this wasn't going to stop the quants pretending that it worked.

Market Price of Risk Again

This might all seem a bit esoteric, but it's of great importance in the story of quantitative finance. For this is possibly the first, or most important, time that quants started cheating. Or maybe let's just call it brushing things under the carpet.

The difference between the traded and the untraded is one of the key distinctions between good models and poor. When the underlying is easy to hedge with, then the Black–Scholes derivation leads to an equation for the value of an option. That's one equation for one unknown. But if we go through the same derivation line by line for an interest-rate product, we now find that we still end up with one equation but two unknowns. In the above example the unknowns would be the one-year bond and the one-month bond. This means that we don't have a unique value for either of them. Instead, we can only value them relative to each other. It turns out that we can value all interest-rate derivatives if we bring in one unifying function – the market price of risk for the interest rate. The hedging argument tells us that all fixed-income instruments should receive the same compensation for taking risk, that's the same market price of risk, since they all have the same risk exposure – interest rates. We are back with Harry Markowitz, just not at that left-hand risk-free dot where we'd like to be, feeling safe and comfortable.

So hopefully – and this is where things get mushy – we can treat this market price of risk as some kind of fixed parameter of the system, which will give the extra piece of information needed to solve our equations.

It looks like we are back on track again. And superficially it does appear that way. Sadly though, this hedging isn't quite so trouble free.

When you read the economics or finance textbooks you get the impression that the market price of risk is something nice. Like three. After all, it's the measure of how much compensation above the risk-free rate one requires for taking a unit of risk. How rational is that? But in practice the market price of risk is unstable. It's also different for each source of risk; each stock has one, so do rates, currencies, etc. And it's not easy to measure.

Figure 5.1 shows a plot[7] of the market price of risk for US short-term rates. It's definitely not a simple three.

This is one of Paul's favorite financial graphs, because it shows what should be blindingly obvious.[8] The market price of risk is not that nice, stable quantity implied by the textbooks. It's all over the shop. One day it's high, one day it's low. Some days it even has the wrong sign – people are paying to take risk. Surely everyone, bar economists, knows that's just kinda how people are. In the figure are labels "fear" and "greed." These are totally unscientific, but we can

---

[7] See Ahmad and Wilmott (2007) for the methodology. Our figure is an updated version of the one in that paper.
[8] You can get your own signed copy from...

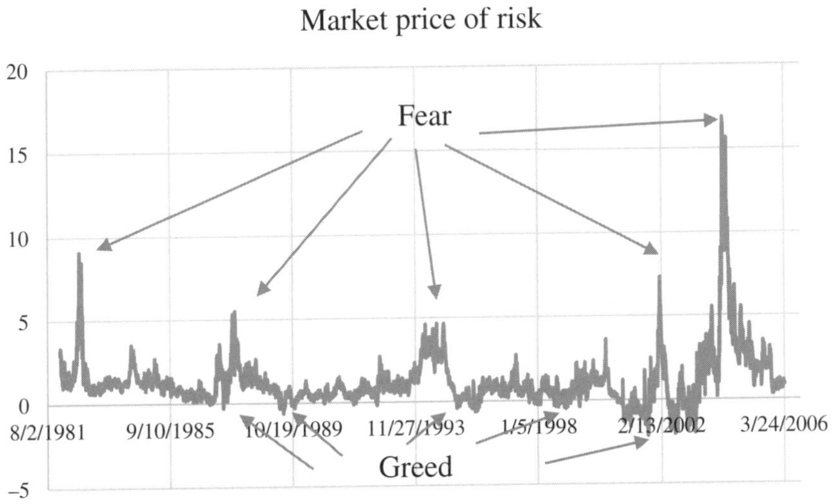

Market price of risk

Figure 5.1   Market price of risk

say that where the spikes are particularly large represents a fearful market, where a greater compensation than usual is required for risk taking. Greed is when the compensation has the wrong sign. That's like buying a lottery ticket, with its negative expectations.

Black–Scholes relies on knowing the volatility, which is already an unstable parameter, but now it has been joined by something even worse. And second, the assumed correlation between the one-year bond and the one-month bond isn't seen in practice; the correlation is far from perfect. The perfect correlation was a by-product of assuming that the instantaneous forward rate was the sole driver for all values. Typically there will be more than one random factor governing a valuation.

It was at this point – as quants issued more and more of these complex, unhedgeable instruments – that they made a sort of collective decision to *not worry*. At precisely the point where they should have. The Black–Scholes model was looking pretty good for traded underlyings, and so they wanted to use it when the underlying was not traded, even though it came with some major drawbacks. It was tempting to look the other way. Let's not frighten the horses when there are so many dollars at stake. Slippery slopes, slippery slopes. The quants had to become masters of cognitive dissonance. Not worrying became part of the job – along with those ill-fitting suits.

Getting Carried Away

If you don't worry too much about the practicality of valuation when the underlying is not traded, then you won't have a problem with derivatives based on the following:

- *Credit.* Businesses are risky. They issue contracts, such as bonds, that are exposed to risk of default (as well as interest rates). Risk of default is not traded, and is hard to model, but has historically been one of the largest concerns of banks. Traditionally it was handled by careful screening of loan candidates, and diversification. But that is a lot of work. Another approach, discussed further below, is tools such as credit default swaps (CDSs). These can be considered a form of insurance, which pay out in the case of "credit events" such as default. To price them, some people build models that take ideas from fundamental analysis, others just treat bankruptcy as a random event triggered by something like a coin toss. Credit derivatives models are therefore dubious.

- *Macro.* A portion of that credit risk is due to the overall state of the economy – bankruptcies go up during a recession. To protect against this, some derivatives use economic variables such as a manufacturing or payroll index as the underlying. Hard to model, and nigh on impossible to hedge.

- *Inflation.* You can have instruments with inflation as the underlying. Again this is not traded. And it's also something that governments try to control, albeit without perfect success.

- *Property.* There are also property derivatives, based on real-estate indices such as the S&P/Case-Shiller Home Price Indices in the USA. These can be used to hedge property risk or speculate on the property market. Although property is traded, it is so illiquid that tradability is virtually irrelevant.

- *Energy.* Energy derivatives have wonderful potential for modeling. Energy is difficult to store, its value changes erratically and to an extreme degree. Hedging is difficult. See the discussion of Enron below.

- *Weather.* Weather has a huge impact on many individual businesses and the economy as a whole. So if you want insurance, you might consider weather derivatives. But you can't hedge weather by buying or selling rain or snow. At least not directly. You can think of fun examples like buying shares in an umbrella manufacturer to hedge rainfall, or using the commodity orange juice as a hedge against the sun. Both are a long way from perfection.

We are starting to see the appeal of quant finance to the mathematician. (And maybe the salary has a slight influence too.) We have mathematical modeling, financial concepts to turn into mathematical principles. We have differential equations and free boundaries. Sometimes we have nice formulas. If we can't find formulas then we have to do some complicated numerical analysis. And complicated can be fun.

It can also be expensive if you get it wrong. Remember that dynamic hedging plays two roles in quant finance. It is used in a mathematical sense to determine the price of an option, as in the Black–Scholes formula. A trader can use the formula without actually buying or selling any stocks. However, hedging can also be used by the option writer as a method to (theoretically) eliminate risk on the option. A bank can issue options while delta hedging at the same time, and make money on the commission. So if instead you are selling an option where you can't trade the underlying, you might be able to come up with a theoretical price using the model, but it is impossible in practice to eliminate risk.

A separate issue is that, while derivatives can be used to reduce risk, just as often they are used as a way to make highly leveraged bets – so models are critical for risk assessment. In the 1990s a number of large companies, such as Procter & Gamble and Metallgesellschaft, experienced huge losses from derivatives trading. The wealthy Orange County in California was driven to bankruptcy by using derivatives to bet on interest rates. In energy derivatives, the undisputed leader was the Houston-based firm Enron. In 2000 it reported revenues of over $100 billion, which worked out at over $5 million per employee.[9] The next year it went bankrupt. But these were just warm-up acts for what was to follow.

From the Sublime to the Ridiculous

Derivatives are obviously not the most stable of financial instruments, and should be handled with extreme care. We'll talk about

---

[9] Ackman (2002).

the importance of good models in detail later, but here we just make a few brief comments.

First of all it's nice if the models are robust and internally consistent. In this category we'd put derivatives with shares, indices, exchange rates, and commodities as the underlying. As long as they aren't multi-asset contracts. At least these underlyings are traded and so the model fudging is minimal. And quants tend to all use similar models here.

Interest-rate models are not great. There are many, many of them. Different people use different models for the same instrument. And the inability to hedge consistently within the model can be a problem. On the down side, there's also the fact that the market in interest-rate derivatives is huge. The potential for a systemic disaster is therefore equally large. On the positive side, however, interest rates are dull, dull, dull. There is usually so little volatility in interest rates that perhaps none of this matters. At least this is true at the time of writing.

Credit-risk models are worse. You can't hedge. You don't know how to model default. Default isn't random, governed by the roll of a die – it's a business decision. There's no data for specific companies, since bankruptcy tends to be a one-off event. Volatility in risky businesses can be huge. And the market in credit instruments is large. Credit modeling is so bad, and credit instruments so dangerous, that it's worth having a closer look at these, in particular the infamous collateralized debt obligation (CDO) instrument.

Before explaining what quants do with CDOs, let's be clear, they are wonderful instruments. It's not that they are frightening *per se*, the worry is more to do with their abuse.

CDOs are a class of financial instrument in the family of asset-backed securities (ABSs). An ABS is a financial instrument whose value or cash flows are linked to a pool of typically illiquid underlying assets. These underlying assets could be things like property rental income, credit cards, student loans, car loans, mortgages, etc. Being pooled together so that you have thousands of student loans in the pot is meant to help with diversification and therefore control risk. Sometimes the ABS passes through a "special-purpose vehicle," a specially created legal entity, designed to obscure risk or hide investments from prying eyes… including those of shareholders.

CDOs were originally invented in the late 1980s, but only really caught on when bankers hit upon the mother lode of risk: subprime mortgages. Consider, for example, the city of Detroit. Today, Detroit has a reputation as the zombie apocalypse of the real-estate world: wild dogs roaming streets of abandoned buildings; gang-run 'hoods where the police fear to tread; brain-eating zombie politicians. Of course it's not that bad, but in 2014 someone *was* offering to swap an "investor special" three-bedroom house for "a new iPhone 6 or a new iPad," which is usually a sign that the market is coming unstuck. A big contrast from ten years earlier, when home prices were booming, as lenders such as Countrywide Financial swamped the area with easy credit, pushing mortgages at anyone who could sign their name – no job or credit history required.[10] Already in 2004 some 8% of houses in Detroit paid for by subprime loans had been seized by the banks, and a similar scenario was unfolding around the rest of the country, but the lenders didn't care. Why? Because they had found a way to repackage the risk, using CDOs, and sell it off to other people. The mortgage on a house in Detroit could end up being owned by a German bank wanting to diversify its holdings.

From the point of view of most observers, this was all to the good. As the IMF approvingly noted in 2006, its regulatory antennae all aquiver: "The dispersion of credit risk by banks to a broader and more diverse group of investors, rather than warehousing such risks on their balance sheets, has helped to make the banking and overall financial system more resilient."[11] They were echoed by Ben Bernanke, who announced the same year that "because of the dispersion of financial risks to those more willing and able to bear them, the economy and financial system are more resilient."[12]

So how did this "dispersion of credit risk" work? The CDO is a clever way of taking the cash flows from many underlying assets, let's say they are mortgages, pooling them all together, and then paying them out in tranches. Investors can choose which tranche to buy, some are far riskier than others. In detail, we might have something like the following:

---

[10]The city was aware of the problem – as one councillor put it, "I don't think there is any doubt that predatory lenders do target the city and its residents" – however, its attempts to regulate the loan industry, for example by imposing a cap on the maximum interest rate, were deemed illegal by the federal government (Krupa, 2002).

[11]International Monetary Fund (2006, p. 51).

[12]Bernanke (2006).

- The payments, interest, and principals of 1000 mortgages go into one pot.

- As the payments go into the pot they pile up and are paid out to investors.

- Those investors with the senior tranche get paid first, then the mezzanine tranche, and last of all the junk tranche. (There would typically be more tranches than in this example.) The further down you are, the higher the risk that the pot won't be full enough, thanks to mortgage defaults, and you won't get paid.

- Each of these tranches comes with a credit rating. The topmost would be AAA, then AA, etc. The higher the credit rating, the greater the cost of the tranche, *ceteris paribus*, or equivalently the lower the expected return. As you go further down the tranches the risk gets higher, and the expected return gets greater. (That's MPT again.)

So far so good. You decide how much risk you can bear, look at whether the corresponding expected return is sufficient, and choose your tranche. As financial investments they are wonderful things.

Hold it Together

However, from a quant finance modeling perspective these instruments are horrendous. In a chapter on credit derivatives in a book published in 2006, Paul wrote "… credit derivatives with many underlyings have become very popular of late… I have to say that some of these instruments and models being used for these instruments fill me with some nervousness and concern for the future of the global financial markets." (This didn't stop him almost losing a fortune in 2008. Idiot!)

One of the models used to value CDOs is the "copula." This is a mathematical idea in probability theory that helps you analyze the behavior of multiple random variables, here the random variables being default. We'll describe and critique this model here, but note that with CDOs it's not so much on any particular model that we can pin blame for the credit crisis that hit in 2008. No, it's more a problem that there's no model that is going to give you a value that you'd be able to sell at while giving you a mechanism for hedging risk.

The copula model tells you about the probabilistic behavior of multiple random variables in terms of the random behavior of the variables individually. Up until now we have concentrated on derivatives such as call options, which have a single underlying, such as a stock. The copula technique gives you a way to generalize that approach to a portfolio of assets. The connection to CDOs is clear, since there are many, many individual underlyings, the mortgages, say. But we only care about the tranches, which are complex amalgamations of the mortgages. Valuing these tranches depends critically on the degree of correlation between the securities. If they are highly correlated, then even senior tranches risk being exposed to a wave of defaults.

The copula method was originally based on an actuarial technique, used to address something known as the "broken heart syndrome." The death of a person's partner significantly increases the probability of their own death over the next year, which affects (lowers by a few percent) the price of a joint annuity.[13] The copula (from the Latin for "fasten together") was a way to calculate the probability of both partners dying at or before a certain age – and therefore the value of a joint annuity – while accounting for this temporal correlation. A Gaussian copula is one that makes use of the Gaussian distribution, which is another name for the normal distribution discussed earlier. (This work surprisingly didn't win its inventors a Nobel Prize, but they did pick up the Society of Actuaries' 1998 Halmstad Prize.)

The quant idea, then, was to simulate default by assuming that individual defaults are similarly correlated. If one owner defaults on his mortgage, the chances increase that the owner down the street will shortly default too. The approach sounds plausible, but it is less clear how you generalize it to a thousand mortgages. The broken heart syndrome deals with individual correlations, but what if risk is contagious? And what happens if the result is a kind of global financial coronary?

There is a very famous, in quant circles, article in *Wired* magazine from 2009 by Felix Salmon called "The formula that killed Wall Street," about the copula model.[14] His focus, as ours has been, was on the correlation behavior between the underlyings. We've done the combination mathematics already in Chapter 3, but let's quickly

---

[13]Spreeuw and Wang (2008).
[14]Salmon (2009).

do another example. There are 1000 mortgages in the CDO, how many correlations are there? The answer is $1000 \times 999 / 2$, and that's nearly half a million. Who is going to try to measure those parameters? Should one go door to door interviewing the mortgagors to see if the ability to pay is correlated among neighbors? Does a simple number like correlation even capture the relationship between Mrs Smith at number 99 and Dr Garcia at number 101? Won't it change in the event of a financial shock? More on correlation anon. But what is the quant gonna do?

Model Abuse

What the quant does is say, "Let's assume that all of the correlation parameters are 0.6."

WHHHAAAATTT?!?!

The quant has taken a subtle and sophisticated probabilistic concept like the copula, with half a million parameters, and through laziness, naivety, apathy, or something, thrown it all away by plucking a correlation parameter out of thin air and assuming it to be the same for all pairs among the 1000 mortgages.

We have seen above that using volatility in Black–Scholes is problematic, because it is unstable. We have remarked that making up a market rate of risk for interest-rate options is a way of sweeping problems under the carpet. But assuming that the inter-relationships in the complex entity known as the housing market can be adequately described through a single number – a kind of market rate of correlation – is taking model abuse to a completely new level.

Despite the criticism of the copula model from Salmon and others, there have been moderately vigorous defenses. The defenses amount to: "We never really believed the model" and "We used far more sophisticated models."[15] That may well be true. But whatever model you use, if you have a CDO with 1000 underlyings you are going to run against the problem of relating the individual underlying assets, and that is a problem far too complex to do at all accurately.

Indeed, the model's simplicity was its main selling point. Simple models aren't just aesthetically pleasing, they also have many other

---

[15]According to Michel Crouhy from the French bank Natixis, "to assess their own risk, banks used much more comprehensive models" (*ParisTech Review*, 2010).

advantages, including being easy to communicate. As with the Black–Scholes model, the copula model soon took on a life of its own. Traders incorporated it into their working practices, using it as a communication device. Instead of implied volatility, traders could quote on implied correlation. Again, implied correlations for related securities – say, the same mortgage pool but different tranches – tended to be inconsistent, with the senior tranches giving a higher implied correlation than the lower tranches, which again should have raised some alarms. But as one trader told sociologists Donald MacKenzie and Taylor Spears, "if everyone had the same model and they all agreed on the same model it didn't matter whether it was a good model or not."[16] In particular, the model could be used by accountants and auditors to value a contract *now*, even though the true value would only be known in the future, after the mortgages had defaulted or not. So if the trader sold a contract for more than the model value, the profit would count toward his bonus. Without the model, "people would be in serious trouble, all their traders would leave and go to competitors."

Skepticism about the copula technique was further neutralized in August 2004 when the world's main two rating agencies, Moody's and Standard & Poor's, both adopted the formula as a metric for valuing CDOs. Just as Black–Scholes led to a huge expansion in option trading, so the Gaussian copula galvanized the trading of CDOs. The endorsement of the credit agencies meant that regulated institutions such as pension funds could pile in. Institutions didn't even have to make their own models, they could just download Standard & Poor's "CDO Evaluator" program.

In 2004, some $157 billion in CDOs was issued. In 2006, that figure had ballooned to $552 billion.[17] The growth in CDOs was facilitated by the use of CDSs. These could be used to insure against default on the loans, which allowed banks to remove risk from their balance sheets. And since these paid off only if an investment defaulted, they could also be used as a way to go short on assets, and therefore as a hedging device. By the end of 2007, the value of the CDS market, in terms of amount insured, had reached roughly $60 trillion, which was about the same as world GDP.

---

[16]MacKenzie and Spears (2014).
[17]According to the Securities Industry and Financial Markets Association.

Hedge funds were having a field day. One firm which did well at this was Magnetar Capital – it "sponsored" CDOs by offering to buy high-paying junk tranches which no one else wanted, and hedged its risk by using CDSs to go short on the upper tranches. This position would pay off handsomely in the event that correlations blew up during a crash, so that defaults reached all the way to the upper (supposedly safe) tranches. Which of course is exactly what happened.

Pass the Parcel

The only realistic approach to valuation is to assume fairly extreme relationships between underlyings in such a way that the prices of CDO tranches become too expensive so that no one would buy them. Although that might be the mature and responsible thing to do from a valuation perspective, it's not going to win the quant any friends among the traders. All they care about is doing the deal to get the bonus. Fingers crossed that they get the bonus before it all goes pear shaped.

Even though there have been defenses of copula and other models for valuing CDOs, we suspect that a lot of this is rewriting history. Paul was there in the audience at many pre-2008 conferences where both academics and practitioners were peddling their models and risk-management software (see Box 5.1). No one was saying don't trade these, they're too dangerous. This would not have mattered if trade in these too-complicated-to-model derivatives was small, but they were incredibly big business. The reason they became big business is the interesting and dangerous part.

As children we would play pass the parcel at birthday parties. A present would be wrapped in paper prior to the party. This parcel would then be passed around a circle of children as music was played. The music was stopped intermittently and the child holding the parcel at that time would remove a layer. The music resumed, the parcel continued around the circle, and eventually the present was unveiled and kept by the child who had unwrapped it. That's sort of what happened with CDOs. But not with a nice present inside.

A mortgage lender would lend money to people to buy their own homes. This is risky for them. But they wouldn't be holding that risk for long. They could pass that on to a bank, who now temporarily held that risk. But not for long. With a little help from their investment banking quant chums they could package this up and sell it on to investors in individual, tailor-made, tranches. And once it was in the hands of the investors, it was they who took all the risk. Unless they insured it with something like a CDS, in which case the risk passed to the insurer.

It became quite the fashionable business. A bit of a bandwagon you could say. And that's really the dangerous part... the size of the market in these instruments. Not being able to value or hedge doesn't matter too much if the trades are small, but once the size gets enormous you get systematic risk that could bring down the whole system. And the size did get enormous, and that's because there was the illusion that these contracts could be valued and hedged, resulting in the biggest false sense of security in history. And it was the dubious quant models that played a key enabling role. The fact that most of the instruments were sold OTC meant that there was no visibility about institutional exposure, until the debts started to be called in.

The largest issuer of CDSs at the height of the crisis was AIG. But even they didn't keep the parcel for long – they were technically broke and passed it on to taxpayers. If you're curious who ultimately underwrote that $1.2 quadrillion worth of outstanding derivatives, it's you.

Box 5.1   Paul Worries

I'd been attending quite a few conferences in the early 2000s. The speakers tended to be the same at each event, so these events became more of an opportunity for catching up with friends and colleagues than a learning experience. The same speakers would give roughly the same talk each time, just adding minor tweaks to their research. I often didn't even bother sitting through the lectures. One topic that kept coming up, through a couple of professors who shall remain nameless, was the subject of copulas. The copula model was being applied to CDOs with reckless abandon. And I couldn't believe that these models were being taken seriously by all the smart people working in the business. As the eminent professors spoke I wondered if they themselves had any worries, or did they really, truly believe in the nonsense they were spouting? I am sure they did. If your ideas are lapped up so eagerly then I suspect you tend to lose any objective perspective, it's only natural. But surely some people in the audience wouldn't fall for this?

I looked around me, hoping to catch the eye of other audience members, maybe we'd indulge in a spot of mutual eye rolling to convey our worries, or at least our lack of gullibility. But no, everyone was paying rapturous attention. I was finally alone. I was Nancy in *The Bodysnatchers* (1978). I imagine it's like being a sane person at a meeting of Scientologists. The copula was the new religion, with an equally dubious scientific basis. The Germans have got the right idea. According to Wikipedia, the German government "views it as an abusive business masquerading as a religion." But sadly, they are referring to Scientology not copulas.

Also, sadly, I didn't realize the full extent of the CDO horror. Although the basic CDOs are great instruments, they are difficult to value and risk manage. I didn't realize the size of the market for them. It was by then absolutely huge.

Some of the instruments that were being talked about were CDO squared, cubed, etc. These are CDOs which are baskets of other CDOs, which are baskets of other CDOs... I jokingly "invented" the exponential CDO, since the exponential function grows faster than any power. I probably could have got people to take this seriously.

Money Crunch

The net effect of financial instruments such as CDOs and CDSs was not a reduction in risk, but a huge expansion in money and credit. We tend to think of the money supply as being something that is controlled by the central bank, while in fact the vast majority of money is created by lending from private banks. As Adair Turner, former Chairman of the UK's Financial Services Authority, notes: "Economic textbooks and academic papers typically describe how banks take deposits from savers and lend the money on to borrowers. But as a description of what banks actually do this is severely inadequate. In fact they create credit money and purchasing power. The consequences of this are profound: the amount of private credit and money that they can create is potentially infinite."[18] When you take a mortgage out with a bank, they don't take the money from the accounts of other clients, they just make up new funds. When economic conditions are good, the price of assets such as houses goes up, and these can be used as collateral for even larger loans, in a positive feedback loop. The central bank only has indirect influence on this process, by adjusting things such as the interbank lending rate.

Of course, banks have to manage their risks, which puts a cap on their lending activities. However, the invention of CDOs and CDSs,

---

[18]Turner (2014).

and their wholesale misuse in the early 2000s, allowed those banks to parcel the risk up and insure it or sell it on to others. Either way they got it off their balance sheets, meaning they could issue more loans, and further inflate the money bubble. The reason the credit crunch of 2007 did so much damage was that it was in fact a money crunch, similar in spirit to the one which John Law unleashed on France in the 17th century, but on a global scale. Quants didn't set out like Law to print money, but that was the emergent effect of their endeavors. Models such as the Gaussian copula, which modeled the financial world as an intrinsically stable system, and didn't account for the effect of things like sudden crashes or contagion between institutions, created a false sense of security. Simple models have many advantages, including as communication devices, but when misused they can also be a way of enforcing a type of group denial.

As MacKenzie and Spears observe, "Perhaps the modelling of derivatives in investment banking always has an aspect of what one of our interviewees memorably called a 'ballet,' in which highly-paid quants are needed not just to try to capture the way the world is, but also to secure co-ordinated action. Perhaps the quant is actually a dancer, and the dance succeeds when the dancers co-ordinate." Unfortunately, this particular ballet had a tragic ending to rival that of *Swan Lake*, when a black swan – known as reality – swam serenely into view.

A particular property of money, which rivals quantum physics for its weirdness, is the way that it is real, in the sense that its appearance has real effects on people and the economy – the housing boom in places like Detroit meant that more Americans could buy a home than ever before – but when conditions change it can suddenly disappear into the ether, as if it had never existed. In the next chapter we look more deeply at how the quant community attempts to use mathematics to tame this mysterious substance, and ask why the results so often end in an explosion.

What Quants Do

"Largely, a waste of time and human potential. It has created jobs, whose value to society is suspect.
Why is it that young, bright engineers end up staring at the screens, looking for patterns in asset prices when they could have far better served the society by solving some real problems?"
—Answers to the survey question:
"How would you describe quantitative finance at a dinner party?" at wilmott.com

"One can predict the course of a comet more easily than one can predict the course of Citigroup's stock. The attractiveness, of course, is that you can make more money successfully predicting a stock than you can a comet."
—James Simons

From the 1980s with the increase in trading in derivatives, through the 1990s with the increasing complexity of products, and then the 2000s with the creation of credit instruments and the shift to high-frequency electronic trading, quants have played an ever-more-important role in banking. The educational requirements for quants got tougher, and, as so often seems to happen, the commonsense requirements dwindled to near zero. Quants are the classical boffins, here outside of academia, who do the esoteric mathematics, write the computer code, quantify a bank or hedge fund's risk, and often design the algorithms that actually make the trades. As it has become cool to be a programming nerd, so it is cool to be a quant (the big salary helps). But will it ever be as cool as being a writer?

In this chapter, we're going to lift the lid a little more on what quants actually do – and just as importantly, how much they get paid. We're going to include some feedback and results from a survey we carried out at wilmott.com, so the message is coming straight from the horse's mouth. First though a little more history to bring us up to date and explain how – with the help of technology – these Masters of the Universe reached their current awesome level of power over the world financial system.

In olden times, like pre-1970s, stock markets were places where human traders could meet up in person to buy and sell shares in companies. In the USA the main stock exchange has long been the New York Stock Exchange (NYSE), founded in 1792 by 24 brokers. For the best part of two centuries it had a near monopoly on stock trading. Traders, in brightly colored jackets to indicate their firm, would huddle in trading pits and communicate their intentions with shouted orders and weird hand signals. In 1972 some competition arrived in the form of the NASDAQ, which began as an electronic quoting system but eventually evolved into a proper exchange. Even there, most trading still took place over the phone. This worked well enough until Black Monday, when many brokers just refused to pick up. In response, a computerized trading platform was soon set up. In the UK, Margaret Thatcher's "Big Bang" opened the London Stock Exchange to electronic trading. Thus began a power shift from humans to machines, and from gesticulating traders to writers of code.

As with the rest of society, finance was getting wired. Instead of men yelling at one another over a crowded floor, trades were increasingly being submitted electronically and handled by computers (so traders could yell at them instead). The process was accelerated in the 1990s by technical factors such as the decimalization of US stock prices – which reduced the minimum tick size from 1/16 of a dollar to one cent, thus making it easier to divide trades into small portions – and improved infrastructure for high-speed communications. And it was only a matter of time before it was realized that computer programs could not just help to process human orders, but also make the decisions to buy and sell in the first place.

In 2001, a few years after their Big Blue computer beat Gary Kasparov at chess, a report from IBM gained widespread media attention when it showed that computer algorithms could outperform humans at trading in simulated markets.[1] Mathematicians and physicists, employed by heavyweight firms such as Goldman Sachs or Deutsche Bank, or specialist newcomers such as Automated Trading Desk (later bought by CitiGroup in 2007) or Renaissance Technologies, were soon racing to develop so-called computer robots or "bots" that could track the markets, look for patterns, and execute orders at a pace that humans could never hope to match.

According to the NYSE, the average holding period for stocks declined steadily from 100 months in 1960, to 63 months in 1970, 33 months in 1980, 26 months in 1990, 14 months in 2000, and 6 months in 2010.[2] By that time trading activity was already starting to be dominated by high-frequency-trading (HFT) firms, which make thousands or millions of stock and option trades every day, often holding them for only a few seconds.[3] Originally these concentrated on simple strategies such as exploiting small discrepancies in prices posted by different exchanges, or reacting to changes before human market-makers had time to update their prices, but over time they became increasingly elaborate. Today sophisticated algorithms – which seem to favor computer-game names like Stealth, Dagger, Sniper, and Guerrilla – automatically jump in and out of positions, competing with one another to make tiny profits on huge numbers of transactions, often trying to feint each other out or jam exchanges with fake orders that are cancelled at the last moment.

The electronification of markets initially promised to make the stock markets more accessible and democratic. Buyers and sellers could be matched in electronic barter networks, cutting out the market-maker middlemen of traditional exchanges (those who post both bid and sell prices and profit from the gap between them). Huge amounts of data on transactions were suddenly available to the masses, in easily displayed formats, at least for a fee. However, even as the main exchanges were opening up, dozens of alternative private exchanges, or pools, were set up to cater to large institutions

---

[1] Das *et al.* (2001).

[2] Harding (2011).

[3] According to the consultancy firm Tabb Group, HFT accounts for "as much as 73 percent of US daily equity volume, up from 30 percent in 2005" (Bailey, 2015).

and hedge funds. These were only lightly regulated, so could choose how much information to supply to users about other trades, and at what price. Some pools were open or "lit," so that trades were freely viewable, but in "dark pools" information was kept secret, or sold at a price to subscribers. Stock exchanges such as the NYSE used to be a closed club, where membership was decided by wealth or privilege; the new system was in theory more open, but in practice access and knowledge were as tightly controlled as ever. The only difference was that now it was the quants, and their computers, who could see what was going on, sending out small buy or sell orders to "ping" the depths, gauge volume, and seek out the presence of large orders. Traditional volume buyers such as mutual funds, or smaller individual investors, were left groping in the dark.

Today, most trading takes places not on trading floors, but in massive computer facilities. The NYSE still has a busy-looking floor on Wall Street, which forms its public face on TV, but the real action takes place in its data center some 30 miles away in Mahwah, NJ. Speed has become so important that the speed of light has become a constraint, with hedge funds paying fees to locate their computer servers close to the exchanges, in order to avoid microsecond delays in order times. Others triangulate their location between different exchanges around the world. In 2010, the HFT company Getco spent $300 million to lay a cable connecting its computers near the Chicago Mercantile Exchange to the NASDAQ exchange in New Jersey, thus shaving a good 3 ms off the 16-ms order time.[4] Microwaves are sometimes preferred, because light is slowed by 31% when it passes through fiber-optic cables, which is irritating if you're in a hurry. Or lasers, which have more bandwidth and are less affected by weather.

Despite its dangers, which we'll discuss further below, algorithmic trading is taking over stock markets around the world (one of the few holdouts so far is China, where humans are protected by government regulations and a stamp duty on trades).[5] According to the US Commodity Futures Trading Commission, "automated traders are on at least one side of 50 percent of trades for metals and energy futures, and almost 40 percent in agricultural contracts."[6] So, who are the brains behind this race of the robots? You guessed it: the quants.

---

[4] Patterson (2012, p. 287).
[5] Mamudi *et al.* (2015).
[6] Massad (2015).

Trading is a statistical exercise, so algorithms and trading strategies must be designed which on average will provide positive returns. At the same time, the massive trading volume means that risk must be tightly controlled, in case it spirals out of control. For example, many hedge funds trade in options which promise a large payoff, but risk must be hedged by owning or shorting stocks – as discussed in previous chapters. And because leverage is often employed to boost returns, attention to downside risk is especially important. Unlike other areas, increased automation has therefore not led to much of a cull in jobs. From coding up trading algorithms, to designing bespoke derivatives, to analyzing and controlling risk, the skills of quants have never been in greater demand. As Jared Butler from the recruitment firm Selby Jennings told the *Financial Times*: "Traders used to be first-class citizens of the financial world, but that's not true any more. Technologists are the priority now. It's easier to hire a computer scientist and teach them the financial world than the other way around."[7]

Quants are no longer just helping to write the story, they have stepped into it themselves like a post-modern author experimenting with new narrative forms. The changing status of quants has made the field highly lucrative – and lured away much of the mathematical talent from areas such as science and engineering. Which brings us to an important topic: salaries.

What do Quants Make – and are They Adequately Paid?

Got a degree in mathematics, physics, engineering, or computer science? For the last 20 years there's been only one job for you. And that's quant finance. Got a degree in finance or economics? It's still the same job, but you're going to have to get some hardcore mathematics on your CV if you're to get it.[8]

---

[7] Wigglesworth (2015a).

[8] Paul went into a branch of his bank, one of his banks rather, recently. The cashier said "You're Dr Wilmott, aren't you? You've got a Wikipedia page." Okay, so the cheque he was holding might have been a clue to his identity. It turned out that the cashier quite fancied getting into quant finance. Although mathematics had been his favourite subject at school he didn't have a degree. Paul was torn between brutal honesty and being friendly but misleading. He opted for brutal honesty while grinning broadly. Not sure it went down as intended.

Why is quant finance such a desirable career? I don't think we are betraying any secrets if we say that the salaries might play a key role here. Let's get these numbers out of the way before we give you the full job description. Keep that envy under control.

Taken from the Jobs Board at wilmott.com:

> Junior Quant 1–3 years' experience / Hedge Fund job in London, $75–99,000
>> Quantitative Research Analyst (Financial Engineer) job in New York, $200,000

Or how about:

> Senior Algorithmic Trading Developer, Hong Kong, $100–150,000.

That's not an annual salary – it's per month.

The record salary for a job advertised on that website is around $2m. That's an advertised job. On a public website. Not the behind-closed-doors, secretly headhunted, privately negotiated salary. *You* could apply for it. And maybe haggle it up a bit.

And that's before the bonus.

You get the picture?

Not everyone is earning such big bucks. At the junior end you'll be a code monkey, implementing other people's models. But at the top end you'll own the fund, and dine with presidents and dictators. Let's break down the jobs into some detail. This list is in a completely subjective order from least interesting to most, not necessarily in order of salary or importance.

- **Junior quant.** As a junior quant you will probably be straight out of university. That probably means you will have done something scientific or financial as an undergraduate, followed by a postgraduate degree in something more specifically in mathematical finance. Perhaps that will be a Masters, increasingly it will mean a doctorate. So you are probably in your mid-twenties. You will have taken quite a chance by pinning your hopes on getting the banking job. A lot of your contemporaries won't have been as lucky as you, many will have ended up in software companies, consultancies, or insurance. Fine places to work, and in many ways better than banks in terms of work/life balance, but still not perceived as being glamorous, if we can use that word. A PhD is not strictly necessary for quant finance work, technically all you need is second-year undergraduate mathematics, but banks do often ask for that qualification. Maybe it shows you can work independently... strike that, this is not the twentieth century any more, PhD students aren't what they used to be... but more probably simply because they can. And if the employer has a PhD himself he's probably more likely to hire someone similar. As part of your graduate studies you will have learned to write computer programs. And to maximize your chances of getting a quant job you will take the coding very seriously. At a minimum you'll be extremely comfortable with the C++ programming language. Ideally you'll be *au fait* with other languages as well. Fashions change in programming, new languages come, and then often go. These days it's Python.[9] You are a code monkey. You'll be tinkering with code that others have written. You'll be implementing models that other people have created. You'll be working long hours, but that applies to everyone in banking.

- **Model validation.** Model validation is, as the name suggests, checking that models are implemented correctly. As discussed further in the next chapter, it's not really about whether those models are any good, sadly. We can't do better than take a few quotations from wilmott.com concerning this least interesting of jobs. One member, katastrofa, says: "Model validation is where quants go to die." Another member, deimanteR, adds some flesh to this: "My impression is Model Validation can be particularly dull in big banks – you will be pressing Shift-F9 mainly. In smaller places you might be developing alternative models that no one uses. Still the best you can hope for. Moving out might be difficult – the longer you stay there the harder is to get out." How depressing is that? (Shift-F9, by the way, refers to the Excel command that recalculates a spreadsheet.) Member Gamal is a bit, just a bit, more upbeat:

---

[9] While typing this paragraph the new programming kid on the block has become "Julia."

"If you like browsing net 8 hours per day, it's a perfect place." Only 8 hours? Model validation is quite a new role in banks, really coming into vogue following the crisis of modeling that started in 2007. Because it lacks any creativity, it's rather dull. And because it's not close to the money (and if anything it can be a source of frustration for those who are) it is very poorly paid, relatively speaking.

- **Quant developer.** This is almost the default quant job, in that there seem to be lots of them around. The job is implementing models in the programming language *du jour*. It is a grand title for someone who is a little bit more senior but is essentially just programming, that's the "developer" bit. In another company, Google for example, you might be called a software developer. As well as being extremely good at coding, you will know something about numerical algorithms. That means you will know about Monte Carlo simulations, and some of the theoretical basis for this. Or maybe numerical solutions of partial differential equations. Increasingly, as discussed below, it may also involve analyzing "big data" and applying machine learning techniques to everything from Internet search terms to weather patterns. If you have anything to do with portfolios of assets or investments, you'll be called upon to write the code to optimize asset allocation.

- **Risk management.** As a risk quant you will be measuring the amount of risk in contracts and portfolios. You won't be the most popular quant in the bank, since you will be the guy telling people that they have to cut down on their risky positions, and thereby probably decrease their bonuses. But look on the bright side, the traders won't want to listen to you anyway.

- **Research quant.** Like unicorns this is a mythical creature, a thing of beauty and envy. Almost. The few research quants still in existence are supposed to invent new models, to improve those that already exist and have perhaps failed. Or maybe you'll be trying to speed up models, or make them more accurate, or uncover new sources of data. You will undoubtedly have a PhD, you will be a whizz at stochastic calculus. It is highly unlikely that your research will be all that different from what others are doing, and although your job will feel a little bit like academia you will have to work much longer hours, and you won't have free rein for much blue-sky research. In a perfect world you would be creating genuinely original models and techniques, but in the real world banks don't like too much originality. You will sometimes publish papers in learned journals, and speak at international conferences. You will become famous among quant newbies who will look up to you. However, if your research turns out to be wonderfully clever but somewhat lacking in the profit arena, then expect to be "let go." Don't despair though, there are plenty of MSc programs that will take you on as a professor in the blink of an eye.

- **Front office or desk quant.** As one of these you are close to the money, and you'll work closely with the traders. Make no mistake, you may have better qualifications and a higher IQ than them, but you are very much lower down in the food chain. Expect to get the blame when things go wrong. A thick skin is needed in this role. But the pay can be good. There'll always be a need for such employees. The coding can vary from simple tweaking of existing programs, to debugging major code, to implementing new models from scratch. The trader doesn't care whether the theoretical foundations for his ideas are sound. Does it make money? Check. Is it fast? Check.

- **Quant trader.** This is the holy grail of quant jobs, managing your own trading book. You are a trader who uses quant tools to assist in decision making, portfolio allocation, etc. It takes a very special type of person to do this job well. First of all you'll have lots of technical mathematical skills, especially statistical. And you'll need nerves to take the risks. You won't be too obsessed with the mathematics. If something works (i.e., makes money) then the possibility of it being incorrect is of minor concern. Hey, if you've got a plus sign where it should be a minus and it's making money then you'd be stupid to correct it. You are pragmatic. And very smart. And since you are probably doing your own programming then you are just some legal paperwork and a few hundred million dollars away from starting your own hedge fund.

We've sprinkled some of the feedback from our informal and highly unscientific quant survey at wilmott.com throughout the book, but here are some statistical findings from the hundreds of people from 47 different countries who endured a detailed, 50-part questionnaire and psychological probing, which we performed in order to get the pulse of the quant community and also as a blatant attempt to get ideas and material.

Average estimated IQ (self-reported!): 122. David once did an IQ test at school. The separate computer-readable answer sheet had two sides, and there was only one instruction, which was to record the answers on the green side first and then the red side. And ever since, his IQ has been one of those statistics with an asterisk by it. (Another test showed he was color blind, but that's not really an excuse.)

95% attended college.

42% have a doctorate.

72% have a professional qualification.

12% are female.

11% think there are gender inequality issues where they work (about as many as there are females, then).

On average they thought the highest tax rate should be 27%.

One-third of respondents thought that their company would consider relocating if taxes were to rise.

70% donated to charity.

66% prefer non-fiction over fiction. We think this book qualifies as 66% non-fiction. Those that like fiction seem to prefer sci-fi.

Movies popular among quants include *The Godfather* and *Dr Strangelove*. One person favored *Happy Gilmore*.

93% describe their recreational drug of choice as "none," and 6% say "aspirin," which may invalidate our other results.

Half of quants are teetotal.

43% agreed with the statement that the efficient market theory is true. We're using the past tense in case we change anyone's mind.

70% agree with the statement that the recent crisis was "Just a warm-up."

The quants' car brand of choice is Toyota.

We also asked about their religion. Sadly, not a single Jedi was among them. Although Pastafarianism is big on wilmott.com.

So, picture a teetotal male, high on aspirin, driving a Toyota, and you won't be far off.

Quants vs. Regulators

We wanted to compare these quant salaries and education levels with those of regulators, but found it hard to get a straight answer about the latter group. The two main financial regulatory bodies in the UK are the Prudential Regulation Authority (PRA), which is a subsidiary of the Bank of England and is responsible for supervising the finances of banks, insurance firms, etc. and the Financial Conduct Authority (FCA), which deals more with things like business conduct and consumer issues (there is a degree of overlap in their responsibilities). We bombarded both of them with Freedom of Information requests, asking them questions about education levels, median salaries, and other topics such as criminal prosecutions, but unfortunately the information content of the responses was rather low. Neither group had anything useful to say about prosecutions against quants, which is unsurprising given that it doesn't seem to be something they go in for. When asked about education levels, the PRA said: "we would need to go through each personal record of the 1241 people working in the PRA to determine whether we hold the specific information about their education such as, where and how each person was educated and to what level." (Seriously? They might actually not know what level of education people working for them have?!!)

The FCA was more forthcoming, and told us that although finding the information about staff education levels for us would be too time consuming, an internal survey did show that 44 of their 2169 employees self-reported having a PhD, with 252 not answering about their education level. Now that's very nice for us, but why were they asking their employees about their education level in an internal survey? Surely they had access to that data. Typically, one asks for qualifications before hiring. And who were the 252 employees who declined to tell their employers their education level? (FYI that's on top of the employees who didn't respond to the internal survey at all, which makes it a deliberate act rather than apathy.) Strange way to run a regulator. Anyway, call it between 2% and an unlikely maximum of 10% of their workforce with PhDs. Compare that with a hedge fund, where typically a third of the employees might have PhDs (and nearly everyone working at the quant end does). And there are a lot of hedge firms to regulate.

For salaries, the FCA told us that the salary range for their regulatory jobs started at £20,000–£40,000 for a Junior Associate. A Senior Associate, who "may act as a team leader or mentor," can expect £46,000–£81,000. Managers get anything from £65,000 to as high as £118,000. The PRA only referred us to their annual report, which stated that remuneration in 2015 ranged from £18,578 to £266,777 for their CEO, with a median of £67,952, but didn't break it down by job category as we had asked.

These are very respectable salaries, and compare favorably with those in science or engineering. But with salaries in quant finance, not so much. We don't like to use the expressions "order of magnitude smaller" or "apparently missing a digit" when it comes to people's earnings, but it's in that ballpark. This says less about regulators than it does about quants – but it means that recruiting the best experts is always going to be a challenge. And it's easy to see the problems that can arise when regulators don't have enough qualified personnel. For example, in a 2015 survey of hedge funds, the FCA wrote: "Value at Risk (VaR) is a measure of the potential loss of a portfolio at a given level of confidence. We asked firms to provide us with their own VaR calculations for their funds."[10] So no chance of fraud there, then (we will show later how such measures are easily adjusted to give the right answer).

Writer-nomics

Working our way down the salary scale, it is interesting, if only for the sake of humor, to compare all this to another, very different occupation of which we both have some experience: writing. Writing is a great job. Writers can make up their own projects and set their own deadlines. They can work from home and have no one to report to but themselves, their readers, and the occasional editor. There are only two catches. The barrier to entry is high, and the pay is a little unreliable. But that's not what you're in it for.

---

[10] See Financial Conduct Authority (2015). The report acknowledges that "VaR is by no means an optimal measure" but uses it nonetheless.

The odds of an unsolicited manuscript being accepted by a publisher has been estimated at about 1 in 10,000.[11] Similar for the chances of having a screenplay turned into a film.[12] Even authors who later went on to great success have had trouble getting a foot in the door. J.K. Rowling of *Harry Potter* fame, for example, only got lucky with her thirteenth publisher. Having a polished CV or a degree from a fancy institution is no help here. Contacts aren't much use either. Being famous for doing something else is better. Acquiring a literary agent is useful, but "is even harder than finding a publisher!" as one publisher informed Rowling, when she later submitted a novel under the pen name Robert Galbraith.[13] You can always self-publish, as we have both done, but the challenge of finding a readership is harder.[14]

And then, even when you get your first work published, that is just the start, because the chances that it will actually sell are minimal, book sales being dominated by a small number of titles.[15] As discussed earlier, neoclassical economics and most risk assessment tools are based on the normal distribution, which is a shame because many important economic phenomena, from sales to stock-market fluctuations to wealth distribution to company size, are better described by a highly skewed power law. If book sales followed a normal

---

[11]Estimates vary but this is a common one. In the USA, it has been estimated that unsolicited manuscripts have a 1 in 15,000 chance of acceptance (Sorensen, 2004).

[12]Morris (2014).

[13]See Rowling (2016).

[14]Paul writes: In 1992 I was part of a small team of people at Oxford and Southampton Universities giving professional training courses in derivatives. We turned the courses into a book, *Option Pricing: Mathematical models and computation*. We presented our work to a few publishers, but the responses were lukewarm, and that's putting a positive spin on it. So we decided to self-publish, which turned out to be a very good decision. We set up an imprint, Oxford Financial Press. My mother and stepfather dealt with orders and supply. (She didn't totally appreciate my idea of having a 24-hour order hotline... when she was a little old lady in a bungalow with a fax machine... taking orders from all time zones.) Even before the book came out people were buying advance copies. Now this was before PDFs, so the advance copies consisted of a pile of A4 pages with the text, and a separate pile of A4 graphs; the purchaser had to cut the images out and paste the two together. (Yes, that's where the expression "cut & paste" comes from, actually cutting and actually pasting. You kids!) And for this they paid $200!

[15]Back in 1994, for example, only five authors – John Grisham, Tom Clancy, Danielle Steel, Michael Crichton, and Stephen King – accounted for 70% of fiction sales in the USA (Sorensen, 2004).

distribution, authors could safely expect to sell, within a certain range, an average number of copies per year. The reality is quite different. It is possible to make good money if you have a bestseller, or sell lucrative movie rights, or win a prestigious award such as the hedge-fund-sponsored Man Booker Prize (the 2015 prize went to Marlon James, whose first book was rejected 78 times before being published). But there is no base salary or steady income, and as a general money-making strategy, writing is not recommended. A 2015 survey of about a thousand published authors, fiction and non-fiction, by the Writers' Union of Canada showed that their average annual income from writing was, er, $12,879 Canadian, or about $10,000 US.[16] Roughly an order of magnitude smaller than regulators, then. The numbers are also in decline, probably because no one (apart from you – thanks!) buys books anymore.[17] Of course the average doesn't mean much, because the distribution is so highly skewed (the median is under $5000 CAD) – but if reliable income is the goal, then definitely go with the quantitative finance if you can.

Writers must also accept that sales are unpredictable, and only partially within their control (though having one bestseller raises the author's profile and increases the chances that the next book will sell well too). They are like a nice kind of economic crash – you never know exactly how big they are going to be, or where they are going to come from. Who would have thought that a 700-page tract on inequality by a little-known French economist would be one of the bestselling books of 2014 (Thomas Piketty's *Capital in the Twenty-First Century*)?[18] Even Miguel de Cervantes, credited with the best-selling novel of all time, was considered a bit of "a loser" in his time according to one historian – his first novel flopped, he spent time in jail, and *Don Quixote* only became a phenomenon after he died.[19] One

---

[16]That includes all sources including royalties, freelance articles, and government grants. Self-publishing contributed 8% of total income (Writers' Union of Canada, 2015).

[17]Canadian authors reported that they were earning 27% less from their craft, after inflation, in 2015 than during the last survey in 1998, and a survey of writers in the UK showed a similar trend (Flood, 2014). Of course the reason for falling sales is that we have become used to getting access to anything for free over the Internet. Who makes money from this? Google, and aggregator sites such as Huffington Post.

[18]Piketty (2014).

[19]Historian Fernando de Prado, quoted in Minder (2014).

reason writers are dangerous is that you can deprive them of money, put them in prison, and they will keep writing.

Many writers support themselves by teaching writing to other would-be writers, at one of the creative-writing programs that have sprung up in universities (or in jails, for that matter) around the world. The economics of this are unclear – hiring a few writers to produce a lot more of them doesn't exactly seem like a long-term solution to the problem. But even if students were told upfront about their salary prospects, it probably wouldn't make much difference. David once attended a meeting for aspiring screenwriters where a writer, who was considered massively successful because he once had a screenplay made into a film, told the audience what the statistical chances were of one of their screenplays being similarly accepted. No one cared, because everyone there thought they were the one with the brilliant and marketable idea. It was like explaining to a quarter-billion spermatozoa that statistically speaking, they are probably wasting their time. (David's idea, since you ask, was a story in which *the Earth* was the villain! It went through some iterations with a production company, but didn't go anywhere, so he turned it into a book, which got him an agent.)

So what does this have to do with quantitative finance (the subject of this particular piece of writing)? For one thing, the economics of writing gives a different perspective on efficient market theory, and particularly the idea that market price reflects "intrinsic value." When Eugene Fama was asked in a 2007 interview to comment on average CEO pay – which in the USA is now 354 times that of an unskilled worker – he said "you're just looking at market wages. They may be big numbers; that's not saying they're too high."[20] By the same argument, average writers' salaries are just market wages. They may be small numbers; that's not saying they're too low. Which may be one reason why writers, like quants, take efficient market theory less seriously than tenured business school professors.

Writers, with their hands-on experience of free markets, also know that the world is not "normal," that there is not a neat relationship between risk and reward, and that markets are affected by powerful feedback effects – so, for example, having a book on a bestseller list encourages further sales, mentions, reviews, and

---

[20]Clement (2007). CEO pay: Kiatpongsan and Norton (2014).

better placement in stores, which in turn drive more sales. This kind of winner-takes-all dynamic is common in many areas. The earnings of visual artists, for example, are in the same ballpark as those of writers, but the distribution is even more skewed – at least if you count dead artists.[21] At the time of writing, the record price for a painting was about $300 million for a particularly fetching (we assume) Gauguin. The purchaser was reputed to be the State of Qatar, but hedge-fund owners are also big buyers. Winner-takes-all applies even to the world of quantitative finance, with the important difference that it is winner-takes-all above base salary plus bonus.

Why then would anyone choose to become a writer, apart from the adulation, the groupies, the thrilling risk, and the occasional free books from publishers? It's a chance to do something authentic, that you believe in. It has "intrinsic value" of the sort that doesn't appear as a number on a pay check. You can do other things at the same time, including banking (T.S. Eliot penned *The Wasteland* while employed at Lloyds). And you can set your own hours.

Blinding us with Science

While some quants like to invest in art, others find science more appealing. David Harding, who founded Winton Capital, has for example generously funded The Winton Programme for the Physics of Sustainability at Cambridge; The Harding Center for Risk Literacy at the Max Planck Institute for Human Development in Berlin; £5 million towards building a new mathematics gallery at the Science Museum in London; and for science writers the Royal Society Winton Prize for Science Books. Winton Capital also funded a science competition to improve on algorithms for the mapping of dark matter, the mysterious, elusive substance which is thought to permeate the universe, as well as areas behind the fridge.[22]

David E. Shaw gave up day-to-day operations of his hedge fund in 2001 to concentrate on D.E. Shaw Research, which carries out biochemistry research. The firm's job ads helpfully point out that of successful applicants, a considerable number have "competed successfully in the United States and International Math Olympiads as well as the Putnam Competition." This is like saying "many of our

---

[21] Hill Strategies Research Inc. (2014).
[22] But maybe dark matter doesn't exist! (Orrell, 2012, p. 202.)

fitness instructors are Olympic medal holders," or "most of our drivers are Formula One champions."

Another heavyweight in the science market is the Templeton Foundation, which is propped up by a $3 billion endowment from the estate of the famed investment manager John Templeton. Each year it hands out grants worth over $100 million, with a significant portion going toward high-energy physics, and in particular supporters of string and multiverse theory. For comparison, the US National Science Foundation's budget for high-energy physics is about $12 million. Whether his foundation is as good at spotting scientific theories as Templeton was at picking stocks remains to be seen. (The physics of string and multiverse theory, as opposed to the mathematics behind it, was critiqued in David's willfully obscure treatise on science called *Truth or Beauty*. Its sales – since we were on that topic – were unexciting everywhere except in China, where the translated version was unaccountably chosen by Xinhua, the press arm of the Chinese state and mouthpiece of the Communist Party, as recommended New Year holiday reading. As we said, unpredictable.)

And then there is James Simons of Renaissance Technology – one of the biggest patrons of scientists since the Medicis hired Galileo as a tutor. Ranked 76 on the 2015 Forbes list of the world's billionaires (another list which follows a power law[23]), he has a personal fortune estimated at $14 billion, and seems intent on giving much of it away to promote a range of scientific research through his Simons Foundation.[24] Its "Mathematics and Physical Sciences" program focuses on computer science and theoretical physics, doling out million-dollar grants to leading scientists. "Life Sciences" supports research on the boundary between physics and biology, including a brain-modeling project known as the Global Brain. "Education and Outreach" features a program aimed at secondary schools and teachers called Math for America. In addition, there is an Autism Research Initiative and a Center for Data Analysis, which explores big data in areas such as genomics and neuroscience. The Foundation even has its own online science magazine, *Quanta*, so employs a few science writers.[25]

While any source of science funding is probably to be welcomed, not everyone is comfortable with the idea that scientific research

---

[23]Orrell (2008, pp. 276–277).
[24]See www.simonsfoundation.org/.
[25]See www.quantamagazine.org/.

is being shaped by the tastes of hedge-fund owners. The Templeton Foundation, for example, has been accused of blurring the line
between science and what cosmologist Sean Carroll called "explicitly
religious activity" (which may explain that weird multiverse stuff).[26]
There is a risk that billionaires may distort the science market the
same way they distort the art market, by turning it into something
like the luxury goods sector. Instead of a Gauguin, or a Jeff Koons,
you can get the latest version of a Theory of Everything. However,
the Simons Foundation seems to be a solid and broad-based extension of public funding for high-quality science. It probably helps that
Simons is an accomplished scientist himself. He doesn't just fund
things like string theory: as a young mathematician, he co-developed
the Chern–Simons theorem, which was popularized by string theorist Edward Witten, and serves as an important mathematical tool in
that area.

Bots

Simons has had an interesting career path, and – getting back to the
topic of quantitative finance – if there is one firm that exemplifies
the field's rise, it is his Renaissance Technology.

After receiving his doctorate in mathematics at the age of 23,
Simons celebrated with two friends by buying Lambrettas and motor
scooting from Boston to Bogota. A few years later, together with
Simons's father, the group teamed up to buy a Columbian floor-tile
factory, as one does. The same year, 1964, Simons started work as a
code-breaker with the National Security Agency (NSA). In 1967, General Maxwell Taylor wrote an article for the *New York Times Magazine* in
favor of the Vietnam War. Simons penned a reply for the same magazine, arguing the opposite. Shortly after he was fired by the NSA.[27]
However, he was welcomed by academia, and was soon appointed
chairman of the mathematics department at Stony Brook University.
There he began to build up what would become a formidable group
of mathematicians.

Simons also dabbled with trading on the side. The Columbian
factory had done quite well, so in 1974 Simons and his partners decided to take out some profits, and invest $600,000 with a

---

[26]Carroll (2005).
[27]Simons (2015).

commodities trader, making leveraged bets on the price of sugar. In the space of a few months, it became $6 million.[28] Figuring he could do this himself, Simons left Stony Brook in 1977 and went into trading full time, setting up a firm called Monemetrics in a strip mall in the Long Island town of Setauket, close to Stony Brook. Two of his first hires were Lenny Baum, a former colleague from the IDA, and a mathematician called James Ax.

Baum was co-inventor of the Baum–Welch algorithm, which is used to build models of hidden Markov processes. A Markov process is an iterative process in which the rule governing the transition to the next step depends on nothing more than the current state. A simple example is a random walk. When you take a step, your position depends only on where you just were, along with the rule for the random step (e.g., the standard deviation of the step size). A hidden Markov process is one that you have lost somewhere on your desk. Or alternatively, it's one where the rules are hidden. There could be something going on in the background, but all you see are the observed states at each step. Baum–Welch is a mathematical process for teasing out the hidden parameters. The algorithm was used in everything from code-breaking to speech recognition, but Simons thought it could work in finance as well. The markets were a giant hidden Markov process; all you had to do was figure out the rules.

James Ax took over the task, and tried applying the technique to futures contracts. In 1988 he and Simons started a new hedge fund call Medallion, naming it after mathematics awards they had won. But the bugs weren't all worked out and in 1989 the fund was losing money. Ax left, went back to fundamental research on quantum mechanics, learned to play golf, took a screenwriting class, and wrote a screenplay for a scientific thriller called "Bots."[29] Simons – whose recruitment skills had been honed at Stony Brook – hired a string of mathematicians to take over. In 1990 the Medallion fund returned over 50% after fees, the first of a long series of stellar results. In 1993 the fund was closed to outside investors, and now serves only as an investment vehicle for Simons and his staff.

We haven't seen James Ax's screenplay – he died in 2006 – but the word "bots" usually refers to the software robots that run automated tasks on computer networks including the Internet. Maybe the *bot*

---

[28]Teitelbaum (2007).
[29]UCSD Department of Mathematics (2016).

is the villain. If so, it is fitting that the co-founder of the Medallion fund came up with the idea, since in many ways the fund resembles a kind of sophisticated robot, its artificial intelligence automatically learning about the markets as it goes along, buying and selling with each millisecond pulse of its digital brain.

Global Brain

In the early 1990s, Simons poached two machine translation experts, Robert Mercer and Peter Brown, from IBM's speech recognition group, by offering 50% more pay (it would turn into a lot more than that).[30] They were soon followed by much of the rest of the group, leading some to complain that Renaissance set the field of machine translation back by five years.[31] The firm's interest in speech recognition also led to speculation that they had worked out a way to listen in on Wall Street conversations. But their approach probably has as little to do with that as it does with string theory (although a number of firms now automatically scan news reports and twitter feeds to divine market sentiment and generate buy or sell recommendations).

The two main components of a hedge fund's strategy are figuring out what the markets will likely do next, and integrating that prediction into a trading platform. Especially for large firms, these are connected since making a significant trade can affect the market. Both steps need to take into account not just expected profits, but also risk analysis and expenses including taxes. Some hedge funds, such as the ill-fated LTCM, take a "convergence" approach where they look for two different assets whose prices are related – for example, stocks of companies in a similar area – but where one appears underpriced relative to the other. They can then buy the underpriced asset, short the overpriced asset, and wait for their prices to converge. Unfortunately, convergence may take forever, or not happen at all. It is like picking bestsellers based on rational criteria such as the performance of similar books, which as we've seen would miss a lot of candidates.

Renaissance's approach is to throw away any preconceived notions and just look for short-term patterns in the data, which may reflect artefacts to do with trading as much as fundamentals. The Medallion fund, for example, appears to be Catholic in its tastes, and trades international commodity futures, equities, currency swaps,

[30]Delevingne (2014).
[31]McGrayne (2011, p. 247).

bonds, mortgage derivatives, and so on. The fund has its own trading desk, which employs about 20 traders. In one year, the firm executes tens of millions of trades, with many of them held for only a few seconds (the firm pioneered many of the high-frequency trading techniques described by Michael Lewis in *Flash Boys*).[32] As Simons told the Greenwich Roundtable in 1999, "we look at anomalies that may be small in size and brief in time. We make our forecast. Then, shortly thereafter, we re-evaluate the situation and revise our forecast and our portfolio. We do this all day long. We're always in and out and out and in. So we're dependent on activity to make money."[33]

Much of this activity takes place in private "dark-pool" exchanges, in order to avoid telegraphing transactions, which would affect prices. Results are also boosted through leverage: the firm deposits money with a broker, say Barclays or Deutsche Bank, who in turn loan further money. Renaissance manages the whole pot for a year, repays the broker its loan plus fees, and keeps the proceeds. The process can be structured as buying an option on a basket of assets, where Renaissance manages the basket and always chooses to exercise the option; and as discussed below, Renaissance argued exactly that in order to qualify for lower tax rates.[34]

The forecast model therefore has less to do with analyzing fundamentals than using machine learning to find patterns in big data and execute on them rapidly. As Mercer tells the story: "RenTec gets a trillion bytes of data a day, from newspapers, AP wire, all the trades, quotes, weather reports, energy reports, government reports, all with the goal of trying to figure out what's going to be the price of something or other at every point in the future… The information we have today is a garbled version of what the price is going to be next week. People don't really grasp how noisy the market is. It's very hard to find information, but it is there, and in some cases it's been there for a long, long time. It's very close to science's needle-in-a-haystack problem."[35]

Another source of information for Renaissance, as revealed in transcripts of a legal case involving former employees, is limit order book data from public exchanges, which list all the orders that are

---

[32]Stevenson (2014).
[33]Lux (2000).
[34]Levine (2014).
[35]McGrayne (2011, p. 238).

in place to buy and sell an asset at particular prices.[36] One of the best indicators of market changes is the activity of other traders. For example, if there is a queue of orders to buy a stock, then a nimble trader can insert themselves into the order by buying the stock and then quickly reselling it – much as a scalper can profit by being first in line to buy tickets at a popular concert. And part of the prediction is knowing what effect one's own trades will have on the market. Any large order will be sensed by other bots, which will try to profit from them, either by selling into them or buying ahead of them. Strategies have to evolve constantly, as copycats appear and markets change.[37] Because most of the trading is carried out by bots, machine learning algorithms have to learn the behavior of other machine learning algorithms, in a kind of regressive loop, as if the markets are becoming self-aware. The complex technical nature of the problem – akin to building a global brain for finance – is why Renaissance hires mathematicians, statisticians, physicists, and other scientists, but not people from a finance background.[38] (It is ironic that Mercer, who now shares CEO duties with Simons and Brown, went into speech recognition, since he seems to fit into the typical quant mold of being somewhat uninterested in light conversation. As he told the *Wall Street Journal*: "I'm happy going through my life without saying anything to anybody."[39])

Creative Finance

While the exact workings of Renaissance are a closely guarded secret, its financial performance is not. In 2008, at the heart of the financial crisis, when the S&P 500 lost 38.5%, Medallion nearly doubled, with a gain of 98.2%. In the decade from 1994 to mid-2014, the fund made an average annual gain, before fees, of 71.8%. (Fees take about half that, but since the fund is employee-owned, they are just paying

---

[36]Burton and Teitelbaum (2007).
[37]"Almost any good viable predictive signal will almost certainly erode over five years. You have to keep coming up with new things. The market is working against you." Simons quoted in Hamilton (2007).
[38]As Simons told an audience at the International Association of Financial Engineers annual conference, "We hire physicists, mathematicians, astronomers and computer scientists and they typically know nothing about finance. We haven't hired out of Wall Street at all."
[39]Patterson and Strasburg (2010).

themselves.) Its other funds that are open to outside investors also posted consistently positive, if less spectacular, returns. (One dud was the Renaissance Institutional Futures Funds, which was closed in 2015 after returning an average of only 2.86% since its establishment in 2007.[40])

Taxes aren't a problem either. In 2015, after four years of intensive legal work, the company got the Labor Department's permission to shield Medallion inside Roth IRAs, which means it can grow completely tax-free.[41] The firm's aggressive tax stance met with controversy in 2014, when the Senate took it to task for using basket options to avoid more than "$6 billion in taxes by disguising its day-to-day stock trades as long term investments," according to Senator John McCain.[42] There seems to be a disconnect between the tight-fisted approach to taxes on the one hand, and the philanthropy of the Simons Foundation on the other. The Foundation presumably believes that it can do a better job of handing out money and promoting mathematics education and science than the government can. It all fits with the idea of rational, efficient markets, where the biggest winners are the most rational and enlightened of all. Or it would, except that co-CEO Robert Mercer's own foundation donated $2.5 million to the Koch brothers' Freedom Partners Action Fund, and $11 million to the presidential campaign of Tea-party candidate Ted Cruz, neither of which are renowned for their pro-science stance.[43] And it also points to a wider contradiction between the interests of firms such as Renaissance, and those of the economy as a whole.

As we've seen, quants add value by calculating prices for financial instruments such as derivatives, which are used by a diverse range of users. But as the OECD noted in a 2015 report, "there can be too much finance. When the financial sector is well developed, as has been the case in OECD economies for some time, further increases in its size usually slow long-term growth."[44] One reason is that, while banks, investment funds, and stock exchanges have an essential role in supplying capital to companies and individuals, most

---

[40]Wigglesworth (2015b).
[41]Rubin and Collins (2015).
[42]See McCain (2014).
[43]Linskey (2014), Lichtblau (2015), Schwartz (2015).
[44]Cournède *et al.* (2015).

of those recipients in practice turn out to be – other financial firms. In other words, banks are funding one another and trading each other's shares and debts in a kind of merry-go-round. And while this activity is profitable, most of it is not inherently productive.

Hedge funds, for example, don't build anything in the normal sense; instead, they take in techniques and experts from other areas and use their skills to take lots of tiny cuts out of markets (like black holes, information goes in, but little leaks out). Something like high-frequency trading is pretty much a zero-sum game: if Renaissance is making billions, then others – for example, people with retirement funds – are losing billions. While it adds liquidity to certain assets, as discussed in Chapter 10, this apparent liquidity is somewhat illusory, and is not a priority for long-term investors.[45] At the same time, it carries a very real risk to system stability – as illustrated by the trillion-dollar Flash Crash of 2010, which began on May 6 at 2:32 EST, and was all over a little more than half an hour later at 3:08. In that time the Dow Jones lost about 9% of its value, but recovered most of that by the end of the day.

As with most financial crashes, the exact cause of the Flash Crash is uncertain and has been blamed on a number of factors – first on an accidental order which triggered an over-reaction, then five years later on a London-based high-frequency trader using spoof sell orders to drive the markets down – but algorithms certainly played a part, since they dominate most normal trading. Many just turned themselves off as prices began to plummet, which is the computer equivalent of not answering the phone. Computers gave markets an even quicker jolt on October 15, 2014 at 9:33 in the morning, when the prices of US Treasuries spiked up by over seven standard deviations, but were back to normal within twelve minutes. An investigation by regulators showed the activity was mostly "aggressive" momentum-chasing algorithms selling to "passive" algorithms that were acting as market makers. In many cases these algorithms belonged to the same outfit – some 15% of the total activity was firms "self-trading" (i.e., selling to themselves), so "no change in beneficial ownership results."[46] Smaller versions of such "flash" events have become regular occurrences, even in

---

[45]Hendershott *et al.* (2011).
[46]Levine (2015).

previously staid markets such as corn futures.[47] While computer algorithms may seem to be the perfect realization of the type of rational behavior imagined by theorists, the fact that computers do not feel emotions such as fear or greed does not mean that the end result of their actions is rational or optimal.

Hedge funds have their place in the financial ecosystem, and their activities have certainly made it more "efficient" in the narrow sense that prices are consistent and there are fewer arbitrage opportunities for other traders; but anyone who thinks that is what they are being paid for probably also believes in efficient market theory and has stopped reading by now (words being cheap, as we've seen). They aren't about wealth creation, they are about wealth redistribution – like taxes but in reverse. In a world where economic rewards are becoming increasingly skewed and asymmetric – where more and more professions are beginning to look like writing – this is not universally perceived as a good thing, as Piketty pointed out in his book. Which is one reason hedge funds channel much of their largesse toward lobbying politicians (and in some countries dominate political contributions).[48] They shape/influence/game elections the same way they do markets.

Another problem, as a paper from the Bank for International Settlements (BIS) notes, is that "a bloated financial sector can also suck in more than its share of talent, hampering the development of other sectors."[49] In countries such as the USA and the UK, a substantial portion of mathematicians from elite institutions go into finance: "people who might have become scientists, who in another age dreamt of curing cancer or flying to Mars, today dream of becoming hedge fund managers."[50] (BIS – known as the central bank of

---

[47]Massad (2015).

[48]See, for example, Stewart (2009). According to the *New York Times*, of the 158 families who were dominating contributions to the 2016 political race, 64 made their fortune in the finance sector. Next was energy and natural resources, at 17 (Confessore *et al.*, 2015).

[49]"R&D-intensive industries – aircraft, computing, and the like – will be disproportionately harmed when the financial sector grows quickly... a sector with high R&D intensity located in a country whose financial system is growing rapidly grows between 1.9 and 2.9% a year slower than a sector with low R&D intensity located in a country whose financial system is growing slowly" (Bank for International Settlements, 2012).

[50]Cecchetti and Kharroubi (2011). Oxford University claims that about 35% of mathematics graduates go into finance (University of Oxford, 2016).

central banks – often seems to enjoy criticizing the financial system which, as much as any organization, it helped design.) And once firms such as D.E. Shaw hire up all the Math Olympiad champions, most of those skills don't get used in a productive way, if at all. The mathematics used by hedge funds can be tricky and sophisticated, but in the scale of things it isn't that deep, as even Simons admits.[51] Instead, as we noted above, degrees from top-flight institutions act primarily as a barrier to entry, and add to the field's aura of mystique. Training people in mathematics only so they end up in hedge funds is therefore rather like creative writing classes: in either case, from a global perspective, it doesn't make a lot of economic sense, but that isn't the point.[52]

Quants, scientists, and writers all share some of the same impulses: to do something authentic and creative; to test themselves; to achieve a kind of freedom. And they are driven by a similar kind of passion and curiosity. As quant Tom Hayes – on charge for manipulating Libor – said on the stand: "when you get it right, it's like solving that equation. It's make money, lose money, and it's just so pure."[53] But if hedge fund owners *really* wanted to help scientists do their work, the best way would be to stop recruiting their top students by offering them eye-watering salaries. A more realistic alternative, of course, is that the financial sector becomes a less dominant source of employment for other reasons. We will return to this topic in the final chapter. We first turn to the role of quants in creating, and maintaining, a different kind of fiction: the sort that consists of mathematical models.

---

[51]"We don't use very, very deep stuff. Certain of our statistical approaches can be very sophisticated. I'm not suggesting it's simple. I want a guy who knows enough math so that he can use those tools effectively but has a curiosity about how things work and enough imagination and tenacity to dope it out." Simons, quoted in Lux (2000).

[52]As Joshua Levine – the computer expert who designed much of the plumbing for electronic trading – told author Scott Patterson, the chase for ever-increasing speed has become an "expensive and needless mess. You could probably find a cure for cancer in a year if you just reassigned all the smart people who are now working on this artificially created and otherwise useless problem" Patterson (2012, p. 229).

[53]Finch and Vaughan (2015).

C H A P T E R

The Rewrite

"The truth is, the Science of Nature has been already too long made only a work of the Brain and the Fancy: It is now high time that it should return to the plainness and soundness of Observations on material and obvious things."
— Robert Hooke, *Micrographia* (1665)

"During emission testing, the vehicles' ECM ran software which produced compliant emission results under an ECM calibration that VW referred to as the 'dyno calibration'... at all other times during normal vehicle operation, the 'switch' was activated and the vehicle ECM software ran a separate 'road calibration' which reduces the effectiveness of the emission control system."
— The US Environmental Protection Agency explains how
Volkswagen calibrated the electronic control
module (ECM) in its diesel cars to pass emission tests.

Quants put values on esoteric financial products by using sophisticated mathematical models to simulate their behavior. Once a suitable model has been selected, it is first calibrated or tuned to existing data. This typically involves modifying various settings within the model, a process which is rather like adjusting the control surfaces of a model airplane, or tweaking the storyline of a screenplay after a screening. The model is then ready for launch. The quant can let it go and stand back to admire its performance. But what if, instead of working as expected, it veers off course and crashes? This chapter looks at the process of calibration, and shows that model tuning is often as much about fixing appearances, or rewriting reality, as it is about performance.

Our focus here will be on one particularly worrying aspect of quant finance modeling. It's not that this is the worst problem in quant finance, it's just one out of many topics we could have addressed. But we pick on this one because of how it not only illustrates a confusion over modeling in finance, but also sheds light on how quants think, how regulators think, and shows how similar yet how different are finance and proper science.

Let's suppose that your job as a quant is to value an up-and-out call option on the stock of a particular company called XYZ. As discussed in Chapter 5, this is like a regular call option, with the difference that if the stock rises so far as to hit some pre-set trigger level any time before expiration, then it "knocks out" and becomes worthless. This feature makes it a little cheaper, but also makes it very sensitive to volatility, since a volatile stock is more likely to exceed the trigger level.

The straightforward way to estimate volatility is to get a time series of past XYZ stock prices, and analyze these statistically in order to quantify the variability in the numbers. The statistics can be as simple or as complicated as you like – but whatever technique you use will have one fundamental problem, namely how do you know that the future is going to be like the past? The volatility you've just estimated is a number from the past. The future may be completely different. And it's the future value of volatility you need to know; since the contract expires in the future, its value depends on how much the underlying asset moves around from now until expiry.

Another way to approach this problem is to try and infer the future volatility from market prices of simpler derivatives, the calls and puts which are traded in large volumes. These vanilla contracts also depend on estimates of volatility; and these are volatilities over the future, precisely where we need them. However, the prices depart from what you would calculate using Black–Scholes, because – as discussed above – traders adjust them to better account for things like extreme events, and because like everything else these options are subject to market opinion and the forces of supply and demand. One way to interpret this is to say that the model is wrong, or that the model is right and the traders are wrong. But another way, if you believe that markets are efficient, is to say that the prices of these contracts – which concern the future – are telling us something important about volatility *in the future*. There's information in them thar options! And just as we can use the Black–Scholes model to calculate the price of a vanilla option based on a known volatility, so we should be able to go the other way and infer the future volatility by knowing the price. Or if that fails, at least our estimate will be consistent with the other options being traded. It is a financial version of Auto-Tune, the audio processor which corrects singers who sound a bit off so they harmonize perfectly with the rest of the band (here again we see the role of models as a coordination device).

So, returning to our example, we still have to value our complex derivative – for which we need the volatility of the XYZ share price. Fortunately, there is a plain vanilla option on XYZ trading on an exchange for $10. We ask the question: "What value of volatility must be used in our derivatives-valuation model so that it gives an answer of $10 for this basic vanilla contract?" Suppose that the answer was simply that we need a volatility of 0.2, usually written as 20%. This is the implied volatility. Now we are all set to value the more complicated up-and-out call, we just use the same 20% value to calibrate our model for that contract. Job done. Or is it?

Blowing Smoke

Calibration is an example of what are called in mathematical circles "inverse problems." In most physical problems, you are usually trying to figure out from a model how something might behave in the future. Weather forecasting would be a good example. But sometimes you want to go backwards. This would be like trying to figure out what the weather was last week, knowing what it is today. Solving such problems can be easy, as when you infer the stiffness of a spring from experiments with weights, or they can be like driving backwards down a highway using only the rearview mirror – the problems may be larger than they appear.

As an example: you walk into a classroom filled with students, the air is dense with smoke… who is the guilty smoker? Given the distribution of smoke in the room, can you go back mathematically to figure out the source of the smoke, the cigarette?

Smoke concentration obeys the laws of diffusion. This is relatively simple second-year undergraduate mathematics. An undergraduate exam question might ask about the distribution of smoke given the position of its source. But we are not asking that, we are asking the inverse: we want to know the source given its distribution. Superficially similar, they are actually very different. In fact, the smoke problem is what mathematicians call "ill posed," meaning that the slightest disturbance to the distribution could make the backwards calculation impossible. The information has effectively been blurred out.

Talking of blurring reality, fans of *CSI Miami* will remember the episode in which the clue to the identity of a murderer was on a piece of fabric torn from the sail of a yacht, but the fabric had become damp and the ink or mark on the fabric had become diffused. H took the fabric back to CSI headquarters, and, using their clever computer wizardry, undiffused the writing. Well, there's a reason why the verb "to undiffuse" doesn't exist,[1] and that's because IT IS IMPOSSIBLE, H. Our faith in CSI was destroyed at that very moment.[2]

Calibration in finance shares some of the problems of the diffusion problem. As described in Chapter 2, share prices can be modeled as diffusing in time as they are jostled around by random currents, rather like a particle of smoke. Option prices tell you something about what traders think the smoke pattern will look like after a certain time. The Black–Scholes model relies for its accuracy on a single key parameter, the volatility, which is assumed to sum up everything you need to know about a security's behavior. So, if the model were an accurate description of reality, then the inverse problem for any option on a single underlying would also always yield a single number. But as mentioned in Chapter 5, the implied volatility tends to vary with factors such as the strike price and exercise time, so that 20% volatility we calculated for one XYZ option might be 25% for another. And to fit the range of option prices with the model, it turns out (see Box 7.1) that we need to assume the volatility depends both on time and the security's current value. The result of the calibration is not a single constant number, but a lookup table. Furthermore, the

---

[1] 34 hits on Google is our definition of not existing here. Update: It's now over 600 hits. What's going on? Has someone leaked a bootleg copy of this book?

[2] We'd like to give our readers the exact episode reference, but sadly googling "CSI Miami" + yacht doesn't really pin it down. And watching all the episodes is out of the question... we are still way behind with *Mad Men* and *Downton Abbey*.

values in the table are very sensitive, and jump around in a way that does not look natural. In a sense, the complexity of the real world has snuck back into the model by transforming volatility from a single number into something much more complicated.

This isn't the end of the world, as there are mathematical ways of "regularizing" or tidying things up – though it is certainly a clue that all is not well. Of more importance is whether calibration in finance has any grounds for justification – or is it just something that quants do because they can, not because it works? Information is the key. Just how much real information about the future is contained in today's option prices? Is it a lot? Do markets know the future? Or nothing? Traders have to trade, and that leads to prices, even if they have no clue what's going on.

Going backwards with the smoke problem is difficult, but at least it can be justified. Financial calibration cannot easily be justified – in fact, as seen next, it is potentially dangerous.

Box 7.1 Total BS

The history of anything in quantitative finance is hard to pin down. If a new model or trading strategy is financially rewarding, then it would be natural to keep it secret, in order to reap the rewards until someone else comes up with the same idea or something better. The other side of this coin is that only the rubbish will be published. It's not quite that simple, because a lot of finance research is done in universities, where the path to promotion is via publication. Also, many quants are wannabe academics (and many academics are wannabe quants for that matter), so they go ahead and publish even the good stuff. Bearing all this in mind, here are a few highlights from the history of calibration in quant finance.

The first nontrivial example is the Ho–Lee model for interest rates, published in 1986. Interest-rate modeling is more complicated than share-price modeling, because whereas there is only a single share price at any time (ignoring the bid–offer spread), there are different interest rates for different times in the future, corresponding to the yields of bonds of different maturities which make up the so-called yield curve. Ho and Lee found it necessary to use a parameter that was time dependent, as opposed to constant, in order to force the theoretical yield curve to match the market yield curve.

This work was followed in the early 1990s by three papers on valuing options when volatility is varying (by Dupire, Derman and Kani, and Rubinstein, respectively). Their research addressed the more complicated problem of calibrating volatility when there were many options, with a range of strike prices, traded on the same underlying stock. Again, different options available in the market give slightly contradictory information in terms of implied volatility, and to make it work the researchers came up, independently and simultaneously, with the idea of making volatility vary with both time *and* share price. A high share price might be associated with a low volatility, and a low share price with a high volatility. The three papers showed how this volatility function could be chosen so that theoretical option values were consistent with all traded option prices. But the cost was that the easily measured and understood volatility parameter that appeared in traditional models had become much more complicated.

Nevertheless, the new model quickly became a market-standard approach to the valuation of complex equity derivatives.

So, just in case there is any confusion, let's summarize how this works. In order to calculate the price of a complex derivative, we need to know the volatility of the underlying. To do that we look at the prices of vanilla options for the same underlying. These do not conform to the theoretical price calculated using the Black–Scholes formula. But it turns out that we can fit them all if we assume volatility is not a constant, but changes with time and asset price. So, we can make everything work within the Black–Scholes framework – even though we know the same approach didn't work for the vanillas in the first place, and volatility is by definition an average rather than an instantaneously measured quantity. Hang on, now we're confused...

Calibrating the Crystal Ball

The complexity of this model meant there were now no nice formulas for the values of options. But that is no problem for the gifted mathematicians and computer scientists writing the code for our volatility model. More importantly, let's do a sanity check. Does it really make sense that future volatility – the amount of variability in a share price – is a function of asset price and time? Remember, this volatility is backed out from the prices of traded options. So does this mean that traders have access to a crystal ball that tells them the future of volatility? Do the market prices know about the next major earthquake, its date, location, and strength? Do options on the shares of agricultural companies, or ice-cream vendors, or umbrella makers, contain knowledge about next year's rainfall, when weather forecasters struggle with next week?

More subtly, note that the volatility that is backed out is given for all asset prices. For example, the calibration might say that volatility will be 23% in six months' time if the underlying share is $68, or 21% if it is $77, or 20.3% if the share is $83. But the calibration never tells us what the share price itself will be. Hang on a minute, your crystal ball can tell us what the volatility will be for all asset prices. Well, wouldn't it be better if it could instead tell us what the asset price will be in six months? Forget volatility. With *that* crystal ball we can make serious money.

Common sense says that this assumption of a non-constant volatility that we can somehow predict is extremely unrealistic. But that's just common sense. Can we show this scientifically?

There are two ways we could try to confirm that this calibrated model isn't going to work. The first is to wait six months and measure volatility on that date. Using the same numbers as above, if the asset price happens to be $68, then is volatility 23% as predicted, etc.? The problem is that measuring volatility on a specific day is itself a tricky statistical problem, because volatility is defined in terms of an average fluctuation over a reasonably long time period, not just one day. Also, we have to wait a frustrating six months.

A much, much easier method is to do the calibration today, then come back in one week and recalibrate (i.e., use the new market prices of traded options to back out the volatility function), compare the new function with last week's, and check if they are the same. Using the same numbers, does the new function still say that the volatility will be 23% if the asset is $68 in six months less one week? Note that we aren't asking whether the forecast volatility is actually correct. No, we are asking the simpler question of whether the forecast is stable.[3]

The answer is almost certainly that no, they are not the same. The new forecast is different from the old forecast. This is a game you can all play at home, but using weather forecasts. Look at the weather forecast for a specific location in one week. Come back two days later and see what the forecast is now, for the same place and date. (Use a location like England, not Fuerteventura where the weather is always

---

[3] Paul jokes during his lectures that he expected this calibrated model to be popular for all of one week, until the first time it had to be recalibrated. He's been making the same joke now for over 20 years. The model is still popular. People still laugh, but it's more out of pity for Paul these days.

the same.) The forecast usually changes. A day later it may have changed again. And this is for the same date and place. You don't even have to wait until next week to see what the weather turns out to be. What does this make you think? The obvious conclusion is that forecasting isn't much good. To be fair, at least we know that weather forecasting isn't that accurate, and we've come to expect forecasts to change. In quant finance the calibrated function is assumed not to change, and a lot of money is bet on that assumption.

Is this what quants think when they do this recalibration? Surprisingly not. If this were a model of a physical process, most scientists would say it's time to go back to the drawing board. Not so in finance. The real purpose of calibration, it seems, is to fix the appearances of the model, and provide what looks like a mathematically consistent story.

In any case, this is now where things start to get interesting. So far it's all been mathematics and models. Now we have to understand how the quant thinks and his motivations, not to mention the thoughts and motivations of his bosses.

Sources of Confusion

The first point is that the average quant is sadly confused about a number of issues, such as randomness. Which is surprising, to say the least. The basic models that quants use assume that share prices are random. They also have models for random interest rates, random everything. There comes a point where they forget what's modeled as random and what's assumed to be fixed.

In the volatility calibration described above we had only one quantity as random, which was the underlying share price. Everything else was fixed. But fixed doesn't necessarily mean constant. We had a volatility function that depended on asset price and time, but it was meant to be a function that didn't change. Confusing? How can something be time dependent but not changing? Easy. Think of the TV guide. There you'll see that what's on the TV is time dependent: one hour there's a chat show, next there's a comedy, then a movie, and so on. But the schedule is fixed. Imagine sitting down to watch *The Third Man* and *Dumb and Dumber* comes on. That's a rescheduling, in finance a recalibration. In finance it is considered okay, in the world of home entertainment less so.

It is very common to hear quants say that because they always recalibrate it means that the model is always right. Yes, it does mean that the model for one fleeting instant gives the appearance that it gets traded option values right. But it's in appearance only. If you ever recalibrate it means either the model was wrong before, is wrong now, or was wrong both times. And if you happily recalibrate without a second's thought then we have to conclude that it's the last – i.e., the model is always wrong. It is like having to recalibrate a weighing scale every time you use it, instead of just once. Maybe the scale is broken.

Another relevant issue, which affects many quantitative finance models, is the question of price vs. value. The quant is called upon to find a value, a theoretical value, for new products. This value depends on the model. But it's not the same as the price. At least for his sake we hope not. No, the price that a contract is sold for ought to be higher than the theoretical value, because that represents profit. Yet traded prices are used for calibration, and you have no idea how much of that price represents the value that is really needed for the calibration.

Here's a simple example of this. Your car is worth $20k. Your annual insurance premium is $1k. Let's suppose this insurance is only for crashing, not third party, etc. The quant would deduce from this that the probability of crashing in one year was 1 in 20, or 5%. He would completely miss the point that the $1k premium includes a substantial profit margin for the insurance company. And barring loss leaders, etc., the probability of crashing for the average person in this situation would be a lot less than 5%. That's price vs. value for you – and another source of model error, and quant confusion. Ironically, the assumption of no arbitrage creates another opportunity for arbitrage (see Box 7.2).

David once worked in a small firm, listed on the stock market, which at its most minimalist point had only four full-time staff (not including part-time board members, etc.). But at the same time there were two fairly active online chat forums discussing the company. So it was possible to get a sense of how much information investors had about what was actually going on. The share price was very volatile, and would occasionally spike or fall because of some news announcement, or a sudden change in sentiment on the part of investors, or an obvious attempt to ramp or manipulate the share price; but in nearly all cases the relationship between the stock quote and what was actually going on at the company – i.e., between price and information – was tenuous or just wrong.

Here's one final example to illustrate just how much information is contained in a market price. Or rather, how little. Do you remember when oil first hit $100 a barrel? It was the beginning of 2008. Do you remember why? What were the economic circumstances? Okay, well make a guess. Something about the situation in the Middle East? Maybe. Demand in China? Could be. Actually no. It was reported that a lone trader bought 1000 barrels, and immediately sold them, at a $600 loss. His goal? To be able to tell his grandchildren that he was the person who first paid $100 a barrel. And how much information is contained here? Not a lot about oil, or the Middle East, or China, but quite a lot about one trader and his family.

Box 7.2   Paul's Hedge Fund

In the hedge fund in which I was a partner, our niche was volatility arbitrage. We forecast volatility and exploited differences between the prices at which options were trading vs. what we reckoned volatility would turn out to be. It was simple actual vol vs. implied vol arbitrage. To remove any market risk, we delta hedged.

It was a simple story and easy to explain. Although it seems quite a basic idea, making money from having a forecast of volatility, it was surprisingly little discussed in the academic literature. Funny how making money and academia are so opposed.

Let me explain one of the subtleties.

Suppose you forecast that volatility will be 20%. But options are trading with an implied volatility of 30%. How can you make money, assuming your forecast turns out to be correct?

The first step is easy, you sell options! They are overpriced. But selling options alone will leave you exposed to market risk – i.e., movement in the underlying asset. To get rid of that market risk, you have to delta hedge. Let's suppose that we are in a Black–Scholes world of constant volatility, no transaction costs, etc., then there's the whole Black–Scholes delta-hedging technique you can use to get rid of that market risk, and there's the famous delta formulas.

Now the only difference between our scenario and that in the textbooks is that people are buying and selling options for the wrong (as far as we are concerned) price.

Here's the question for you. When we delta hedge using the Black–Scholes formulas, do we plug 20% or 30% into the place where the formulas need volatility?

In a nutshell, we are saying that options are mispriced and asking how we can make money from this mispricing. An innocent enough question. But it turns out that when we had our hedge fund there were fewer than five papers on this topic. There were tens of thousands of papers based around time-dependent volatility, stochastic volatility, calibration, and assuming that all market prices were correct. But fewer than five on the mathematics of how to make money from volatility arbitrage.

Can there be any other business besides derivatives in which the first assumption is that there's no money to be made? I've written quite a few business plans over the years, and I can't recall ever saying we wouldn't make money.

You'll have to read Ahmad and Wilmott (2005) for the detailed answer to the delta-hedging question, but the idea that almost every quant in the world was assuming no arbitrage was helpful to our fund sales pitch. While everyone else was assuming no arbitrage, it meant less competition for our fund and explained why options could be consistently mispriced. If everyone believes in something unquestioningly, then no one is going to be trying to disprove it, and in this case options could stay mispriced forever. And investors knew that perfectly efficient markets was a nonsense and so appreciated our story.

Model Risk

Because the model's theoretical output is briefly the same as the market's option prices, people are fooled into thinking that the model is right. And in being right, there's no risk in the valuation. Unfortunately, this could not be further from the truth.

In quantitative finance there's always a question about the accuracy of models. This is termed "model risk." There are many, many forms of risk, all of which the responsible bank will try to measure and if necessary reduce. However, if we are constantly recalibrating it means that we never get to see the risk in the volatility model. Certainly it is possible to see how bad the model is by seeing how much our table of future volatilities changes at each recalibration. But there's not much incentive to do this, as we'll see later. Worse, there are some models that can go straight to valuation of derivatives without ever going through the step of formally calculating the calibrated quantities.[4] This means that you never get to see the model error, it remains hidden somewhere in the bowels of the model.

---

[4] An example is the Heath, Jarrow, and Morton interest-rate model.

As discussed further in the next chapter, one reason why mathematical modelers in general prefer to use simple models is because the assumptions and their associated risks are more transparent. One of the great appeals of the Black–Scholes model is its parsimony. The tendency of an asset price to fluctuate is summed up by a single number, the volatility. But when we attempt to back out volatility from market data, and use it to value a derivative, the single number is replaced by a lookup table that mutates with time. It is no longer correct to say that the volatility is a single parameter – it is a whole series of separate parameters, which apply for different prices and dates. A simple concept – an asset's volatility – has been transformed into something that is highly complex, and the model risk has become intractable.

This goes to the heart of the danger that derivatives can pose to the financial system if used incorrectly. Engineers can build a complex system like an airplane out of hundreds of thousands of parts, because they understand the rules that describe the behavior of the parts within a certain regime, and they make sure that those parts operate within that regime. The motor that actuates the rudder is designed to be able to withstand the forces that it will experience; the landing gear can support the stress of a forced landing; the flaps can handle the stress when extended; and so on. As a result, the airplane responds in a predictable fashion to its controls. But financial derivatives, and therefore much of the financial system, are cobbled together from components such as implied volatility, which are highly unstable and unreliable – so you can bet the whole is as well.

Flying Blind

It might seem that these problems are reasonably obvious, and it is true that the more sophisticated banker is aware of them (though such people are sadly not as common as you'd expect for such a highly paid job). However, for institutional reasons his main aim is not to debunk the model – after all, there is no bonus for that. Instead, it is to justify the use of the calibrated model, to himself, to his boss, to risk managers, regulators, and investors. There are strong incentives to go with the flow. Two main justifications are commonly used.

The first is that the method may not be perfect, but it is always possible to hedge the derivatives using exchange-traded vanillas, which mitigates the risk. This isn't too bad a justification – as long as it's right. Unfortunately, it's not only hard to estimate the model risk from this sort of hedging, it's also something that people take on faith, and they rarely try to estimate the remaining model error in practice. (It's also a bit like saying we are using scales to weigh something rather than a spring. Scales will work whatever the force of gravity, because they measure weight directly against known quantities rather than indirectly via a spring. This may be the perfect justification, but can we have some more research on this please?)

The second, more scary but very common, justification is: what else can we do? The banker says: "We need to trade, we need a model, this is what we've got, there's nothing better, we use it." Leaving aside the question of whether there is a better model, this justification makes you wonder about the morals here. Is it true that they "need" to trade? Isn't there the option of trading simpler products? It could even be counterproductive. If you want to trade but a risk manager says there's too much risk, that you can't, well, there goes your fee. Trading is much easier if you don't know the risks involved. Don't ever forget it's OPM – other people's money.

Without an understanding of model risk, the financial system is flying blind, the controls are not responding as expected, and we are headed for a crash. In the next chapter, we consider the fundamental cause of model risk, of which calibration problems are just a symptom – namely the category error of treating a human system as a mechanical one.

8

No Laws, Only Toys

"The forecast," said Mr. Oliver, turning the pages till he found it,
"says: Variable winds; fair average temperature; rain at times."...
There was a fecklessness, a lack of symmetry and order in the clouds,
as they thinned and thickened. Was it their own law, or no law, they
obeyed?

—Virginia Woolf, *Between the Acts*

"For every expert there is an equal and opposite expert."

—Arthur C. Clarke

Mathematical models in the real sciences are based on fundamental physical laws and principles. Mass and energy are conserved, to name two obvious examples. But there are no such laws in finance. Financial models are necessarily more qualitative than quantitative. But this doesn't stop the quant thinking he's a scientist. After all, he's more than likely had a scientific education, so it's tempting to think that in going from physics to finance he has merely changed from denim and sneakers to suit and oxfords. He sees an idea like the efficient markets hypothesis and thinks he's back in the quadrangle with Dirac. Sometimes his belief in the models is simple naiveté, sometimes it is physics envy. Either way, it's dangerous to have too much faith in the models. But does the field need less physics – or more?

One great skill in life is to be able to distinguish between problems and opportunities. Going further, surely every motivational speaker tells us that there are opportunities within every problem? "In the middle of difficulty lies opportunity," said Albert Einstein. He also said, "You think you've got problems. You should see mine!" Large parts of Kipling's *If* are devoted to precisely this attitude. Miguel de Cervantes said, "As one door shuts another door opens." Perhaps it was when they were shutting the cell door on him. (Paul's stepfather says, "As one door shuts another door closes," somewhat less optimistically.) And this is precisely how quantitative finance should be approached.

We've already seen – and we'll discuss it more below – that quantitative finance does not have any of the fundamental building blocks that are throughout the physical sciences, the Newtonian laws for example. Or the perfectly reproducible chemical reactions. In 1991, back when he was chief economist of the World Bank, Larry Summers proclaimed: "Spread the truth – the laws of economics are like the laws of engineering. One set of laws works everywhere."[1] But there are no "laws of economics." Nothing is reproducible. They say you can't argue with physics, but you can certainly argue with economics.

Is this a problem?

Hell, no! It's an opportunity!

This is how science works. You see something, perhaps in nature, perhaps in industry, perhaps in finance, that you'd like to understand. You formulate some hypothesis about what's going on. That hypothesis ought to explain what you are seeing, but then so could many theories. Therefore, you seek out new situations that you haven't seen before for which your theory is relevant and see if your hypothesis can predict what happens. If your theory is good at predicting such new results – ideally in as parsimonious a way as possible – then it's a point in favor of your theory. If it's no good then you need to tweak your hypothesis, or maybe even go all the way back to the drawing board. (If your theory is consistent with *anything* – i.e., it's unfalsifiable – then it's not very useful. See string theory.)

The parsimonious bit is important. You could (well, you couldn't, but you know what we mean) have a giant spreadsheet table listing the gravitational forces between all the bodies in the universe. You could argue that this was a theoretical model of the universe. The

---

[1] Hedlund (2011, p. 20).

table would take the form of a square matrix, with the number of rows and columns being the number of such bodies.[2]

How does that compare with the simple formula that the gravitational force between two bodies is proportional to the mass of the bodies (m_1 and m_2) and inversely proportional to the square of the distance r between their centers of mass?

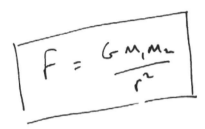

$$F = \frac{G\, m_1 m_2}{r^2}$$

See what we mean by parsimonious? No need for that spreadsheet.

It's important to note that the "laws" have a zone of validity, just like human laws. Hooke's law for springs, for example, says that the force needed to stretch or compress a spring is equal to a constant number multiplied by the extension. Engineers apply it to compute an object's response to a force. However, the formula is a linear approximation which works better for some materials than others – it is not much use for concrete (too brittle), or human tissue (if you pull on your ear lobe, it stretches easily at first but soon becomes very resistant), or rubber (when you blow into a balloon, it is hard at first, then easy, then hard again). Newton's law, meanwhile, is an approximation to Einstein's theory of general relativity, which accounts for the curvature of space-time. According to philosopher Roberto Mangabeira Unger and physicist Lee Smolin, it may be that no laws are completely fundamental and eternal, but themselves evolve with time – as if the universe is learning as it goes.[3] For the purposes of modeling, we'll say that a law is a relationship that has been extensively tested and can be treated as fixed and certain within a certain domain.

To summarize, then, the key elements of this process are reproducibility, prediction, and simplicity. Plus knowing where the model breaks down.

---

[2] But, damn, that would only work at an instant in time. The bodies would move and the gravitational forces would change.

[3] Unger and Smolin (2015).

- *Hooke's law for springs.* Applies for materials only within a certain range – and if you stretch anything too far, it will break.

- *Newton's law of gravity.* Seems to apply everywhere in the visible universe, subject to Einstein's corrections. Unless of course the gravitational force ascribed to "dark matter" is actually due to Newton's law breaking.

- *Conservation laws.* In his *Principia*, Newton assumed that, while one substance might conceivably transmute into another (he was an alchemist as well, after all), the total amount of mass in a closed system should remain constant.[4] Einstein later modified this by showing that energy was another form of mass. Another such principle is conservation of momentum (mass times velocity), which Newton showed was a consequence of his laws of motion.

Even if you're not a mathematician, you can see that these fundamental mathematical models are simple. There's no spreadsheet the size of the universe here. And they just feel right.

A Clue

Quantitative finance does not have any fundamental laws. There's no such thing as conservation, for example. If a share price falls 50% in one day, then half the company's value has just disappeared. If there are no laws, then we might try to rely on statistics. We can still build up a solid model. But if the statistics are not stable, then our model might be limited in accuracy. That's finance.

Consider that old chestnut, the "law of supply and demand." This states that the market for a particular product has a certain supply, which tends to increase as the price goes up (more suppliers enter the market). There is also a certain demand for the product, which increases as the price goes *down*. If you plot these two functions – supply and demand – as a function of price, then they form an X pattern, one line going up and the other down, intersecting at a single, correct price. This simple relationship – first illustrated by Scottish engineer (and inventor of the cable car) Fleming Jenkin in his 1870 essay "On the graphical representation of supply

---

[4] Newton and Chittenden (1846).

and demand" – does capture a key insight into the way markets work, in a way which has been described as "gratifying and aesthetically pleasing."[5] The market value of a product cannot be determined simply by adding up the costs of production and including a profit margin, because if no one wants the product, there won't be a market for it. Conversely, you can't back out all such information just by knowing the market price – something that will be news for many quants who routinely do exactly that for key quantities such as volatility.

But while the supply and demand picture might capture a general fuzzy principle, it is far from being a law. For one thing, there is no such thing as a stable "demand" that we can measure independently – there are only transactions. When a transaction takes place, the buyers and sellers are necessarily in balance (as Bachelier pointed out), and while it may be the case that potential buyers outweigh potential sellers, or vice versa, at any time, this is extremely hard to quantify. Also, the desire for a product is not independent of supply, or other factors, so it isn't possible to think of supply and demand as two separate lines. Part of the attraction of luxury goods – or for that matter more basic things, such as housing – is exactly that their supply is limited. And when their price goes up, they are often perceived as more desirable, not less. This is why the "law of supply and demand" is frequently trotted out to explain why something just happened after-the-fact – as in "this year the price of oil went down because demand decreased" – but is less useful for making accurate predictions (see oil price forecasts). And when someone asserts, for example, that "price is the intersection of two curves, supply and demand," they are referring to an imaginary thing they have never seen outside their economics textbook.

The "no-arbitrage principle" doesn't quite work either, and for similar reasons. In theory, one should be able to deduce the price of an option from the price and volatility of a stock, on the basis that any departure from that price would create an arbitrage opportunity. But in practice the price of the option is also affected by its own supply and demand, by fear and greed, not to mention all the imperfections such as hedging errors, transaction costs, feedback effects, etc. The role of assumptions such as no arbitrage is again to simply put fuzzy bounds on the relative prices among all the instruments. For example, you cannot have an equity price being 10 and an at-the-money call option being 20 without violating a simple arbitrage. The

---

[5] DeMartino (2010, p. 175).

more realistic the assumption/model, and the harder it is to violate in practice, the more seriously you should treat it. The arbitrage in that example is trivial to exploit and so should be believed. However, in contrast, the theoretical profit you might think could be achieved via dynamic hedging is harder to realize in practice, because delta hedging is not the exact science that one is usually taught. Therefore, results based on delta hedging should be treated less seriously.

However, while there are no fixed laws in financial modeling, there are clues that can point us in the right direction.

Or rather, there's one clue. In the whole of quant finance there is only really one peg onto which we can hang our modeling hat.

The one clue to modeling a share price is... drum roll... we don't care about the share price. (Shurely shome mishtake, ed.)

No, really. We don't care about the price of a share, its numerical value in dollars, pounds, or whatever. No, there's nothing special about $1, or $100, or 10 cents. At least not in absolute terms. Yes, we do care that the share price is now 10 cents since it was $10 when we bought it. But that's a relative thing. The absolute value of the share price doesn't matter, but its value relative to the past does matter.

Think of it this way. If you've got $1000 dollars to invest and the stock is $1, you must buy 1000 shares. If it's $10, you must buy 100 shares. In both cases you have $1000 in stock to start with, and it's how that $1000 changes that you care about. All that you really, really care about is how much the share price has gone up, or gone down, in relative terms. In other words, all that matters is its return. A similar observation inspired Osborne, in his paper on Brownian motion, to note that the model should track proportional price changes (one way to do this is to use a logarithmic scale).

Back to Basics

Why is this an important clue for us modelers? Because it means that in any model we build up we should first study data for the returns, and then model these returns. Suppose, for example, we are trying to model the expected returns of the Dow Jones over a certain time period. Then we could start by plotting some data as we did in Figure 2.5, which showed a histogram of the 100-day returns. One approach would be to use this histogram directly to calculate the probability of a price change within a certain range. Note that even by doing this, we would already be making a couple of critical assumptions. One is that the distribution is stable, so in statistical terms the future will resemble the past. Another is that what happens each period is independent of previous periods, so there is no memory (see also Box 8.1 below).[6]

But it's hard to do any mathematical analysis without equations. So what the mathematician does is to say "Hey, that distribution of returns could be represented by a formula." And this is where the mathematical modeling comes in, and further assumptions are made.

Some mathematicians will say "It looks like the normal distribution to me, boys!" Which is great, because the normal distribution is easy to work with and has some great properties. Others will say "No, it looks more like [insert favorite (and therefore probably quite complicated) probability distribution here] to me."

The second group would probably be closer to the truth, since their distribution would be a better fit to the empirical distribution. But their distribution might be so complicated as to limit the usability of the model. The power-law distribution, for example, has no well-defined mean, and is extremely hard to calibrate accurately because the sample of extreme events on which this process depends is by definition small.

In almost all practice it is the normal distribution that is used. So, by a natural process, we end up with a simple random walk of the sort discussed in Chapter 2 (see Figure 2.3). It's the statistical equivalent of fitting a nice straight line to the data. But note how, by choosing the normal distribution, we have already gone from a potentially accurate, albeit unwieldy, model to a toy model.

Even though it's a toy model, it contains a couple of useful ideas that can then be used throughout quantitative finance. These two ideas are just the two parameters in the normal distribution – the average, which tells you the expected return, and the standard deviation, which tells you the volatility.[7] As we've seen throughout

---

[6] The assumption of time independence is quite good if you look at quantities like serial autocorrelation – that is, the correlation of prices with the past. And very few researchers assume anything else. (PW is one, natch.) However, if you look at the days before and after the 1987 crash you will see a large number of statistically unlikely moves in the S&P 500, not just the biggy of October 19th. Clearly, at crisis times, there is some history effect.

[7] There's some scaling to be done to get the common "annualized" quantities, the annualized expected return and the volatility. Since the data is daily you need to multiply the expected return by the number of data points in a year, around 252, and the standard deviation by the square root of the number of business days in a year.

this book, these are very useful, intuitively understandable concepts. But we have to remember their zone of validity. By using the normal distribution, we are saying that extreme events such as Black Monday, or the Flash Crash, or financial crises in general, have effectively zero chance of happening. We are also assuming that the rate of return, and the volatility, will remain constant (recalibration apart).

If these limitations don't trouble us, then as shown in Chapter 3 we could push the idea a little further. Plot risk against reward for a large number of assets. Come up with the idea of a "capital market line," which draws a straight line through the data, just like Hooke's law. Begin to think of the market as a giant weighing device that stretches returns as you pile on risk.

In derivatives, the volatility is the most important stock parameter. Indeed, we've seen that the expected return doesn't affect the value of an option at all according to the Black–Scholes theory. Volatility is something quite easy to understand, it's how jumpy the stock price is. It's so easy to understand that traders even talk about the value of volatility on the understanding that there's a one-to-one correspondence between the value of volatility and the value of vanilla options. A toy model has led to a good grasp of how options behave, but its variables and parameters – the characters in the story – have also started to take on a life of their own.

A Model for Interest Rates?

Emboldened by having created a toy model that's so-so accurate for stocks, we can ask if perhaps this stock-price model is also good for other financial quantities.

The model we have just built up says that the share-price *return* is normally distributed with a certain mean and a certain standard deviation. And those two parameters don't depend on the level of the stock. Equivalently, it's like saying that the stock *price* evolves from one instant to the next with a mean that is proportional to the stock price and a standard deviation proportional to the stock price.

Now, let's see if we can apply similar ideas to modeling interest rates, as a first example of applying the model elsewhere. Can we just replace "share price" in the above with "interest rate"?

Is this a good model: "The interest rate evolves from one instant to the next with a mean proportional to the interest rate and a standard deviation proportional to the interest rate"? Emphatically no! It's instructive to see why.

First of all, stocks tend to keep rising. Not steadily, the volatility makes them bounce around, but in the long run (e.g., Figure 2.5). That's if they survive the long run. Or the company steadily gets worse and the stock falls, and falls. This characteristic is seen in the lognormal random walk model we've built up. If the expected growth is big enough, then the stock will grow over time. If too small, then it will fall. Therefore, if you apply this model to interest rates, they too will either rise indefinitely, or keep falling. Even if the growth rate is set to zero, the expected deviation from its starting point of a random walk could become arbitrarily large. And rates just don't do this in practice. They go up, then come down. They go down, and then rise up. Any model should capture this behavior.

We can do this within the framework we've built up by simply making the expected return and the volatility of interest rates into some function of interest rates. This is easily seen by looking at the expected return. If we make it negative for high interest rates, then high interest rates will tend to fall. If we also make it positive for low rates, then low rates will tend to increase. This is called mean-reverting behavior. In such a model interest rates go up, then fall, then fall, then go back up, just as we see.

But here's our modeling problem. Which function of rates is positive for low values of the rates but negative for high values? Are you kidding? There are an uncountably infinite number of such functions. Which is the right one?

See the problem? In modeling the stock we had to have the expected return function proportional to the stock to get the behavior that the level of the stock didn't matter, only its return. That left one parameter in the expected-return function, the coefficient of proportionality. We have little clue as to what the functional form should be for interest-rate expected growth. And we haven't even started to look at the volatility behavior of rates. Or the question of whether there is a stable value for the mean that we are supposed to be reverting to.

And it's the same problem for anything else we try to model. Credit risk, volatility, etc.

The only half-decent, yet still toy, models in finance are the lognormal random walk models for those instruments whose level we don't care about. That's equities, indices, exchange rates, commodities.[8] This is why almost everyone is using the lognormal random walk model for these quantities, but there isn't a standard model for interest rates, everyone uses something different. There's no bollard on which to moor our interest-rate modeling boat. But that doesn't mean we can't make some progress. For inspiration, we can turn to an area with a different history and set of approaches – mathematical biology.

Box 8.1 Memories

Even the assumption that the level of the stock price is irrelevant can be questioned. Here's what can happen in practice. And we'll also show you how to make small changes to the model to allow for reality.

A stock is hovering around $100. It has a volatility of 20%. The company starts to struggle as competitors enter its market. The share price falls over the course of a year to $60. At the same time, volatility rises to 30%. Now that shouldn't happen according to the classical constant-parameter lognormal model. Volatility doesn't vary with stock price. But in reality, investors are nervous about the future of the company now that its share price has fallen and this is seen in increased volatility.

However, it's not the stock level now – the $60 – that matters. No, it's that what is now $60 used to be $100. The market has a memory for this stock. In the language of the behavioral economists, investors are anchored at the $100. They see that as the natural level for this company. Now what will happen is that if the company stabilizes, the market will forget about the $100. It will start to think of $60 as the natural level, at which point the volatility will also fall back to 20%.

This is clearly different from the memory-independent classical lognormal random walk model. But that model is easily tweaked to incorporate such anchoring. All you have to do is introduce a memory variable, some average of the stock price in the past, and then make the volatility a function of the ratio of the current stock price to this average.[9] This is still a toy model, but it captures not only the empirical results but also a little bit of the human as well.

Memory? It's another psychological topic that has crept into economics, and maybe one day we'll see more of it in finance.

A Role Model

In the mid-1980s one of the hottest mathematical topics was that of mathematical biology. There's no better way to describe this subject

---

[8] Yes we do care about the level of these if we have to buy them to run our car, for example, or feed our children. But as investments, we don't care.
[9] Wilmott *et al.* (2014).

than to skim through the contents of possibly the best book on mathematical modeling (and not just in biology) ever written, *Mathematical Biology* by Jim Murray. The edition to which we'll refer is the first, published in 1989. To date this is the only mathematics book that Paul has ever read in bed. We would recommend this book to anyone doing modeling in any field whatsoever – even, or perhaps especially, quant finance. It is highly inspirational, and also covers many different mathematical fields.

The first four chapters are about population dynamics. For example, modeling how the population of the spruce budworm changes due to births and deaths. The resulting model shows how the population can have one or three steady states, depending on parameters in the model. (One is tempted to think of interest rates as a financial quantity that might also exhibit steady states, states that change depending on parameters such as official policy.) We are up to page 7 of Professor Murray's book. From page 8 we learn about delay models. In practice, there is a delay between the birth of a budworm and it reaching maturity and in turn reproducing. (Hmm… a change in interest-rate policy might be flagged by the policy makers but with a delay before implementation. It's not different to see parallels between mathematical biology models and finance.) The delay models are also relevant in some diseases, for example Cheyne–Stokes respiration (we are on page 15). This is not related to populations, but the delay is due to a time lag between a change in the level of carbon dioxide in the blood and its observation in the brain. (Time lag? Observation? "News"! Makes us think of everything financial, after all, it's news which drives much of the change in market prices. And today there are several vendors selling data feeds of news, search terms on Google, and twitter trends precisely so people, or their text-reading algorithms, can get one step ahead of the news.)

Page 29 introduces us to age distribution. People are born, get older, die. Can we figure out the number of people at any age? Yes. Not deterministically perhaps, but probabilistically yes. This is a subject well covered by actuarial science.[10] On page 41 of Chapter 2

---

[10] It's interesting to observe that for the last 10 or 15 years, actuaries have been trying to get into quant finance. Why? They have relevant skills, and they quite like the pay packet. Sadly, although the actuaries are keen to learn mathematical finance, there is no sign of the quants wanting to learn the (probably more useful) skills of the actuary.

we are shown how a simple population model, first developed by ecologist Robert May, leads to the nonlinear logistic model and chaos. In Chapter 3 we have interacting populations, for example the classical lion–gazelle-type models. The lions eat the gazelles, causing the gazelle population to fall. The lions have nothing to eat, their population falls. This allows the gazelle population to build up. As does the lion population in response. (Now, if that isn't a toy model of how interest rates and inflation dance around we don't know what is.) Such models help in the management and conservation of species, helping to determine, for example, whether culling is beneficial.

Seventeen more chapters to go (including appendices and index, the book is 696 pages long). Reaction kinetics, coupled oscillations, chemotaxis, animal coat patterns, epidemics, etc. But we've made our point. There is a richness in mathematical biology, in the subjects addressed and the mathematics used, that ought to be seen in mathematical finance.

The above are almost all toy models. None can predict with pinpoint accuracy the dynamics of the bumble-bee population, and they can't tell you exactly how many spots there will be on a leopard. But all can be used to explain what is seen in nature, and all can be used to help in the control of species where necessary, to aid in the development of pesticides, to fight against disease, or to aid conservation, etc.

Many of the modeling ideas could be used to advantage in finance, economics, government policy making, etc., which seem relatively stuck in the past. As Robert May told the *Financial Times*, "The more I hear about financial economics, the more I am struck by its similarity to ecology in the 1960s."[11] But we bet there are more mathematical biologists wanting to learn the relatively straightforward subject of quant finance than there are quants wanting to learn the tools of mathematical biology. Incidentally, Jim shows how a random walk leads to the diffusion equation, the mainstay of quant finance, in pages 232 to 236. That's five pages. Finance authors can take an entire book to do this simple job.

Is mathematical biology still a science? Sure. You don't need perfect models to be a science – otherwise hardly anything would qualify.

---

[11]Quoted in Cookson *et al.* (2009).

Biological models might simplify very complicated processes, and be qualitative rather than purely quantitative, but they still give useful insights into mechanisms and behaviors.

Why are these toy models? In very few of the models in Jim Murray's book are there any reliable physical laws. The main exception being those based on chemistry. In Section 15.2 we see a model for pattern formation in butterfly wings based on the diffusion of morphogens through the wing. Now, the diffusion equation can be very accurate but given that the wing coloration is happening at a cellular level, and with the complex geometry of the wing and the veins, we cannot expect the model to give anything other than the gross features of the pattern.

In just this one field of mathematical biology we see a great variety of mathematics. And it is precisely because there are no fundamental laws that researchers have the freedom to use whatever mathematics they fancy. And that is what makes mathematical biology as a research field such a joy – the total, uninhibited freedom one has to model in whatever way works.

In the decades since Murray wrote his book, the techniques used in computational biology have expanded to include things such as network theory, complexity theory, and the machine learning techniques discussed in Chapter 6, which are ideally suited for analyzing and searching for patterns in large quantities of data, such as genomes. Now, we aren't saying that we should be transferring technology *en masse* from mathematical biology to quantitative finance. No, that would be silly. Yes, we, seasoned mathematical modelers that we are, can find parallels between things in biology and things in finance literally as fast as we are typing, but that was just an intellectual exercise. We are saying that quantitative finance could benefit from being approached in a similar manner.

Embrace the fact that the models are toy, and learn to work within any limitations. Focus more attention on measuring and managing resulting model risk, and less time on complicated new products.

In fact, the same could be said of life in general. We all carry our mental models of reality around in our head. We all try to shoehorn experience into our preconceived structures. But only by remaining both skeptical and agile can we learn. Keep your models simple, but remember they are just things you made up, and be ready to update them as new information comes in.

Reasons to be Mathematical

If all finance models are inevitably toys, then why do abstract fields such as measure theory (which generalizes measures such as length or area and is used in advanced probability theory) have such a stranglehold on the subject? Why go to such lengths to rigorously prove over and over again what is quite frankly obvious to any seasoned mathematician? Why is the subject so insistent about maintaining the appearance of mathematical exactness? There are a number of reasons:

- *Envy.* Mathematical biologists are comfortable working with toy models. They tend to be people from a solid mathematics background and know their strengths and weaknesses. They are quite at ease with themselves. In contrast, most people working in quantitative finance come from finance or economics or computer science. And quant finance is their big break, they can now proudly tell their parents that they are proper mathematicians. But only if they can fool people that the mathematics is hard enough. Measure theory can be very hard. It's quite abstract. But it's also something that is seen in the first year of an undergraduate mathematics degree. However, being abstract gives it a kudos that more practical mathematics, applied mathematics, doesn't have. It's like the Emperor's new clothes. Okay, we'll be the little boy in the story: "Look, Mummy, they're only doing first-year math!"

- *Education.* Masters programs in mathematical finance have almost all been made in the same image. We can see the scenario 20 years ago at a meeting of the mathematics faculty at one of the less prestigious universities. The chairman gets to the part in the agenda were they are to discuss a new degree program in mathematical finance. The chairman asks the faculty members if they know anything about the subject in question. None do. Okay then. "Anyone know measure theory?" A few shy hands go up. "Then let's rebrand the measure theory courses as mathematical finance. Let's rock'n'roll!" Except the chairman wouldn't say "Let's rock'n'roll."

- *Inertia.* Inertia is the wrong word for this. But what we mean is that there's no incentive to incorporate more or better mathematical models into this business. There is so much money in derivatives and banking generally that all you need to make a ton of money is to not get into any trouble and just cream your percentage off the top.

- *Credibility.* At the same time, the fact that there are massive amounts of money at stake is scary and means that you want your model to be based on something that is solid, or at least conforms to agreed standards. You also want to be able to talk in a convincing way about risk analysis. The expression "toy model" is unlikely to play well. In this respect, finance is more like engineering. But engineers rely on well-tested results such as Hooke's law to make their calculations; they know to build in a margin of error, and they are keenly aware of where their models break down.

- *Consistency.* Finally, a related reason why finance has evolved the way it has is that the subject's mental DNA – to employ a biological metaphor – is based on fixed ideas, imported from economic theory, about the way the world works. While economics does not have conservation laws, it does have its economic principles. These include the ideas that investors have similar power and access to information; that they act rationally and independently to optimize their own utility; and that as a result, markets are drawn to a stable equilibrium. The advantage of these highly restrictive assumptions is that they allow economists to develop theoretical models which link the micro level of the economy (e.g., the behavior of individual investors) to the macro level (e.g., market statistics). Instead of a collection of modeling techniques developed for special cases, as in computational biology, the result is a single, consistent, and above all authoritative story.

The problem is that, in the quant's mind, the effect of all this intellectual baggage is that the toy model looks like a real model based on sound principles. He begins to believe that "one set of laws works everywhere." As a result, the toy model gets used outside its zone of validity. An example is the assumption that market returns follow a normal distribution, when in fact empirical evidence shows that they don't, not really. Models based on such idealized assumptions are useful within a certain context, but – like the software packages used in engineering – should carry warning labels to the effect that they are hazardous if applied inappropriately.

These restrictive assumptions have never been adopted in computational biology or ecology, for the obvious reason that they don't work. Ecosystems are non-homogeneous and asymmetric, which is what drives changes and diversity. (In an economist's version of a jungle, all the animals would be white mice.) And in biology, the only systems that are stable are dead.

Quantum Finance

In any case, while it is often said that finance models itself after physics, it is more accurate to say that it has modeled itself after Newtonian physics, which is not quite the same thing, being a little out of date. At the start of the 20th century, physics was shaken to its roots by the quantum revolution. This showed that matter is not made up of billiard-ball particles bouncing off one another, but instead is fundamentally dualistic. Subatomic entities such as electrons behave in some ways like particles, and in other ways like waves.

One implication was that it was impossible to make accurate measurements for subatomic systems. The Heisenberg uncertainty principle, which stated that we can't know both the momentum and the location of a particle to complete accuracy, seemed to say that we could make no precise predictions. However, quantum mechanics did allow physicists to make probabilistic statements which specified the *chance* of an event, such as the probability of an atom of uranium emitting a particle of alpha radiation (useful in designing atomic bombs).

At the same time, though, it was found that the quantum nature of particles added a rich layer of complexity to atomic interactions, giving them, we could say, a life of their own. As a result, we can't divine much about a material's properties by analyzing its components. An example is water: when it freezes, it expands instead of contracting, which means that ice floats on water rather than sinking to the bottom (useful for life in lakes). But that remarkable property can't be predicted or modeled from a knowledge of water's atomic structure, because it depends on the amazingly complex interactions between water molecules.[12] It is better described as an emergent property of the system.

---

[12]Castelvecchi (2008).

In finance there is a similar situation. Consider, for example, the nature of money. Standard economic definitions of money concentrate on its roles as a "medium of exchange," a "store of value," and a "unit of account." Economists such as Paul Samuelson have focused in particular on the first, defining money as "anything that serves as a commonly accepted medium of exchange." This definition is similar to John Law's definition of money as a "Sign of Transmission." Money is therefore not something important in itself; it is only a kind of token. The overall picture is of the economy as a giant barter system, with money acting as an inert facilitator.

However, as David has argued at great and some would say inordinate length elsewhere, money is far more interesting than that, and actually harbors its own kind of lively, dualistic properties.[13] In particular, it merges two things, number and value, which have very different properties: number lives in the abstract, virtual world of mathematics, while valued objects live in the real world. The tension between these contradictory aspects is what gives money its powerful and paradoxical qualities. A money object such as a dollar bill is a physical object that can be traded, valued, and possessed, but unlike other things in the economy it has a fixed, numerical price. Prices for other things emerge from the use of these money objects – just as the properties of water emerge from interactions between molecules.

Of course, something like an electronic transfer, or a bitcoin, does not resemble the Newtonian idea of a self-contained object – but then neither does matter when viewed from a quantum perspective. The real and the virtual become blurred, in physics or in finance. And just as Newtonian theories break down in physics, so our Newtonian approach to money breaks down in economics. In particular, one consequence is that we have tended to take debt less seriously than we should (more on this in Chapter 10).

Now, in the 1950s, when quantitative finance was in its infancy, the fact that things had moved on in physics was not a problem – it was an opportunity! Unfortunately, quants didn't take it. Or rather, they took the wrong one. Instead of facing up to the intrinsically uncertain nature of money and the economy, relaxing some of those tidy assumptions, accepting that markets have emergent properties that resist reduction to simple laws, and building a new and more realistic theory of economics, quants instead glommed on to the idea

---

[13]Orrell (2016a), Orrell and Chlupatý (2016).

that, when a system is unpredictable, you can just switch to making probabilistic predictions. The efficient market hypothesis, for example, was based on the mechanical analogy that markets are stable and perturbed randomly by the actions of atomistic individuals. This led to probabilistic risk-analysis tools such as VaR. However, in reality, the "atoms" are not independent, but are closely linked, like the molecules in water. The result is the non-equilibrium behavior, such as sudden phase changes and turbulence, observed in real markets. Markets are unpredictable not because they are efficient, but because of a financial version of the uncertainty principle.

As discussed in Chapter 2, the great advantage of probabilistic predictions is that they sound authoritative, but are hard to prove wrong because to do so takes a great deal of data. If you say there is only a 5% chance of a market crash, and there is indeed a crash, then you can just say it was bad luck. Theories are almost impossible to falsify. Finance therefore took exactly the wrong lesson from the quantum revolution. It held on to its Newtonian, mechanistic, symmetric picture of an intrinsically stable economy guided to equilibrium by Adam Smith's invisible hand. But it adopted the probabilistic mathematics of stochastic calculus. The result was that, instead of a financial version of $E = mc^2$, we got an uncontrolled global credit bomb.

Order and Chaos

To summarize, markets are not determined by fundamental laws, deterministic or probabilistic. Instead, they are the emergent result of complex transactions. They constitute a living system, not a dead one. While it is often said that the economy is ruled by fixed laws – one sample headline reads: "China learns it can't control the laws of economics" – it would be more accurate to refer to the wildness of the economy. This changes the way that we see financial modeling. In particular, money should play a central role, similar to that of a biologically active substance.

One of the more obvious properties of money is that it has a profound effect on human psychology. Neuroscientist Brian Knutson, who investigated this in a series of experiments, said that "Nothing had an effect on people like money – not naked bodies, not corpses. It got people riled up. Like food provides motivation for dogs, money provides it for people."[14] (Observe quant behavior just before feeding bonus time.) It therefore seems bizarre that economics and finance, since the time of Adam Smith, have treated money as nothing more than an inert medium of exchange. For example, the models used by policy makers usually don't even include a banking or finance sector – which makes banking crises rather hard to predict.[15] But only by omitting money could theorists maintain the pretense that the economy was an orderly, rational, efficient system.

Of course, merely strapping a financial sector onto traditional models will not necessarily make them more predictive or useful. The more apparently realistic you make a model, the less useful it often becomes, and the complexity of the equations turns the model into a black box. The key then is to keep with simple models, but make sure that the model is capturing the key dynamics of the system, and only use it within its zone of validity. Models should be seen as imperfect patches, rather than as accurate representations of the complete system. Instead of attempting to replace traditional theory with a better, more complete "theory of everything," the aim is to find models that are useful for a particular purpose, and know when they break down.

Another approach is to go the Renaissance route, abandon the idea of mechanistic modeling, and just let the computer look for patterns in data. The resulting models may be more parsimonious than a fully mechanistic model, but are a black box in the sense that the equations do not typically correspond to easily understood mechanisms. They therefore lack some of the advantages of simple mechanistic models, such as the ability to test hypotheses, or make qualitative predictions for situations where prior data is not available. However, they are better suited than mechanistic models for handling the massive amounts of financial and other data which have become available in recent years.

Perhaps the best approach is to use a mix of techniques, while being aware of the advantages and disadvantages of each. The *worst* is to pretend that toy models are actually fundamental laws of the universe – and then bet a quadrillion dollars on them. So this is where abstract ideas about models have very real implications. If you think

---

[14]Levy (2006).

[15]As former Deputy Governor of the Bank of Canada, William White points out: "An important practical aspect of these models is that they make no reference to money or credit, and they have no financial sector" (White, 2013).

models are just useful approximations to the far more complex reality, you tend to be more careful about using them.

As discussed earlier, one of the main motivations in financial modeling, apart from pay, has been aesthetics. We are attracted by the beauty of our models, and come to think that they are true. The move from a Newtonian, mechanistic approach to a complexity approach can therefore be viewed in terms of an aesthetic shift. Instead of independent atom-like investors, we have connected networks. Instead of static equilibrium, we have dynamic motion. And instead of linearity and symmetry, we have nonlinearity and asymmetry.

So now that we have shown some alternative, if more humble and limited approaches to financial modeling, will the banks and universities be racing to update their models? Certainly not – because whether dealing with investors, regulators, or the public, or even just for making money, accuracy isn't really the point. What counts is the impression of accuracy, which is much better served by a model in which the economy is at equilibrium, and risk can be precisely calculated, than one in which the economy is far from equilibrium and risk is essentially unquantifiable. This will become clearer in the next chapter, where we turn to another kind of asymmetry – the balance, or lack thereof, between risk and reward – and how quants have learned to exploit it at the expense of investors.

How to Abuse the System

"No.3 Commando was very anxious to be chums with Lord Glasgow, so they offered to blow up an old tree stump for him and he was very grateful and said dont spoil the plantation of young trees near it because that is the apple of my eye and they said no of course not we can blow a tree down so it falls on a sixpence and Lord Glasgow said goodness you are clever and he asked them all to luncheon for the great explosion. So Col. Durnford-Slater D.S.O. said to his subaltern, have you put enough explosive in the tree. Yes, sir, 75lbs. Is that enough? Yes sir I worked it out by mathematics it is exactly right. Well better put a bit more. Very good sir.

And when Col. D. Slater D.S.O. had had his port he sent for the subaltern and said subaltern better put a bit more explosive in that tree. I don't want to disappoint Lord Glasgow. Very good sir.

Then they all went out to see the explosion and Col. D.S. D.S.O. said you will see that tree fall flat at just the angle where it will hurt no young trees and Lord Glasgow said goodness you are clever.

So soon they lit the fuse and waited for the explosion and presently the tree, instead of falling quietly sideways, rose 50 feet into the air taking with it ½ acre of soil and the whole young plantation.

And the subaltern said Sir, I made a mistake, it should have been 7½ lbs not 75.

Lord Glasgow was so upset he walked in dead silence back to his castle and when they came to the turn of the drive in sight of his castle what should they find but that every pane of glass in the building was broken.

*So Lord Glasgow gave a little cry and ran to hide his emotions in
the lavatory and there when he pulled the plug the entire ceiling,
loosened by the explosion, fell on his head.
This is quite true."*
    —Letter by Evelyn Waugh to his wife (31 May 1942).

"The guys who made the world go kablooey."
    —Answer to the survey question: "How would you describe
        quantitative finance at a dinner party?" at wilmott.com

Any system, whether it's financial, business, social, or governmen-
tal, ought to be set up so that the natural selfish or cooperative actions
of individuals can benefit the organization as a whole. An alternative is that the system encourages a certain type of selfish behavior
that harms the whole. Guess which of these two is the current financial system? In this chapter, we'll see how the bonus system based on
using other people's money encourages dangerous practices such as
concentration of risk, and the selling of things for less than they're
worth. And that's just the legal stuff. We'll see the gray area in which
models can be used to hide risk, and to encourage risk taking. We'll
expose just how dangerous it is to rely solely on the numbers, without any sanity checking. And we'll show how mistakes – deliberate or
otherwise – can make the ceiling fall in.

In earlier chapters we have introduced you to some of the ele-
gantly beautiful math that forms the basis of quantitative finance. We
have shown how these methods allow quants to derive prices for all
kinds of complex derivatives. We have given some flavor of their working practices, their amazing salaries, and their blind spots. So now, it's
time to see if you, the reader, have actually been paying attention –
and if you have what it takes to work in the exciting world of quantitative finance. Can you put this learning into practice? Can you think
like a quant?

Or maybe you are a quant? In which case, this is your chance to
prove you deserve that magnificent pay package and rid yourself of
any lingering traces of "imposter syndrome"!

We are going to set you three exercises. You must answer them
as if you were working in a bank or a hedge fund. You can draw

inspiration from classical economic ideas, from behavioral finance, from your own experiences. There are 30 points up for grabs.

Exercise 1: The Newbie Trader

Scenario: Imagine that you have just finished your PhD in modeling credit risk and probability of default. Your work was so groundbreaking and relevant that you walked into a job at a large bank and into their credit-instrument department. This department has a couple of dozen seasoned traders and you, the newbie, are going to be joining them. The pay is okay, but it's the potential bonus that makes this your dream job. You are being introduced to the other traders: "Hi, I'm Ralph, I went to MIT and I trade CDOs." "Hi, Ralph." "Hey, I'm Charles, I went to NYU and I trade CDOs." "Hey, Charles." "Yo, dude, I'm Paul. I went to Stanford and I trade CDOs." "Yo, Paul." And even Larry (he of Harvard) trades CDOs. You are surprised that everyone seems to have the same strategy. And you know from your studies that CDOs are dangerous, and that at most there's a 60% chance of making money with them. Meanwhile, your research has given you some trading ideas that are 80% likely to pay off. That's why you were hired, right?

Question: What do you trade? Do you follow the better strategies that you've been researching for the last four years, or do you follow the herd and trade CDOs like everyone else?

Hint: What does classical finance tell you about eggs and baskets?

Write your answer and justification here:

Correct answer: You trade CDOs, of course! Diversification is for suckers! (Apologies for trying to mislead you with the hint, it won't happen again.)

Explanation: First you have to ask yourself what you are trying to achieve here. There are many things you might be interested in, such as how much money you make, not getting fired, a pleasant working environment, making your parents proud, doing the best for the shareholders. The best strategy for the first four of these goals is achieved by doing the same strategy as the rest of the credit team.

How much money do you make? Well, we know that the vast bulk of your pay will be in the form of the bonus. And to get the bonus you need to be a good trader. So if you follow your strategy then you'll be profitable 80% of the time, and therefore get a bonus 80% of the time. Right? No. Bonuses are typically assessed on the performance of both you individually, and the entire team. So you will only get a bonus if both you and the entire desk make money. If all the rest of the credit team lose money, then there ain't going to be bonuses for them... or you. There's just no money, lads. Do the math. Assuming that their trades and yours are independent, then the probability of both you and the others making money is $0.8 \times 0.6 = 48\%$. Less than half of the time. Whereas if you join them in trading CDOs, you have a 60% chance of making money and getting a bonus.

If you are part of the herd, it also decreases your chance of getting fired. You are already in a dangerous position being last in. But if you also lose money with your crazy ivory-tower ideas then it will just be a matter of time before one morning you find your card reader won't open the door, and the receptionist asks you to wait in the lobby while someone brings your things. (In finance, job security is tenuous to say the least, which is why everyone is in such a hurry about their bonus.)

Being part of the herd, rather than being a bit unusual, is also good for self-esteem in your working environment.

Money, (relative) security, a nice working environment... every mother's dream for her baby.

In contrast, it is true that the bank's interest and the shareholders' interests are best served by as much diversification as possible. Especially diversification that actually increases expected return. But who cares about shareholders?

Points: Give yourself 5 points for the correct answer. Also, 1 point for each of the above (or similar) five angles to this question. For a total of 10 possible points.

This is not just an academic exercise, but it is nice to see this simple idea illustrated with numbers. The concept behind those numbers is as elementary as the concepts behind Markowitz's portfolio management, you're just trying to optimize something different.

This might not strictly be an abuse of the system, since the newbie trader is just doing what's best for him. Selfish it may be, but it's not his job to look after the shareholders. That's for the bank's directors.

What we have here is a fault within the system, a fault that encourages putting all eggs into one basket. And as is so often the case, it could well be your eggs that are put at risk. They're your eggs in someone else's basket. It's simply a case of incentives being aligned with potentially bad outcomes. We are always hearing how bonuses encourage people to work harder. But it's more likely that they encourage that hard work to be whatever makes the most bonus, not what is most beneficial for the system as a whole. And traditionally, and legally, it's the shareholders who are supposed to be the ones ultimately benefitting, since they are the ones taking the financial risk, the risk of serious downside.

Does this matter? Does this really happen in practice? You bet. We chose the example of CDOs for a reason, since they became such an enormous business in the run up to the crisis of 2008.

Exercise 2: The Hedge Fund Manager

Scenario: You are a clever statistician. Thanks to your reputation, you have been able to set up a hedge fund. A small part of the assets under management are your own, but this is a negligible portion of your wealth (most of which is tied up in property, Manhattan, the Hamptons, Barbados, ..., and some Damien Hirsts); the rest is other people's money. You have a statistical model of various complex assets. Your model tells you that some instrument, let's say a put option, has a theoretical value of 10 cents. But that theoretical value is based, like classical quant theory, on an average. Actually, the contract could end up being worth zero or $100. The contract has a maturity of one month.

Question: What should your strategy be? Do you buy the contract or sell it? And for how much?

Hint: What would Oscar Wilde do?

Write your answer and justification here:

_____

_____

_____

_____

_____

Correct answer: Sell as many and as often as possible for 5 cents! Oscar Wilde would have made a great hedge fund manager!

Explanation: In *Lady Windermere's Fan,* Cecil Graham says "What is a cynic?" to which Lord Darlington answers "A man who knows the price of everything, and the value of nothing." We know the theoretical value of the contract, it's 10 cents. And everyone knows that you should aim to buy something for less than fair value, and sell for more. That's just plain business sense. Even if you are making jam in your kitchen, you add up the cost of the ingredients, the fruit, sugar, and pectin, the fuel used, the packaging, jars, lids, labels, marketing, transport, etc., and divide by the number of jars produced, and that's the very least you must sell each jar for. Think of this calculation as giving you the theoretical value of a jar of jam. It's not unlike valuing a derivative, where the delta hedging with the underlying takes the role of making the jam from its ingredients. If you sell the jam for less, then you are going to go out of business. Rarely do you aim to make a loss. One notable exception is the supermarket loss leader, where the cheaper-than-fair-value product is the lure to get you into the shop. And really that loss is a cost that should be allocated to your advertising budget. But surely hedge funds try to make money everywhere, there's no role for loss leaders in rational high finance.

The contract in question is special in that it has a very skewed payoff. Almost always it pays off zip at the end of the month. But every now and again it pays off $100. Now, for the average of zero and $100 to be $0.1, you need to have a very small chance of getting the big one. Just solve

$$100 \times p + 0 \times (1 - p) = 0.1$$

for p, the probability of getting $100. That's a probability of 0.001, or 1 in 1000. Each month there'd be a 99.9% chance of getting zero. In 10 years there's only an 11.3% chance of getting a nonzero payoff.[1] The average lifespan of a hedge fund is three years. Sorry, but buying these contracts, even if you could get them for a couple of cents, way below their fair value, is not a viable business, you won't even make that three-year average.

No, a better business is to sell them. If you sell them then very, very rarely will you have to pay out that $100. So, virtually every month you will collect the premium. Obviously you'll sell them for

---

[1] That's $1 - 0.999^{120}$, where 120 is the number of months.

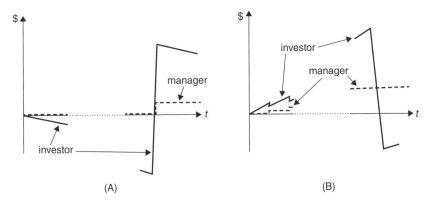

Figure 9.1   Two extreme strategies: (A) successful for both investor and manager in the long run; (B) successful for the manager, but ultimately catastrophic for the investor

as much as you can. Or rather you'll sell them for whatever optimizes your income. Assuming that you'll sell fewer the higher the price, then there might be an optimal value for the price and a maximum income. But crucially it doesn't matter whether the price you sell them for is above or below the fair value. Let's see why this is.

Take a look at Figure 9.1. Strategy A is to buy for less than fair value, assuming such a thing is even possible. The investor, the solid line, loses year after year, decade after decade. Eventually the contract pays off and his P&L makes it into the black. And that's when the manager gets his performance fee, typically based on a percentage of the profit. But what investor is going to have the patience to wait for this to happen?[2] Long before this, the investor will have taken their money out and you will have closed down your fund.

Now look at strategy B. This is selling for less than fair value. The investor's P&L is rising to start with. At the end of every year 20%, say, of the year's profit goes to the manager as his performance fee. His P&L increases in annual jumps. (There's an equal and opposite fall in the investor's P&L.) Eventually the big one hits and the investor loses, big time. We've represented the fact that the sale price is less than fair value by having this investor P&L fall far below the starting

---

[2] Nassim Nicholas Taleb has a fascinating twist on this. If the strategy is presented as an investment, then no one would go for it. However, presenting it as an insurance, so that the big payoff happens in compensation for something bad elsewhere, ensures it is perceived differently. Everyone expects to lose on insurance and this will not be offputting.

value of zero. Meanwhile, the manager's P&L has been increasing annually. And even though the investor ends up losing, the manager, of course, doesn't have to hand anything back.

Clearly, what's good for the investor and what's good for the manager can be very different, even though the manager is compensated for his success. In Chapter 2 we told the story of John Law in Venice, betting his 10,000 pistoles against the chances of any comer rolling six sixes (expected payout 0.21 pistoles). In the modern version, you can happily increase the prize to 100,000 pistoles, so the long-term odds are against you – but you don't care because it's not your money.

Points: Give yourself 2 points for saying you should sell these contracts. And 8 points if you said you could sell them for less than they are worth.

This is definitely abuse. You could argue that the results of Exercise 1 were just unfortunate or unintended, but to knowingly sell something for less than its value in order to profit from someone else's misfortune is definitely immoral. The performance-related pay again has unintended consequences, but we've shown how a devious mind might easily exploit this. It also requires a plausible "story" for the fund. Why are they selling for less than it's worth? Or perhaps, like some Mafia accountant, they have the books/model for public view and the private books/model for internal use.

There is a slightly toned-down version of this situation. Imagine going into your hedge fund office and looking at your model's predictions. On this day your model says that there are no new trading opportunities, all contracts have negative expectations. Okay, so you won't be putting on any new trades today. Never mind, the weather's good, might as well go to the golf course, perhaps pick up some new business among the members. Next day, same story. All contracts are losers. And it's the same for the rest of the week. The month. Uh oh, what's going on? Maybe this will be a temporary blip. Or maybe your model has just broken, the market has changed, there's been a regime shift. The decent and rational thing to do is to stop trading, tell investors, and check (or, if necessary, redesign) your model. Unfortunately, if you stop trading, even with the best and most logical of reasons, your investors will take their money out and invest it elsewhere. However, equally logical and equally best, at least for you, is to keep trading while you do the redesign. Even if that means buying contracts that have negative expectations. Investors are used to funds occasionally losing money. They expect it, even if they don't exactly like it. They could tolerate several months of small losses without withdrawing their money. Again, the incentives of the hedge fund are not aligned with the best interests of the investors.

In Chapter 5, we spoke about the market price of risk, which is the amount that investors demand in return for accepting risk. Usually it is depicted by a line sloping upwards in the risk–reward diagram, so expected return increases with risk. But in this example, the graph has the wrong sign – investors are *paying* to take risks. They just don't know it.

Exercise 3: The Risk Manager

Scenario: You are a risk manager in a bank. You have been asked by a trader to measure the risk in a portfolio of assets. The problem with this portfolio is that it's not clear how diversified the portfolio is. It's possible that all of the assets are independent of each other, but you could imagine times when they become more correlated. You give a number to the trader, your estimate of the risk. It's clear from his facial expression that this number is too high, perhaps there's a limit to the risk he's allowed to take.

Question: What action do you suggest?

Hint: What's the quant equivalent of playing the man not the ball? Write your answer and justification here:

_____

_____

_____

_____

_____

Correct answer: You must have made a mistake. Go back to your calculations and "correct" them to show that there is less risk! (We gave an example of this from a real trader back in Chapter 3.)

Explanation: Let's be clear, the trader is the boss. Without traders there's no bank. We aren't talking about a Mary-Poppins-and-Dick-Van-Dyke-style bank here. The bank exists for the trader, and it is risk management's job to provide the justification for the traders' trades. Obviously not in theory, but in practice. The theory is that risk management is supposed to quantify the risks and the probabilities on the downside, and thereby show how to reduce that risk to

Table 9.1   Volatilities and correlations using two recent years of data

Stock	Volatility	Correlations				
		JNJ	AAPL	PG	IBM	CCE
JNJ	0.14	1	0.14	0.638	0.316	0.402
AAPL	0.259	0.14	1	0.181	−0.005	0.037
PG	0.143	0.638	0.181	1	0.192	0.303
IBM	0.18	0.316	−0.005	0.192	1	0.47
CCE	0.16	0.402	0.037	0.303	0.47	1

The ones on the diagonal represent the correlation of a stock with itself, which is 1. The negative correlation between IBM and AAPL (Apple) is because they tend to move in opposite directions.

acceptable levels by hedging, diversifying, or simply closing positions. However, the practice is that risk-management tools can be used in more nefarious ways.

How easy is this to do? We're not experts, but it only took minutes with real data to figure out plausible ways to game the numbers.

Let's take some real data. In Table 9.1 are the volatilities and correlations for five US stocks using two years' worth of data.

Now suppose that we hold $100 in each of these stocks. We can easily calculate the standard deviation, a measure of risk, over the next year, say.[3] This calculation gives us a standard deviation (risk) of $55. This is not acceptable. Our limit is $50.

The natural, and indeed probably morally correct, response is to cut back on one or more positions to reduce the $55 down to $50. But that means a smaller portfolio and smaller profits. Not to mention it also means that the risk manager holds some power over the trader. No, let's rethink those numbers.

Suppose we work with four years' worth of data? Surely two years is just too small a data set; think of the possible statistical errors. If we go back four years, we get the parameters in Table 9.2

Now we find that the risk is $52. Bugger, so close! (Of course, it could have been that four years of data made things worse, maybe we'd then look at one year of data, which after all is more recent. Muahaha!)

---

[3] There are quite a few assumptions in this calculation, but a simple formula is $\sqrt{T \sum_{i=1}^{5} \sum_{j=1}^{5} W_i W_j \rho_{ij} \sigma_i \sigma_j}$ where T is the time horizon (here 1 year), the Ws represent the dollar amount in each of the five shares, the σs are the volatilities, and the ρs are the correlations.

Table 9.2   Volatilities and correlations using four recent years of data

Stock	Volatility	Correlations				
		JNJ	AAPL	PG	IBM	CCE
JNJ	0.132	1	−0.001	0.542	0.22	0.392
AAPL	0.253	−0.001	1	0.173	0.217	0.116
PG	0.133	0.542	0.173	1	0.103	0.285
IBM	0.158	0.22	0.217	0.103	1	0.419
CCE	0.159	0.392	0.116	0.285	0.419	1

Notice that the volatilities all just happen to be lower using the larger data set, but only marginally so. In contrast, the correlations have changed quite a lot. Hmm... that gives us an idea. Clearly, correlations are moving around a lot (true). And who is to say that the correlations we've measured are statistically accurate (also true). And, you know, there's clearly a trend here (er, hang on a sec'). Inspired by these thoughts, let's tweak the correlations. Let's change them by 0.1, that's of the order of magnitude of the movement/error/trend. And by doing this we can get the risk down to a mere $46. Below the risk limit. Job done.

And you know what? It also means that the trader can now even increase his positions by almost 10%!

None of this is difficult to do. Think of all the different ways there are to measure volatility and correlation, using moving windows, weighted in various ways, using daily, weekly, monthly, etc. data. It's almost impossible to have a data set in which you are confident anyway.

The end result of this is a (temporarily) happy trader. But you're smarter than him, no? And if you're really clever then you'd go one step further. You'd fiddle the risk figure to make it as bad as possible to start with; that is, going in the wrong direction. When you then reduce the risk to acceptable levels, you'll get even more credit (more bonus?). Using the above data, two years, and adding in a margin for error, we can get the risk all the way up to a starting value of $60. Now we can boast a reduction of almost a quarter.

Points: Have 5 points for realizing that if you want to keep your job you'll have to fiddle the numbers, and 5 points if you could think of an example.

Of course, such fiddling is not something you want to make a habit of. Or at least, be subtle about it. If there's a forensic quant looking at your numbers he might easily spot a pattern. But equally, this simple experiment took us minutes to conduct using a spreadsheet and Excel's Solver add-in, and we're almost certainly not making six figures with this book. (At least the authors aren't.) Had we been compensated sufficiently, who knows how low we could get the risk with a day's work?

In another context, someone at Volkswagen clearly thought it worthwhile to do something not dissimilar when they adjusted the behavior of their diesel engines during test conditions so as to make emissions look lower. This is their cunning "defeat device." The act of monitoring risk seems to cause people to adjust the way that risk is measured rather than reducing the risk, in an evil Heisenbergian way.

On the subject of being subtle about it, suppose you've got a kinda justifiable way of adjusting parameters to reduce the risk, then you can just automate the procedure. That gives you two levels of cover. A regulator has to first find the fiddling (but it's hidden deep inside the code), and then prove that the fiddling is malicious.

You know what we've just reinvented? Calibration! Calibration is a simple way of hiding model risk; you choose the parameters so that your model superficially appears to value everything correctly when really it's doing no such thing. Instead of doing the boring "road calibration," you can go for the exciting "dyno calibration," which allows extra performance at the expense of a little unseen risk. And since regulators are actively encouraging banks to calibrate, you are absolutely safe. Here we see the advantage of having a flawed model that needs constant adjustment in order to fit the data. If you want to understand how regulators think, you couldn't do better than study Inspector Clouseau in the Pink Panther movies.

We can take this idea a lot, lot further.

On the wilmott.com forum there are always students asking for mathematical finance research topics:

> "Hi, We are required to write up a dissertation for the summer term as part of our MSc in Financial Mathematics & Computation. Any suggestions on how/where I can start if I want to come up with a topic on my own? Thank you."[4]

---

[4]Yes… on your own.

We have one for you if you are interested. It's about building a mathematical model for some instrument, let's say an interest-rate product so we'll need an interest-rate model. You have to design a rates model with the following characteristics.

1. It must be simple enough to use in practice.

2. It must be possible to calibrate this model, and recalibrate if necessary, to as many liquid instruments as possible.

3. It must be possible to optimize parameters in the model with the following goal: to maximize the contract's value at some time in the future, specifically at bonus time.

4. It doesn't matter whether the model matches statistical data for how interest rates behave.

5. And how well it performs in terms of making money is irrelevant.

6. Also irrelevant is how it performs after bonus time.

You can see where we are going with this. Cash flow can be irrelevant for profit. Profit can depend on perceived value and in some cases a mathematical model. So your bonus can be linked to a number you've made up. No chance of abuse there then! And after bonus time, you'll probably move on to an even better paid job at another bank so you're not concerned how the model performs.

Given the intellectual limitations of anyone monitoring your model, why not go the whole hog and try to make as much money for yourself as possible? Make this the topic of your PhD thesis and that quant job at Goldman Sachs is yours.

Anyway, it's now time to assess your performance. Add up the sum of your scores. If the answer is:

0–9. You recently completed an economics degree.

10–19. Please try harder.

20–29. Good effort! You definitely have a future, even if the world financial system doesn't.

30. Hah! We just included this to tell if you *cheated* by looking at the answers! Bonus star.

Triple-A

Now, we don't want to give the impression that quantitative finance is necessarily more corrupt than other areas – vehicle emission controls, say, or politics. However, quantitative finance is unique in a couple of respects. One is the scale of the problem – it's one thing to do a favor in return for a handout, it's another to blow up a quadrillion-dollar credit bubble and charge commission on it. The other is the way that quants can avoid charges of corruption. The financial crisis of 2007/8 may have been partly caused by quants, but hardly anyone went to jail for their role, except in Iceland, which is a complete no-go zone for quants (in the UK, zero bankers received a custodial sentence; in the USA, one did; in Iceland, 26 did).[5] And this is where the models show their more sinister side.

The common thread in the three test questions above is the industrial-scale abuse of mathematical models in order to optimize the quant's interests rather than those of the client.

- Using flawed but industry-standard models because they are safe, for the quant.

- Selling products which are destined to eventually blow up, but only after the manager has collected his fee.

- Adjusting the model to give the desired result.

In each of these cases, the model is there less to elucidate the truth, than to provide a plausible story for a particular course of action. Quants use the apparently objective, detached, and impartial nature of mathematical formulas as a kind of concealment, but also as a stamp of certification.

Consider again the example of CDOs, which played such an important role in the financial crisis. These relied on collecting a large number of instruments such as household mortgages, repackaging them into separate bundles, and assigning each bundle a specific investment grade. The resulting products were then sold off to investors around the world. The process was therefore like sausage making – the inputs were a lot of messy parts, but the outputs were easily traded, plastic-wrapped products with a tailored degree of risk.

---

[5] See Eisinger (2014).

Key to making this work was the copula pricing model. Originally invented by quants, it was also adopted by rating agencies such as Standard & Poor's. Both groups had an incentive to provide favorable ratings – quants because they were selling the products, and rating agencies because the quants were their clients. According to a US civil complaint against S&P, the company's internal S&P documents showed that model results were adjusted to give the right (i.e., triple-A) answers. As Tony West from the US Justice Department put it, "It's sort of like buying sausage from your favorite butcher, and he assures you the sausage was made fresh that morning and is safe. What he doesn't tell you is that it was made with meat he knows is rotten and plans to throw out later that night."[6]

That landmark case ended in a 2015 settlement, where S&P did not admit to violating laws on those mortgage deals. However, they did agree to pay $1.37 billion, with about half going to the Justice Department and the rest being divided between 19 states and the District of Columbia.[7] For comparison, the firm claimed that it made about $900 million on the deals. No individual was punished or found to be at fault. Which is a little strange, when you think about it – how big would the fine have been if someone had actually done something wrong? Models are the perfect get-out-of-jail card.

Defeat Device

It still seems remarkable that an industry which is so important to society can get away with manipulating models in this way, with only the occasional profit-denting fine to worry about. But one of the advantages of mathematical models, if defending them is the aim, is that they can only be understood by a relatively small number of experts. The only people debating copula models in the early 2000s were those working in that particular part of the financial sector. At the same time, mathematical equations can seem imposing to those outside the field, which grants a degree of immunity. While journalists, anthropologists, film makers, and so on have investigated the banking industry to great effect, they usually have to get their information secondhand from anonymous sources (the non-anonymous

---

[6] See US Department of Justice (2013).
[7] Martin and Grossman (2015).

type get fired) and tend to avoid getting into the nitty gritty of the equations (it's hard, and makes lousy TV).

Again, this problem is not unique to finance. In the early 1980s, a paper by Will Keepin and Brian Wynne showed that a model used by nuclear scientists to predict future energy requirements was drastically overestimating the need for nuclear power plants – not to mention the nuclear scientists to design them. As Keepin described it, the model was so flexible that "It was a bit like the Wizard of Oz… Some guy was pulling on levers and making a big show, but it was a show determined by the little guy behind the curtain."[8] In physics, authors such as Lee Smolin and Peter Woit have written about the sociology of university departments, where promotion is based on fitting in with what Smolin describes as "groupthink" about correct modeling approaches.[9]

However, this still doesn't seem to quite explain what is going on in finance. Few journalists or readers care much about string theory, but they are certainly interested in where their money is going. So barriers which might put off a detailed investigation of a university physics department surely won't dissuade someone bent on an exposé of quantitative finance. Quants may be afraid to speak to journalists because they will lose their jobs, but so are most professionals, and whistleblowers still appear. So how is it that the finance sector – after nearly blowing up the world financial system through its miscalculations – can continue to escape serious scrutiny? What makes it special?

The answer to this question, we believe, lies in the fact that only finance has learned to fully exploit the power of the ultimate defeat device – which as any math-phobe will remember from school is mathematical equations. It doesn't just use formulas to dazzle – it imbues them with a kind of higher moral authority. It makes them into a consistent *story*. And by doing so it has achieved a remarkable degree of buy-in not just from those working in the field, but also from regulators, academia, the media, and the general public.

Whenever you make a mathematical model of a process, you are moving the system to the abstract plane of number. It seems to become objective and rational, free from the vagaries of human

---

[8] Ray and Anderson (2000, pp. 273–275).
[9] Smolin (2006), Woit (2006).

behavior or emotion. But quant finance (with its economist apologists) goes further, because it manages to transfer these properties to the system itself. Market prices are seen as objective, rational, and intrinsically fair. If the price of a commodity, a currency, a stock, or a complex derivative spikes or plunges, that's just the system at work. To criticize quantitative finance is therefore to criticize the markets themselves, which makes no sense because they are as objective and impartial as a physical phenomenon. It is as effective as yelling abuse at a storm.

In an area such as engineering or biology, one can argue about a particular model and use experiment as a guide – the model and the system are seen as separate things. But the dominant lesson of mainstream economics, with its assumptions of stability, efficiency, and rationality, is that market price and value are one and the same.[10] Models based on this theory are therefore seen as inviolable. The only human factor comes in during calibration, which can always be interpreted as human error. There is little account for the fact, not only that the models are wrong, but that their use can affect the system itself.

Consider, for example, the testimony that Alan Greenspan provided to the House Committee of Government Oversight and Reform in 2008. "In recent decades, a vast risk-management and pricing system has evolved, combining the best insights of mathematicians and finance experts supported by major advances in computer and communications technology. A Nobel Prize was awarded for the discovery of the pricing model that underpins much of the advance in derivatives markets. This modern risk management paradigm held sway for decades. The whole intellectual edifice, however, collapsed in the summer of last year *because the data inputted into the risk management models generally covered only the past two decades, a period of euphoria"* (our emphasis).[11] He went on: "Had instead the models been fitted more appropriately to historic periods of stress, capital requirements would have been much higher and the financial world would be in far better shape today, in my judgment." So according to Greenspan,

---

[10] As physicist J. Doyne Farmer and economist John Geanakoplos note, "Economic theory says that there is very little to know about markets: An asset's price is the best possible measure of its fundamental value, and the best predictor of future prices." Farmer and Geanakoplos (2009).
[11] Greenspan (2008).

there was nothing wrong with the math – some over-enthusiastic young people just plugged the wrong numbers into the formula, and blew out all the windows. The global financial crisis, in other words, was all due to a naive and innocent calibration error.

Of course, while the media and the general public might be willing to go along with this story, there should be at least a few academics who can see the flaws in the model. Such experts have in fact been around for a long time, and are collectively known as heterodox economists – or more colloquially as cranks. Despite being taken slightly more seriously since the crisis, and aided also by the recent shift toward empirical data-driven approaches in the social sciences, they generally don't win important prizes or get invited to the White House for policy meetings, and their intellectual edifices are the mental equivalent of shanty towns surrounding the gleaming high-rent downtown core of mainstream economics.[12] Now, are we saying that money in the form of, for example, grants and consulting opportunities could possibly affect the intellectual output of university economics departments, and decide who gets power and influence? Or that the influence of wealthy benefactors on economists did not stop with Adam Smith (Box 1.1)? Well, how many other fields have their "Nobel Prize" paid for by a bank? As economist Barry Eichengreen notes, university economists "do not object to the occasional high-paying consulting gig. They don't mind serving as the entertainment at beachside and ski-slope retreats hosted by investment banks for their important clients." The result is "a subconscious tendency to embrace the arguments of one's more 'successful' colleagues in a discipline where money, in this case earned through speaking engagements and consultancies, is the common denominator of success."[13] (The 2010 documentary film *Inside Job* did a revealing take on economists' supporting role in the crisis.)

Finally, there are the regulators. We'll discuss this topic more in the next chapter, but here is what author and journalist Joris Luyendijk wrote about it, after conducting a series of interviews with people in the financial sector after the crisis. "Perhaps the most terrifying interview of all the 200 I recorded was with a senior regulator. It was not only what he said but how he said it: as if the status

---

[12]There are some exceptions, such as Kingston University in the UK, where the economics department is headed by heterodox economist Steve Keen.
[13]Eichengreen (2009).

quo was simply unassailable. Ultimately, he explained, regulators – the government agencies that ensure the financial sector is safe and compliant – rely on self-declaration; what is presented by a bank's internal management. The trouble, he said with a calm smile, is that a bank's internal management often doesn't know what's going on because banks today are so vast and complex. He did not think he had ever been deliberately lied to, although he acknowledged that, obviously, he couldn't know for sure. 'The real threat is not a bank's management hiding things from us, it's the management not knowing themselves what the risks are.'"[14]

Well, other industries are complicated as well, but regulators somehow manage to cope. And since the financial sector, unlike most lines of business, has the power to destroy the world economy, you would think it deserves especially close attention. However, part of the economic story which policy makers such as Greenspan bought into was that finance is inherently efficient and therefore self-regulating – so it is no surprise that regulators lack the resources or even the motivation to dig a little deeper. As Ben Bernanke reassured Congress in 2006, "the best way to make sure the hedge funds are not taking excessive risk or excessive leverage is through market discipline."[15] And anyway, who needs fallible, human regulators when the mathematical models used by quants can compute and control risk automatically.

This trust in the system – or confusion of the reality with the model – is what Adair Turner called "regulatory capture through the intellectual zeitgeist." Abandoning it would put regulators "in a much more worrying space, because you don't have an intellectual system to refer each of your decisions."[16] (That is, it would no longer be enough to politely ask hedge funds to self-report their VaR.) One respondent to our survey described attending a finance conference two years after the crisis, with the leaders of the major banks and regulatory officers from G20 countries. The take-home message was: "We don't want any more regulation, as it kills financial innovation. What is the use of state treasury departments? They are for the good of the financial sector. We need them for these bad days."

---

[14]Luyendijk (2015).
[15]US House of Representatives, Committee on Banking and Financial Services (2000).
[16]Tett (2009).

Quantitative finance has therefore pulled off a truly amazing stunt, by bringing all the relevant players together on the same page. And here again we see the connection between making models and writing fiction – both involve creating a universe that people can believe in. The difference is that quants spin their stories out of mathematical formulas. In the next chapter, though, we show how the story is at risk of falling apart.

CHAPTER 10

Systemic Threat

"I was looking for an opportunity to use my skills and knowledge. This is an interesting firm."
—Former Chairman of the Federal Reserve Ben Bernanke
accepts a position as senior adviser to the $25 billion
high-frequency trading firm Citadel in 2015.

"Sunlight is said to be the best of disinfectants; electric light the most efficient policeman."
—Louis Brandeis, *Other People's Money and How the Bankers Use It* (1914)

Because of the bankers' insistence on treating complex finance as a university end-of-term exam in probability theory, many of the risks in the system are hidden. And when risks are hidden, one is lured into a false sense of security. More risk is taken so that when the inevitable happens, it is worse than it could have been. Eventually the probabilities break down, disastrous events become correlated, the cascade of dominoes is triggered, and we have systemic risk. A risk to the whole financial system. None of this would matter if the numbers were small relative to world economic output, but the numbers are huge. The infiltration of derivatives into society is like an inoperable metastasized cancer. Underneath many of the most innocent of human financial arrangements there's likely to be a complex structured financial product, with some banker taking his cut. And ultimately it's your money he's taking his cut from. And when a bank goes bust, the stock market collapses, and house prices tumble, it's your bank account, your shares, and your house equity that suffer. This chapter shines some light on the murky depths of finance and politics, and asks if we've moved on since John Law first dazzled the French monarchy with his system.

In the summer of 2010, Paul was contacted by Her Majesty's Treasury to ask if he would like to join a project related to high-frequency algorithmic trading. The email referenced the volume of trading in equities generated by automated computer algorithms, and the May 6, 2010 Flash Crash that wiped a trillion dollars off the value of US stocks, fortunately only for a few crazy minutes. The UK government was worried about high-frequency trading having a similar impact on the UK financial markets, and was setting up the project to examine this possibility.

The UK government has organized many of these "Foresight" reports on a variety of important topics. With input from experts from industry, academia, etc., they have in the past looked at topics as diverse as "Exploiting the electromagnetic spectrum," "Infectious diseases: preparing for the future," "Reducing risk of future disasters: priorities for decision makers," and naturally quite a few on climate change and sustainable stuff. The topic on which Paul was to be asked to comment turned out to be "Future of computer trading in financial markets: an international perspective."

Paul was naturally delighted to be asked to advise Her Majesty's government. Finally, appreciation for his expertise and hard work. The knighthood was almost certain to follow. "Is it possible? Dare I even think it?" he thought, "A… peerage?!" Not to mention an opportunity to help prevent a crisis before it happened, rather than seeing it unfold from the outside.

And so began a series of meetings and exchanges of thoughts. Paul was shown a list of all the (other) eminent people who were being approached for their opinions, more anon.

Paul explained his worries about feedback effects, and bandwagons, and how computer trading broke the connection between share price and company value (the whole purpose of markets). Having been in on various discussions on this topic before he knew that the commonest defense of such trading was the provision of liquidity, Paul gave his reasons for why "playing the liquidity card" was totally fallacious, and only fooled people who didn't think very deeply.

Paul was asked to put together a list of "drivers," important points for discussion.[1] We've already seen most of these points in this book already.

1. *Incentives, moral hazard, and feedback.* Does computerized trading facilitate coordination among traders whether deliberate (moral hazard) or via an evolutionary process? The current system of incentives for bankers encourages the taking of risk. Does coordination or competition among traders (man or machine) lead to an increase or a decrease in market risk? (Is the feedback positive or negative?) Will there be an increase in, or a new kind of, systemic risk in the markets? What new form will market movements take, will there be an increase in volatility or an increase in jumps? Should incentives be changed?

2. *Innovation and regulators.* Regulators always seem to be on the back foot with respect to monitoring or even understanding new products, strategies, and structures. They do not move as quickly as banks or funds. How can regulations be designed so as to remain future proof? Regulators are not paid as much as bankers, and this may result in a lower caliber of regulator. How can regulators be given more bite or made to genuinely worry banks (rather than just being an inconvenience). Should regulators be better educated, so as to know the difficult questions to ask of the banks?

3. *The structure and purpose of exchanges.* What are the fundamental purposes of exchanges? And how should they be designed now that the connections between them (in terms of latency and speed) have become part of the computerized trading game? Should there be competing exchanges subject to market forces? If so, how will that competition interplay with the computerized trading, and will that add to or decrease old and new risk factors? Or should exchanges be a public service, perhaps not for profit? And if so, should this be at a national or international level?

4. *Taxes, minimum holding periods, etc.* Should there be any disincentives to short-term trading? Possibilities are taxes per trade,

---

[1] Paul couldn't bring himself to call these "drivers," it seemed like such management speak.

minimum holding periods, and restrictions on stock lending (and therefore limits on short selling), among others. What are the pros and cons of such "frictions"?

5. *National vs. international.* How important is international cooperation on computerized trading? Restrictions imposed in one country will probably encourage financial institutions to move to a more friendly nation. Is this true? And does this matter if, for example, it leads to a more stable economy? Is there a natural and healthy fraction of a country's economy that should come from finance, or is more simply better?

6. *Value vs. price.* The purpose of the markets is to enable companies to raise money to grow and benefit society. This requires the prices of stocks in the market to relate to fundamental values, with some subjectivity to encourage trading, so that those trading can fairly estimate rewards and risks. If prices and values are too far out of line, then the market becomes a casino. Is there a natural holding period for stocks so as to keep value and price in some alignment? Does computerized trading cause any dislocation? How quickly does a company's "value" change?

Foresight

At the meetings, various solutions were discussed. One that Paul remembers clearly was the suggestion that exchanges could implement circuit breakers in the event of a crisis. This is simply the idea that should markets fall by $x\%$ in y minutes, then the markets would be closed for z minutes. Paul laughed at this. He said that he thought hedge-fund managers would enjoy triggering such events. They'd put it into their computer algorithms and would inevitably find a way in which to benefit from them. Even if *we* couldn't think of how profit could be extracted from a market-cooling mechanism, that was just because we weren't as clever as the fund managers. Paul tried to explain that you had to understand the mentality of these people. You have to be more of a Miss Marple than a Sherlock Holmes. Paul said that he predicted hedge-fund managers would be in favor of circuit breakers.

And then nothing happened.

A year went by. Paul assumed that this was just how committees worked – inefficiently and slowly. Apart from the Oxford University Ballroom Dance Club in the 1980s, Paul had avoided committees like the plague. Anyway, Paul had plenty of other business matters to keep him off the streets. But then he got curious and sent a follow-up query.

Another meeting followed. It was explained to Paul that he was seen as being a little too academic. "The knighthood is on hold then," thought Paul. But they were ever so polite. One thing Paul took away from these meetings was how incredibly charming civil servants are, even when telling you your services are no longer required.[2] Later in 2012 the final report came out. You can find it easily online.

To put it briefly, the finding of the experts was that everything is fine. There is nothing to worry about. High-frequency and computer trading are nothing but good for everyone. Nine proposals had been made for pruning the impact of HFT, seven were deemed unnecessary or problematic.

Of the remaining two, one stood out. The experts were in agreement that circuit breakers were a good idea.

When he first read this Paul did that thing where you pretend to lick your finger and make a mark on an imaginary blackboard. "Yes," he thought, "I may not be as clever as these people at moving the markets, but I can read their minds!" Miss Marple rules!

Paul then went into his investigative mode. He does this whenever he sees stupidity or smells something fishy. He looked at the list of people on the "High Level Stakeholders Group," those whose advice was sought. (The group from which he had been dumped.) He noticed a pattern. He then rummaged through his old emails to find the original make-up of this panel.[3] Now, Paul isn't going to reveal the names he was originally given. It's bad enough that this book and the blog he wrote at the time have effectively ruled out him ever getting that knighthood or peerage, but he doesn't want to fall foul of the Official Secrets Act.

---

[2] But Paul didn't like to miss an opportunity, so he arranged for a couple of these civil servants to get places on his Certificate in Quantitative Finance (CQF) course at a seriously reduced cost. The idea was that it could only be beneficial if those in control of things had a better understanding of how they work. Although face-to-face they agreed to joining the CQF program, of course they never did.

[3] We hope you are visualizing this. It's going to be a key scene in the film of this book.

At the start of the reporting process in 2010 the membership of the High Level Stakeholders Group was balanced between those within the finance industry and independents outside it. By the time this panel had been "reconfigured," it was dominated by banking insiders. Over two-thirds were from the financial services and over half of the panel had links to high-frequency trading. The Bureau of Investigative Journalism reported "… a well-placed source close to the Foresight team said the High Level Panel 'is dominated by providers, not by users'. The three- to four-hour meetings, the insider said, 'tended to be dominated by industry… It is a concern that the group is like that.'"[4]

And you know what's most disturbing? This manipulation of the panel was not even subtle. Presumably the government got the answer it wanted, and the dominance of the City of London in the financial markets was assured.

This is why we've opened this chapter on systemic risk with this story. Sure algorithmic trading is a systemic risk, but a larger one is toothless governments and regulators, or worse, governments and regulators whose interests are also aligned with those of the traders. Take our earlier examples from Chapter 9 out of the bank and onto the world stage. The amount that a hedge-fund manager can make in a couple of years is potentially enough on which to retire extremely comfortably. For that reason one can imagine that the business model is to get as much out, as quickly as possible, from any bandwagon, before its inevitable reversal. So if you are a hedge-fund manager and you happen to find yourself on any government advisory panel, just keep saying "There's nothing to see, move along now" for the short time that the bandwagon is rolling. You can be sure that regulators and governments will be trundling along behind your bandwagon, but at a snail's pace, giving you enough time to fill your boots.

Okay, having dealt with those in charge, let's look at the science and psychology of other aspects of systemic risk.

The MacGuffin

The next systemic risk after the cupidity and stupidity of governments is the role of bandwagons in high finance. Bandwagons beget bubbles, and bubbles beget crashes. Bubbles are not allowed

---

[4] Ross *et al.* (2012).

according to efficient market theory, but speaking of bubbles, that one popped a while ago.[5]

Bubbles need something underlying on which to pin unrealistic prices. Alfred Hitchcock used the word MacGuffin for a device to keep a plot moving along, something that really did not matter in the final analysis: the [Spoiler Alert] stamps in his *Charade*, the briefcase in Tarantino's *Pulp Fiction*. And that's all that's needed to get a bandwagon going, and where there's a bandwagon, there's money. Some examples:

- Tulips, for God's sake.

- Louisiana gold (John Law's Mississippi Company).

- The Internet! (It'll never catch on.)

On October 19, 1987, aka Black Monday, there was a MacGuffin as well – but this time the glowing object in the briefcase was a mathematical model. With their secret formula to eliminate portfolio risk, the firm LOR had found a way to make a bubble out of that same risk (see Box 10.1). And that's what burst in 1987. Twenty years later, the problem was the risk that was packaged up and hidden inside CDOs. Today, it is the risk that has been created by high-speed algorithms, all based on similar models, all racing to be the first to do the same thing.

Indeed, algorithmic trading may represent the ultimate MacGuffin – because even if someone opens the case, they still have no idea what's inside. The code could take the form of a genetic algorithm that has evolved to supposedly find the best method of forecasting, or a neural network so complex that even the creator doesn't know what's going on. As discussed in Chapter 8, this is a disadvantage if you want to understand or communicate the workings of the model. If you've got a black box making all the decisions based on some statistical analysis of share price moves over the last few seconds, and no one is allowed to look inside the box, and maybe even the manager doesn't know what the code is doing, then how much is there to say? "We've backtested it using… years' worth of data. It works. End of."

---

[5] As Eugene Fama told the *New Yorker* magazine in 2010, after the collapse of the housing bubble, "I don't even know what a bubble means" (Cassidy, 2010). In 2015 he repeated the claim to the Swiss paper *Finanz und Wirtschaft*: "I don't think there is any concrete evidence of bubbles. A bubble to me means something that has a predictable ending. But nobody has ever been able to identify any predictability in financial markets." Again, this conflates unpredictability with efficiency (Gisiger, 2016).

But for the marketing pitch what counts isn't the technical explanation or the equations – it's the story and the promise that the box represents. Maybe the story is about macroeconomic conditions, or some inefficiency in the market, or faster execution of trades. It's got to be convincing and simple. And ideally true. And so it all boils down to your skills as a salesman. Market the heck out of it, raise funds, trade, and pray that it works. It if doesn't, then blame regime shifts.

The recent move to black box/algo trading means that there is less need than ever for any scientific basis for trading or modeling. Now finance has been distilled into the purest form of business, possibly zero-content, pure showmanship.

Don't get us wrong, we know that salesmen are the most important people on earth, without whom we'd still be living in caves. And since we've mentioned caves we ought to mention Gary Dahl, the inventor of the pet rock, talk about salesmanship! Black box trading is to the 2010s what pet rocks were to the 1970s. In either case, you're buying a story.

Box 10.1   Business Model

The common factor of all financial bubbles, or bandwagons in general, is positive feedback, which amplifies swings both up and down. Perhaps the most basic example is the credit cycle. During a boom, asset prices rise, which boosts sentiment and increases collateral for loans (positive feedback). Credit therefore rises in tandem, until a crisis point is reached. Growth slows, then stops, then goes negative, loans are called in, leading to a crash and a destruction of value. And then you start again from scratch. Or that's the way it's supposed to work, in practice the economy is "rescued" by the central bank (the Fed has its back). This is why global debt levels have grown fairly consistently over the past few decades, with only the occasional dip during a downturn, to reach unprecedentedly high levels.

While the eventual collapse of that super-bubble probably won't be the fault of quants *per se*, there is another type of feedback prevalent in quantitative finance. The first time this became noticeable was in the 1980s, with the popularization of portfolio insurance, which (as discussed in Chapter 4) was based on the idea of replicating options by buying and selling futures contracts. A very simple model of this feedback was developed by Wilmott and Schönbucher.[6] It showed that replicating a short position, as in portfolio insurance, would lead to

---

[6]See Wilmott and Schönbucher (2000), but also 1995 as a thesis and conference proceedings. We saw in Chapter 4 how there's a concept called the delta of an option, which is how many shares have to be bought or sold for hedging. If we are replicating

positive feedback and increased volatility – in other words, systemic risk, of the sort brought home on Black Monday.

But there is a more subtle problem. Because, even if portfolio insurance did inadvertently create the event that it was designed to protect against, this doesn't mean that it was necessarily a bad *business* model. It was akin to selling a drug which treats a disease, but at a societal level increases the prevalence of the disease (see over-use of antibiotics). If the crash had been less dramatic, and portfolio insurance not been put forward as a possible cause, then firms such as LOR selling the product could actually have done rather well out of the resulting fear and increased business. We'll never know. But as with all the risk-management techniques we have discussed in this book, a side effect is to increase the propensity for risk, which leads to more instability, and more demand for risk management, in a self-perpetuating loop.

Today, of course, there is far more money riding on the models than in the 1980s – and when it comes to positive feedback, size matters. Indeed, another example of positive feedback is the relationship between the financial sector and regulators. As the sector increases in size, it gains more influence over the government; this allows it to change regulations in its favor, which allows it to grow even larger, and so on, until it becomes Goldman Sachs.[7]

---

an option then we need to sell or buy the same number. As the share price changes then so the delta changes and we have to rebalance. And how much the delta changes is related to a quantity called the gamma. If you recall your calculus from school then you'll know that the delta is the first derivative of the option value with respect to the asset, and the gamma is therefore the derivative of the delta with respect to the asset, or equivalently the second derivative of the value with respect to the asset. Gamma measures how quickly the value is accelerating. A supply-and-demand effect combined with that demand depending on gamma results in a volatility that also depends on gamma. And crucially, volatility will increase or decrease depending on the sign of gamma. When convertible bonds are first issued they are issued at a discount to encourage people to buy them. Hedge funds tend to be big buyers, and their strategy can be to make a profit from this mispricing by hedging the bonds against market movements. Amusingly, the signs are different from the portfolio insurance case and result in negative feedback, reducing volatility and therefore reducing the value of the convertible bond. Serves them right!

[7]Gandel (2013). Sometimes called Government Sachs, because of the remarkable ability of its alumni to go straight into senior levels of government, perhaps related to the fact that the firm is a leading corporate donor to political campaigns (Baram, 2009). It is even better represented at central banks. Four of the Federal Reserve's 12 regional banks are currently headed by former Goldman Sachs executives. Only five banks have voting power, in a rotating fashion, and in 2017 ex-Goldmanites will

But High-Speed Trading Provides Liquidity!

The main defense of high-speed algorithmic trading is that it adds liquidity to the market. And that this is a good thing, and therefore such trading is also a good thing. This is a completely false argument. It fails in at least three ways, and it points toward yet another source of systemic risk, which goes to the heart of what markets are about. To get away with this feeble excuse it relies on people not thinking too deeply…

First, let's suppose that it is true: yes, there's greater liquidity and transaction costs are reduced by all that lovely liquidity. So you'll save a few cents here and there. But who cares about those few cents? Only others working in high finance care. The man in the street doesn't care. He buys or sells shares every few months, if that. He doesn't care two hoots about saving a few cents. He's either made or lost a much larger sum than that in that time. It's only the high-frequency boys themselves who care about the cents. But if, thanks to bandwagon/feedback effects, the market has crashed, or volatility has increased, then the man in the street could have lost a fortune. "I'm sorry you lost your life savings in a flash crash but, hey, you can console yourself with a nice latte, small mind you, thanks to lower transaction costs." There's a saying for this, "Penny wise, pound foolish."

Second, what counts isn't the spread you see between buy and sell prices, it's the actual price of the transaction. So if the price is being moved around, for example by algos jumping in and out of the queue, then you might end up paying more even though the quoted spread seems small.

And finally, even if liquidity improves on average, that doesn't mean it will be there when you need it. The moment that the algos start seeing something out of the ordinary that they can't profit from, then the plug gets pulled. Precisely the moment you want to get out of the market, there's no market to get out of.

The purpose of a formal market is less about instant liquidity than reliable price discovery. With a work of art, you don't really know what it's worth until you sell it. A large house is similar. With a mid-terrace

---

hold four of these votes. Together with Mark Carney at the Bank of England and Mario Draghi at the European Central Bank, this means that interest rate decisions for much of the world's economy are made by people who came from a single firm. Nothing to see here, move along.

house among lots of similar houses then you might have an idea, if a similar house has sold recently. But with shares, and currencies, and many commodities, you have a much better idea of how much something is worth thanks to exchanges. And that share price in the market ought to bear some relation to some concept of the true value of the underlying company. Of course, company valuation is a tricky business. But if the share price and a plausible company valuation are too far out of line, then things can get strange.

For a brief period during the 2010 Flash Crash, Accenture shares traded for a few cents, down from around $40. As mentioned in Chapter 6, the crash lasted only a few minutes before the market returned to normal levels. Not everything fell. Some shares, including Apple, rose to six-figure amounts, before falling back. Fortunately the Flash Crash was short lived, and also so extreme as to be obviously an anomaly, but smaller versions of such events have become a recurrent phenomenon. In 2014, according to the US Commodity Futures Trading Commission, there were about 35 "flash" events involving the West Texas Intermediate crude oil contract alone.[8] Instead of aiding price discovery, HFT is doing the opposite. Call it a new kind of pricing risk, on which more below. Those in favor are the exchanges, which benefit from the volume, and the algo firms themselves. And of course the regulators and politicians under their sway (Box 10.2).

Box 10.2   PW's Blog, November 11, 2011

The Tobin (or Robin Hood) tax was proposed decades ago by the eponymous Nobel Laureate (that's James Tobin, not Robin Hood) as a means of stabilizing currencies via a small tax on all transactions. Every few decades the idea comes back, although no longer confined just to foreign exchange. There are various reasons why it keeps being dismissed, reasons such as infeasibility, elimination of incentives, requirement for the initiative to be global, etc. One assumes, though, that it's the political clout of the bankers that is the real reason why this has not been adopted. My sense is that the time might now be right for the adoption of the Tobin tax, thanks to the valid fear over high-frequency trading and thanks to the widely held low opinion of bankers. Countries are going to have to learn to cooperate thanks to the recent financial crises, and what better place than a tiny little tax? And the technology is in place.

---

[8] Massad (2015).

But there's the question of how tiny is tiny. Tobin himself said "let's say 0.5%." It wasn't meant as a well-thought-out number, and it's certainly far too high given typical bid–ask spreads. So what is a better number?

Trading happens for a number of reasons. Let's focus on just two, hedging and speculation. Hedging is generally considered to be a good thing, as it is meant to reduce risk. Speculation can be good or bad. In my opinion it's bad when it happens at such a high frequency that the relationship between the share price of a company and its value becomes irrelevant to making money. So let's say we want a tax that's big enough to hamper the shortest-term speculation, while small enough not to affect hedging.

The mathematics of hedging of derivatives in the presence of transaction costs goes back to Hayne Leland (1985) for simple calls and puts. Later this was extended to incorporate any derivatives by Hoggard, Whalley, and yours truly. Out of this work comes a simple non-dimensional parameter related to costs, volatility, and hedging frequency that tells you how much your hedging will affect your P&L. It's all in *PWIQF2* if you want the details.[9]

Supposing that you wanted to have less than 1% effect on the profitability of a derivative (and that number is open to discussion, but is easily well within the margins of model error), and supposing you hedge every day in a market with 20% volatility (again, two numbers that you are free to dispute or change), then the tax could be at most 0.008% of the value of each trade. Around one basis point.

Would this level affect good hedging? No. Would it affect speculation over the medium and long term? No. Would it dampen short-term speculation? You bet.

A Million Billion Dollars

HFT is an example of systemic risk that arises directly from the models used by quants. In addition, there is a more general form of risk which has to do with the size and structure of the financial system. We've mentioned a few times that the notional value of all financial derivatives is over a quadrillion dollars, which everyone can agree is a large number. Now, notional value isn't the same as the amount at risk, because it represents the value of the underlying asset. For example, consider an interest-rate swap between two people, one earning interest at a fixed rate of 5% on a million dollars and the other earning interest at a variable rate, currently 4%. If they arrange to swap those income streams, then the notional value of the swap is

---

[9] *Paul Wilmott on Quantitative Finance*, 2nd edn, John Wiley & Sons.

a million dollars, but the actual value of the swap itself will be much less – around 1% of that (it corresponds to the difference in the interest rates, which will change with time). So, describing the swap as a million-dollar derivative seems to exaggerate its size.

But now consider a CDS, which (as discussed in Chapter 5) is used as a form of insurance against a firm going bust. Here the notional value is the amount insured. So if the firm *does* default, then the notional value becomes very real – as companies such as AIG discovered during the crisis. Or imagine that, in the interest swap example, one of the parties goes broke and the other discovers that they are legally responsible to replace that income stream. Again, this amounts to ponying up the equivalent notional value.

Credit events, as they are known, are part of the risk of doing business, and instruments such as CDSs are supposed to insure against them. But unlike proper insurance policies, whose writers are highly regulated and for obvious reasons need to maintain adequate reserves, financial derivatives are subject to none of the same regulatory scrutiny. Furthermore, because derivatives are often traded over the counter, rather than through a central exchange, it is impossible to see the net exposure throughout the economy to events such as defaults, or to know how many firms or individuals will be affected. We therefore have a situation where risk can be assessed at the individual level, for particular instruments or institutions, but not at the global level. Since the crisis, there has been some attempt to move derivatives trading to central clearing houses where exposure can be better monitored (e.g., the Dodd–Frank Act in the USA), but much of the risk still remains in the shadows.

Also, while derivatives can be used to insure individual parties against risk, what they are really doing at a system level is transmitting risk. Indeed, a main reason for their popularity is that by appearing to offload risk, they allow the purchaser to take on even more risk – and potential profit – somewhere else. But when a problem such as a bank failure occurs, the high degree of connectivity in the economy means that its effects rapidly propagate through the rest of the system, as loans are called in and risk tolerance deteriorates. Just as the high volume of international traffic is the best friend of viral pandemics, so our globalized financial system has prepared the perfect ground for financial contagion. The network is highly connected, but it is impossible to see where the connections are, or to turn them off in a crisis.

With complex systems, there is usually a trade-off between efficiency and robustness. Increasing bank reserves makes banks less profitable, but also more secure. Introducing friction into the system – for example by putting regulatory brakes on HFT – will slow the markets, but also make them more transparent and reliable. And imposing a degree of modularity on the financial system – say by restructuring large global banks into smaller, more local entities – would reduce efficiency but also the likelihood of contagion. As ecologists such as Robert May have pointed out, robust ecosystems such as food webs tend to be organized into separate, weakly connected subnetworks.[10] However, the banking system has only become more concentrated since the crisis, as weaker banks were taken over by the survivors.

Perhaps the greatest structural risk to the financial system, though, is – the financial system. Or rather, money itself. As we've seen, money and debt don't play much of a role in mainstream economics. This is related to the fact that money has traditionally been treated as an inert medium of exchange, rather than something with powers of its own.[11] The so-called dynamic stochastic general equilibrium models favored by macroeconomists, for example, model the entire global economy, except for the finance part. Models are a way of interpreting the world, and if something is not in the model then we tend not to see it. This blind spot toward money and debt helps explain why we have let debt become so large – rather like a newbie subprime housing customer, lured in by teaser rates, but on a more magnificent scale. According to a 2014 report from McKinsey, global debt has reached almost $200 trillion, up by 40% just in the seven years following the crisis.[12] Debt is inherently destabilizing, for the simple reason that during an economic downturn, debts don't decline as well – they just grow mathematically over time. Leverage also amplifies the effect of price changes and feedback loops.

One solution would be to… actually, we don't have a solution (apart from the obvious ones, default or debt forgiveness). But a first step will be to rethink our models – not just the mathematical ones, but the entire way in which we see the economy.

---

[10]May *et al.* (2008).
[11]Orrell and Chlupatý (2016). As economist Stephanie Kelton (2012) notes, "Money, debt and finance don't even fit into many economic models."
[12]McKinsey Global Institute (2015), Sedghi (2015).

The Bionic Hand

Discussions about regulating or fixing the system usually return to the old debate over free markets, and whether state interference helps or hinders progress. Opinions on this have long been shaped by the picture – our collective mental model – of the economy as a fundamentally stable and optimal system, controlled by the negative feedback of the invisible hand. For Adam Smith, this process not only led to market prices stabilizing at an optimal "center of repose," but ensured "ease of body and peace of mind" for kings and beggars alike. Neoclassical economists fleshed out the story with mathematical equations, and tried to prove it by making what amounted to symmetry assumptions about things such as fairness and stability. Other theories – such as the efficient market hypothesis, with its rational, independent investors driving prices to equilibrium – are essentially updated elaborations of this theme. Quants put it to work by modeling asset prices as a probabilistic, mechanistic system, spreading and dispersing in time like plumes of smoke but without the annoying turbulence. Money throughout was mostly treated as just a metric, rather than something of importance in itself.

Today, Keynesian economists promote government attempts to stabilize markets, and central banks tinker with them at will. However, the touted ability of properly managed markets to drive prices to their "natural" level remains the lynchpin of mainstream economics, and much quant finance, and even markets themselves, because it means that those prices correspond to something solid and reliable, instead of just being a transient, emergent phenomenon of the world economy. Portfolio management assumes that prices encode a relationship between growth and risk. Financial derivatives are valued on the basis that markets set prices correctly even for things like volatility and correlation. Without such assumptions, the calculations just don't add up. To quote Blaise Pascal (on the perils of home renovation), "our whole foundation cracks and the earth opens into the depth of the abyss."

Smith's idea that selfishness at the individual level can paradoxically lead to positive societal outcomes wasn't a new one, even in the 18th century – as Czech economist Tomáš Sedláček points out, it has been around in one form or another since antiquity – but he put the story into a form and language suitable for the industrial age.[13] The world was experiencing an economic boom unlike anything ever experienced before – a truly singular event in human history – and Smith was its Poet Laureate. Even now, the invisible hand remains conflated with the ideas of economic efficiency and technological progress. On the one hand, it drives prices to an equilibrium level where no firm makes excessive profits; but on the other hand, it also drives innovation and evolution, by acting as a kind of Darwinian selection mechanism for the markets. High-frequency trading, in the words of one commentator, is a way of "giving Adam Smith's invisible hand a bionic upgrade by making it better, stronger and faster like Steve Austin in the *Six Million Dollar Man*."[14]

But as we know, the story is more complex than the one portrayed in the standard model. Algorithms share similar models so are not independent; power and influence distort the playing field by allowing privileged access to market information; positive feedback loops accentuate sudden changes and make the system unstable; and having robots mindlessly compete does not automatically benefit society. There may be tiny savings in transaction costs, but as shown above these are little compensation for the true costs, in terms of both profits and financial stability. It is hard to believe in "no arbitrage" when a major portion of the economy depends on exactly that. The financial sector protects its turf through its influence in power centers such as Washington and London, and pushes for bailouts when it screws up. If this is the bionic invisible hand, then it has the economy by its throat – less Steve Austin than the Peter Sellers character *Doctor Strangelove* (we're sticking with old pop culture references).

If we see high-frequency trading not as the perfect realization of the invisible hand, but as an emergent property of the financial system, which itself has emerged from a nexus of cultural, political, legal, technological, and other factors, then things become more complicated and nuanced. Unrestricted competition in the system can be good when it is between relative equals, but bad when it leads to excessive concentration of power; cooperation can be good when it leads to the productive sharing of ideas and resources, but bad when it becomes a bandwagon. And just because something

---

[13]Sedláček (2011).
[14]Watson (2011).

emerges – be it a trading strategy or a tumor – doesn't mean we want to keep it.

The System (John Law feat. Isaac Newton)

As we have seen in this book, high-frequency trading can be viewed as the latest step in the long evolution of quantitative finance. The principal characters in the story, in descending order of distance from the money, have been bankers, quants, economists, and scientists – with a fair degree of overlap and crossover between them. Some scientists become quants, some quants become bankers. Some bankers fund scientists, some economists are scientists. But all have important roles.

While Smith idealized Isaac Newton, he had no time for John Law, with his idea of "multiplying paper to almost any extent... the most extravagant project both of banking and stock-jobbing that, perhaps, the world ever saw." But today our financial system owes less to the former than the latter. Instead of Newton's gold standard, with its clearly defined units of value weighed out in precious metal, we have Law's fiat currency, only on a much larger scale. And in place of Newtonian stability, the dominant theme seems to be chaos and uncertainty. However, our financial institutions still look and behave as if they were in the gold-standard era. Remarkably little has changed, on the surface, at the Bank of England or the Federal Reserve, or in university economics departments, since that time. The system is Law's, but Newton serves as the straight man, the public face of reason. The role of economists since Smith has been to channel Newton, and give the system the gold-standard stamp of certification.

And the role of quants? Everything was fine, back when they were just making calculations and valuing derivatives and doing a better job than their competitors of balancing growth and risk. But something changed – they became too big. Beginning in the 1980s, their models first influenced, then took over, the system, creating unanticipated feedback loops between the models and reality. In the early 2000s their CDOs and CDSs literally made money, Law style, by allowing banks to lend out more and more credit, which consisted of new money, and charging commission on the process. When their schemes – their quantitative seizing – cratered, the central banks stepped in to fill the hole with quantitative easing. This at least reinflated asset prices to roughly where they were, but global debt levels inflated too.

The crisis didn't slow quants down. Instead, they turned markets into a plaything for algorithms. No longer content to just analyze markets, quants – or at least their robot avatars – actually *became* the markets. But the danger is that their cover has been blown. The old story about markets being stable and self-correcting looks more uncertain with each disaster and every flash crash. The idea that we all behave like independent atoms no longer appeals in an age of social networks and complexity theory. Newton has left the building.

And here we have the biggest systemic risk of all. Money is a way to attach number to the concept of value, and markets are a way to make sure the numbers have meaning. Because number is involved, it is easy to get sucked into the idea that the economy is a physical system, governed by mechanical laws. But maintaining that fiction, that illusion of validity, requires an epic amount of denial – a recalibration of reality. Number is – literally – only half of it, only one side of the coin, because money and markets also depend on human factors such as trust and belief. So for the system to function, the story – the bond between number and value – has to hold. Break that, and we are back in John Law territory, where the miraculous "system" is revealed as a Wizard-of-Oz-like fraud.

While algorithms are good at many things, one skill which continues to elude them is the ability to understand stories – or make up new ones (which is why humans are still employed to write screenplays and books, and even trade stocks). And in a world where robotic, twitter-fed algorithms race to react to the decoded mutterings of equally robotic central banks, finance appears to have lost the plot.

So the question is, how does this end? Can quants turn it around, or will the straight man become the fall guy? After all, if most of the trading is being done by algos, how are the humans going to react the next time things really go wrong? In an unequal world, that's called political risk – and the outcome might be worse than Law's exile in Venice.

Answers to wilmott.com, please. We'll wrap this up with some thoughts on reforming the field we call quantitative finance – and ask if it needs to become more qualitative.

Epilogue: Keep it Simple

"It's a great topic you have chosen and I fully support your intention on preventing the next crash. But I feel that the world is controlled by a bunch of morons that either just want as much money and power as possible for themselves – or are afraid to question the status quo. I think that the solution lies in educating the people of our planet on how it works so that we together can create a new system where the power is more distributed (as opposed to concentrated) – I am certain such a system is much less likely to crash. With a currency that means something and cannot just be diluted by a government to boost the economy's statistics and please the markets and thereby the few in monetary power. I think you get my point – good luck with the book! Use your famous names and great intellects [and good looks, ed.] *for the future good of humanity :)"*

"How to prevent economic crises?, how to have a long-term stable global economy?, are we complicating a simple thing (economy and its study)?, what should an individual do to shield from inconsistencies of the economy?"

"Qualitative analysis also needs to be included."
　　—Answers to the survey question: "What topics should
　　definitely feature in the book?" at wilmott.com

Human beings learn, or are supposed to learn, from past mistakes. Building codes, fire codes, engineering codes, and safety codes of all sorts carry within them the memory of past disasters. Boiler explosions were common in the 19th century, until their designers started to follow pressure codes. In finance today, even insurance companies blow up, which takes some of the security out of having insurance. So how can we reform the rules of financial markets to make them more boringly reliable, and is that even possible? This final section proposes some principles that a financial engineering code should include or reflect.

"Keep it simple, stupid – KISS – is our constant reminder." Thus spoke Lockheed engineer Kelly Johnson, who long served as the firm's Head of Advanced Development Projects.[1] His projects – which included what was in 1964 the world's fastest and highest-flying aircraft, the SR-71 Blackbird – pushed the limit of performance; but he knew that an overly complicated mechanism was both more likely to go wrong and more difficult to repair (especially if you were in the middle of a battle).

The world financial system, unfortunately, does not appear to have been designed with the same principle in mind. Instead of being simple and clear, it is complicated and opaque. Rather than a high-performance jet, it is more like something that you would deliberately crash behind enemy lines in order to confuse the enemy. It might be based in theory on elegant equations and symmetry laws, but the actual implementation, with its infinite calibrations and adjustments, is a confounding mess. As discussed earlier, it is both too big to fail, and designed to fail. So how can we make it safer for those directly and indirectly affected by its activities?

Since equations are at the heart of quant finance, we'll start with the quant equivalent of the KISS principle, which is what Paul calls "the math sweet spot." He has used this idea throughout his lectures, and sales pitches for the Certificate in Quantitative Finance.[2] We then give handy, actionable, and above all humble, advice to everyone else in finance, telling them how to do their jobs.

Quants: The Math Sweet Spot

You see different levels of mathematics in quant finance. Some people try to dumb the subject down. There are plenty of textbooks that kid you into thinking that there is almost no mathematics in the subject at all. But dumbing the subject down is not good. You cannot price sophisticated contracts (and yes, some of them can actually be useful) unless you have a decent mathematical toolbox, and an

---

[1] Rich (1995).

[2] He also blogged about this in April 2008. And since we're mathematicians, which means we are deeply lazy (mathematics was invented to save work), we present here a shortened, and improved, version of that blog post.

understanding of how to use those tools. But then there's the opposite extreme.

Some people try to make the subject as complicated as they can. It may be an academic author who, far from wanting to pass on knowledge to younger generations, instead wants to impress the professor down the corridor. He hopes that one day he will get to be the professor down the corridor who everyone is trying to impress. Or maybe it's a university seeing the lucrative quant finance bandwagon. Perhaps they don't have any faculty with knowledge of finance, certainly no practical knowledge, but they sure do have plenty of people with a deep knowledge of measure theory.

It's the latter group that is a great danger. This sort of mathematics is wonderful, if you want to do it on your own time, fine. Or become a finance professor. Or move into a field where the mathematics is hard and the models are good, such as aeronautics. But please don't bring this nonsense into an important subject like finance, where even the best models are rubbish. Every chain has its weakest link. In quantitative finance the weakest links are the models.

There is a math sweet spot, not too dumb, not too smart, where quants should focus. In this sweet spot we have basic tools of probability theory, a decent grasp of calculus, and the important tools of numerical analysis. The models are advanced enough to be able to be creative with new instruments, and robust enough not to fall over all the time. They are transparent, so the quant, the trader, and the salesperson can understand them, at least in their assumptions and use.

Because the models are necessarily far, far from perfect, one must be suspicious of any analytical technique or numerical method that is too fiddly or detailed. Being blinded by mathematical science and consequently believing in your models is all too common in quantitative finance.

To Paul, who teaches and uses the stuff, this is the reason why quant finance is interesting and challenging: not because the mathematics is complicated, it isn't, but because putting mathematics, trading and market imperfections, and human nature together and trying to model all this, knowing all the while that it is probably futile, now that's fun!

Regulators: Go Full Iceland

We've had a few laughs at the expense of the regulators in this book. But regulators are those best placed to get financial engineering and all those complex products back on the straight and narrow. We don't think it can be too hard.

There are a few basic principles that need to be adhered to, first and foremost the idea of transparency. We don't really need to say much about this, since it's already at the top of every to-do list for finance. Except to point out that transparency sounds nice, but practically no one who works with money actually wants it. Money likes to hide in the shadows.

So to do their jobs, regulators need to go on the attack. No more reacting to events. They are not police who have to wait until a crime is committed. And again, unlike the police, they can and should use profiling... some financial institutions and people have a bad reputation, and the regulators should let rip on these. There've been some bizarre individuals at the very top of the banking ladder, people who really should not be in charge of a pair of scissors let alone people's life savings. Who can forget Paul Flowers? Paul Flowers BA (Hons) FRSA FRGS. Local councilor endorsed by Labour leader Ed Miliband, Methodist minister, rising to become a non-executive director of Co-operative Bank. We are keen for people with a variety of life experiences to be appointed as non-execs, but his private life experiences, running parallel with his public life, included cocaine, methamphetamine, allegations of hiring rent boys, hiding child abuse, and a conviction for a sex act in a public toilet.[3] To the newspapers he became, rather wonderfully, the *Crystal Methodist.* When asked by a Treasury Select Committee to outline his qualifications, earned during his sole four-year spell at a bank, he replied: "I took the exam of the Institute of Bankers. I completed part one and the best part of part two of those exams before I became a Methodist minister. I would judge that experience is out of date in terms of needs of contemporary banking." However, he didn't resign until 2013 when it was noticed that the bank had lost £1.5 billion.

The near collapse of HBOS in 2008 was blamed on a "colossal failure of management."[4] So far, so standard. But one of those executives, the Chief Executive no less, was Sir James Crosby. He managed the clever trick of, for a while, simultaneously also being the Deputy Chairman of the regulator, the Financial Services Authority. Although no one has said that he acted improperly in regulating himself, other than being a colossal failure that is, it beggars belief

---

[3] Burn-Callander and Quinn (2013).
[4] Treanor (2015).

that anyone should consider it a good idea for a banker to be at the same time a regulator. To his credit, after the initial report on HBOS was published in 2013, Mr Crosby did relinquish 30% of his pension, and his knighthood.

We could probably name a few bad apples ourselves. Fear of litigation prevents us. And that's yet another book in itself: how the legal profession protects the guilty against the innocent. So while on the subject, let's suggest decent protection for whistleblowers.

As well as hunting out bad'uns, regulators need to go on the offensive in interrogating the banks. Researchers can help out with this. Start providing regulators with ammunition, difficult questions for the banks to answer. A visit from the regulators should strike fear into the bankers, and not just be an inconvenience. Let's have more reverse stress testing. What's that, you ask? It's like a role-playing exercise for bankers, or something that lateral-thinking expert Edward de Bono might have come up with. It goes like this. The bankers have to put themselves in the position of having lost billions of dollars and then, as a show of creativity, come up with as many explanations as possible for how this could have happened. And then they have to plug the gap. Let's have some fun with this... Bank A can reverse stress test Bank B. Great amusement can be had by all. If you've seen Steve Martin in *Roxanne*, the scene where his character comes up with 20 imaginative insults for his large nose, then you'll know the sort of creativity that might be required. What do you mean, bankers don't have any imagination?[5]

If the regulators feel they don't have the necessary skills, or resolve, they can be sent to an intensive boot camp in Iceland, where – according to urban legend – bankers who go astray are buried in the ground up to their neck, urinated on, and left to ferment for several months (or is that an urban legend about their tasty national dish, hákarl?).

Economists: Wake Up

We've also had a few laughs at the expense of mainstream economists. Of course, it's easy to criticize, less easy to propose alternatives. But we don't need to, because there are many alternative

---

[5] We have been told that Edmond Rostand's play *Cyrano de Bergerac* contains a similar scene. We weren't cultured enough to know this.

ideas being developed all the time (we mentioned a few in Chapter 8). The problem is that these don't get the attention they deserve, because since at least the time of Adam Smith the power structure of the field has been warped by its very subject matter – money (or what should be the subject matter; as mentioned, money isn't something they study much). Adair Turner talked about "regulatory capture through the intellectual zeitgeist," but to take it another step, the intellectual zeitgeist has been captured by finance.

We predict that in a hundred years' time, historians will see theories such as the efficient market hypothesis as being as embarrassingly wrong as other ideas that hung around well beyond their best-by date, such as the story that planets rotate in crystalline spheres around the Earth. In the meantime, if mainstream economists want to shake their image as the Medieval theologians, or useful idiots, of the quant finance world, they need to ask how rewards from the financial sector in the form of grants, consulting gigs, and so on have shaped their field, and helped to align their core teachings so perfectly with the needs of that same sector. Or at least they should be open about their incentives. As economist Richard Denniss told the CBC: "Economists are often pretending to be impartial. They're often pretending to be putting their intellectual credibility forward in defence of something, and if they just want to be sales people then they should admit that. They should come clean with journalists, they should come clean with politicians, they should come clean with public servants, and say look I am here on behalf of someone, my opinions are irrelevant, these are the opinions I am presenting to help my client get their way."[6]

There also needs to be a proper accounting for the role academic economists played in the crisis. As economist George DeMartino notes, the profession "failed to meet its obligations to society by failing to promote and sustain a diversity of views among its members over matters that are terribly complex and important." Its response was instead characterized by "a herd mentality about the right way to think about financial markets and financial regulation; a dismissal of theory, evidence, and argument about the dangers associated with unregulated asset markets; and perhaps most important, a severe overconfidence among the most influential economists about the

---

[6] Kennedy (2016).

extent of economic expertise."[7] Above all, most economists failed to stand up when their insights were needed. Confronted with a $1.2 quadrillion derivatives bomb, all they did was play with their models. Instead of sucking up to money, or adopting the hands-off "not my problem" approach, academic economists should take a leaf from organizations such as the Union of Concerned Scientists, and speak truth to power – even if it means saying "I don't know."[8] Economists have an ethical responsibility, and it is not just to protect their turf and their egos.

We believe that economics is in for a period of rapid change, but it will take time for this to work through to actual practice. In the meantime, policy makers should take economists' incentives into account when listening to their advice about things like high-frequency trading (thanks for the input, Ben!). And while they're at it, they might also ask why everyone around them appears to have worked at one time or another for Goldman Sachs.

Banks: Learn to Fail

Anyone who has lost money at the hands of identity thieves will know that getting your money back is fraught with worry and paperwork. That's supposing your bank gets beyond thinking *you* are the criminal. Your savings are wiped out, surely the bank just has to unwind all of the disputed activity?

In the 2010 Flash Crash, most trades at crazy prices were unwound. Wouldn't it be nice if banking could borrow some ideas from the PC world and do a simple "Restore" to a previous state? David actually got a bank to do this once, after his mother was mis-sold a mutual fund.[9] But let's take this further. In this crazy old world, don't you sometimes wish to "Boot to Safe Mode"? Especially with no networking. I know we do. Of course this would probably only be feasible over very short time periods, but if we could reboot back to around 2005 that would be even better.

---

[7] DeMartino (2010, p. 171).
[8] Heterodox economists do speak up all the time of course, but in most countries they have little impact on the national discourse. In Canada, for example, you wouldn't know they exist unless you went looking for them.
[9] Writing this article helped: "Are corporate banks stretching themselves thin?" (Orrell, 2016b).

Another idea that bankers can borrow from engineering, or for that matter biology, is the idea of a controlled shutdown. When cells in the human body are damaged, they are targeted for apoptosis, a process in which the cells are taken apart and the constituents recycled for use elsewhere. Cells in a cancerous tumor have found a way to disable apoptosis, so can divide without limit. However, cells at the center of the tumor become necrotic, which means they fall apart in an uncontrolled manner. When banks fail today, their death is similarly necrotic. The collapse of Lehman Brothers, for example, left over a million derivatives transactions outstanding, and a legal mess that took years to clear up.

Regulators are increasingly demanding that banks draw up "living wills," with instructions on what should happen in case of failure. However, as Dennis Kelleher from the lobby group Better Markets said: "The acid test is whether these are in fact credible plans. In the past they have submitted plans with all sorts of provisions and conjectures, but they didn't mean anything because they weren't credible."[10] So regulators must learn to say sorry, we're targeting you for apoptosis.

Traders: Why Does My Bonus Have a Minus Sign in Front?

Here's a word you don't hear often, malus. Unless you are a gardener, for whom it's a genus of apple trees. But if your fingers are green from counting your money rather than planting fruit trees, it's a word you ought to get familiar with. It's the opposite of a bonus, it's a penalty for performing badly. And it's something we believe should feature more prominently in banking circles.

The opportunity to become filthy rich is central to capitalism. And sometimes it can legitimately be at the expense of others, as in when you sell them something they actually want. But, just as in modern portfolio theory, that filthy rich return should be accompanied by an equally large risk. Owners of small businesses take enormous risks, especially when starting out. And when those businesses become large, the risk increases. And often they fail, and the risk is realized.

---

[10] Jopson and McLannahan (2015).

This is not what happens in banks. Nor for the CEOs of major corporations for that matter. Bankers, and quants, are massively compensated for a relatively simple job. And there is currently rarely any downside when losses are made. The worst that happens is that they lose their job. No bonuses need be returned. Even the word "compensated" carries connotations suggesting they are doing a difficult job and we should be jolly appreciative of them. No, we beg to disagree, you are doing a straightforward job, but a job that's as close to picking money off a money tree as it is possible to get. As John Cryan, co-CEO of Deutsche Bank, observed: "Many people in the sector still believe they should be paid entrepreneurial wages for turning up to work with a regular salary, a pension and probably a healthcare scheme and playing with other people's money."[11] (And as someone whose job usually carries a pay package in the region of $7 million, he knows what he's talking about!)[12] According to former investment banker Sam Polk, "It's one of the most stable career paths available. Once you get to the level of making $1m a year, you rarely dip below it. Hedge fund managers who leave Goldman talk about how risky it is, but it's all upside."[13]

But it's not just bankers. How often do you hear the multi-millionaire CEOs of major companies being described as "businessmen"? No, they're not businessmen. They just happen to have friends in the right places, they scratch each others' backs and appoint each other to various boards. They are private-sector politicians. Just google these execs, look at their CVs, and see just how few have ever risked their own money, or ever started their own business. If you, dear reader, run your own business, perhaps it's a corner shop, or as a consultant, or plumber, then you are more of a businessman than they are. Don't let them get away with calling themselves businessmen any longer. John Ralston Saul nailed it in his book *Voltaire's Bastards* back in 1992: "Our business leaders hector us in the name of capitalism, when most of them are no more than corporate employees, isolated from personal risk."[14]

If "compensation" in banks remains at such an unjustifiable level, then we strongly recommend the wide, and regulated, introduction

---

[11]G. Farrell (2015).
[12]McGee (2016).
[13]Quoted in McGee (2016).
[14]Saul (1993, p. 12).

of maluses as part of the pay system within the financial community. And for CEOs while we're at it.

We'd say that full public disclosure of bankers' earnings might also help, but we're worried that would turn it into even more of a competition.

Journalists: Watch Out for Saboteurs

When investigating the financial sector, or talking to bankers, journalists are hampered by the fact that no one gives them a straight answer, and the system is incredibly confusing. For example, suppose they attend a conference on high-frequency trading. At the end of it they will probably emerge with an appreciation of the topic's complexity, and a headache, but little in the way of firm understanding, let alone guidance. They will ask themselves, at the bar afterwards, what the point of the conference was in the first place. And they will wonder why investigations seem to drag on for ever but achieve nothing.

One reason is that, unknown to them, many of the participants at such events are actually engaged in a subtle form of sabotage. Journalists therefore need to learn how to detect such activities. They can do no better than resort to the CIA's *Simple Sabotage Field Manual*, from 1944.[15] This includes useful tips for everyone from arsonists to factory workers. Much of it reads like an excerpt from *Bad Housekeeping* magazine, or standard practice in the Orrell household: "Leave saws slightly twisted when you are not using them. After a while, they will break when used... In putting air into tires, see that they are kept below normal pressure, so that more than an ordinary amount of wear will result." More relevant here is the section on General Interference with Organizations and Conferences, which perfectly describes the approach adopted by industry and government experts alike:

1. Insist on doing everything through "channels." Never permit shortcuts to be taken in order to expedite decisions.

2. Make "speeches." Talk as frequently as possible and at great length. Illustrate your "points" by long anecdotes and

---

[15] CIA Office of Strategic Services (1944).

accounts of personal experiences. Never hesitate to make a few appropriate "patriotic" comments. [It's vital for the economy!]

3. When possible, refer all matters to committees, for "further study and consideration." Attempt to make the committee as large as possible – never less than five.

4. Bring up irrelevant issues as frequently as possible.

5. Haggle over precise wordings of communications, minutes, resolutions.

6. Refer back to matters decided upon at the last meeting and attempt to reopen the question of the advisability of that decision.

7. Advocate "caution." Be "reasonable" and urge your fellow conferees to be "reasonable" and avoid haste, which might result in embarrassments or difficulties later on.

8. Be worried about the propriety of any decision – raise the question of whether such action as is contemplated lies within the jurisdiction of the group or whether it might conflict with the policy of some higher echelon.

Above all, "Hold conferences when there is more critical work to be done." If these all fail, saboteurs can resort to General Devices for Lowering Morale and Creating Confusion. These include "Give lengthy and incomprehensible explanations when questioned," "Act stupid," or in a total emergency "Cry and sob hysterically."

Bankers are masters in this area. Consider, for example, HSBC, one of the world's largest banks, whose managers – when its lucrative sideline in money laundering came under investigation by the US Justice Department – adopted a strategy which was referred to in internal documents as "Discredit, Deny, Deflect, and Delay" (plus sob hysterically, presumably).[16]

Journalists can counter these techniques by copying from the same play book. A first step is to reorient their thinking "in the direction of destruction." As an example, if an interviewee is reciting propaganda, it is "quite easy to overmodulate transmissions of talks... so

---

[16]S. Farrell (2015).

that they will sound as if they were talking through a heavy cotton blanket with a mouth full of marbles." Sorry, can you say that again – HFT is what now? No conflict of what again?

Educators: Quantity and Quality

A few years ago the Royal Statistical Society asked some UK Members of Parliament a simple question in probability: "A coin is tossed twice. What is the probability of getting two heads?" Only 53% of Conservative MPs got the answer right. But even worse, only 23% of Labour MPs knew the correct answer. But at the same time, over 70% of each party expressed confidence when dealing with numbers.

We've moaned quite a bit about the state of education in banking and quantitative finance. We'd like to see better education, specifically in more mathematical tools and techniques, to broaden out the subject from its increasingly narrow and narrow-minded specialization. A more skeptical and scientific (by which we mean the classical hypotheses and testing) attitude has to be encouraged. If something fails to work, it must be thrown out. The principle is clear. But putting this into practice is daunting. For not only are the practitioners badly educated, they, like the MPs, have an unrealistic view of their own abilities. Until a critical mass of self-awareness is reached, there will be no change.

At the same time, mathematical and technical skills are not enough! Let's broaden it even further. Quantitative finance is about numbers, but that doesn't mean it is the same as physics or engineering. The economy is not a machine, it is a living, organic system, and the numbers it produces have a complicated relationship with the underlying reality. So we want the field to be supplied with mathematicians who can also recite Shakespeare. Or at least read books. And if you think that's asking too much, just see our next recommendation.

Politicians: Create an FAA for the Financial System

The financial system has a number of parallels with another human activity that is dangerous, involves almost everyone in the developed world, and is highly regulated, as banks should be.

The Federal Aviation Administration (FAA) administers all US civil aviation matters. Their remit includes pilot certificates, air traffic control, technology, environmental effects, and safety.

In many ways, the FAA covers activities that are not dissimilar to what goes on in banks. Air transport and banking are both necessarily global; there are issues concerning safety (e.g., crashes); technology, both old and new, is important; and then there is the trustworthiness and competence of those involved.

But aviation has got its act together in a way that banks can only dream of. There is collaboration between aviation authorities around the world to the extent that an accident investigation would find many different countries assisting. Should there be an accident then there is the Black Box to help explain what happened to prevent future accidents. Should an accident reveal problems with a type of plane then those planes get grounded all around the world, pretty much immediately. And should there be a new form of terrorist attack then new security measures will immediately be implemented.

In the same way that the FAA has some control over technological matters, there should be greater control over new financial instruments. Banks should have to prove need for the product, and competence in its valuation, and crucially its hedging and risk management. That's before the contract ever gets traded.

Pilots are routinely tested, for flying abilities and also for medical and drug problems. There is also some psychological testing, which will probably increase in the future. Online you can even find information about individual pilots and their qualifications. At most, bankers are sometimes required to take basic multiple-choice exams. The contents of which are instantly forgotten once the exam has been passed. There is little requirement for maintaining and upgrading skills, so that those older bankers who have risen to the top do not have any clue what the youngsters are doing below them.

And air traffic control ensures that all planes don't try to land at the same airport at the same time. The clear parallel is that there should be control over concentration risk, so that all banks don't jump simultaneously onto the same trendy bandwagon.

Of course, the finance sector will argue that this is bad for the finance sector (as opposed to customers), because all that tedious regulation will make it shrink. But that's the idea!

The fact that these or other reforms were not implemented in the drawn-out aftermath of the last epic financial crisis might lead one to conclude that we have missed our chance for good. But if the system continues on its current path, then the next crash, and the next call for reform, will be even stronger.

I Solemnly Swear...

In late 2008, Paul – along with many other quants, and for that matter much of society – was pondering the state of the financial system. Together they had looked into the abyss. And although Paul knew that there were plenty of bad apples in banking, he also knew that the vast majority were either just confused, out of their depth, or not as smart as they thought they were. Perhaps Fama didn't know what a bubble was because he lived in one. Bankers, economists, academics, and quants each have their own bubbles. By keeping the real world out, these bubbles protect them from blowback from their actions. But they also prevent them from seeing the consequences of their actions.

Paul thought that perhaps quants ought to have some guidelines, something to – from time to time – give them a reality check. Emanuel Derman had been having exactly the same idea. So, between them, and drawing inspiration from Karl Marx and Hippocrates, at the end of 2008 Emanuel and Paul wrote the Financial Modelers' Manifesto. It was published in *Business Week*. It was summarized in Scott Patterson's *The Quants*, and Derman's *Models.Behaving.Badly*. And from there it even found its way onto Jon Stewart's *Daily Show*. (Oprah mysteriously didn't bite.)

The full text is available online, but we include here the main part, which is the Modelers' Hippocratic Oath. Similar principles could apply to most forms of mathematical modeling that impact society, from transport forecasting to weather prediction:

~ I will remember that I didn't make the world, and it doesn't satisfy my equations.

~ Though I will use models boldly to estimate value, I will not be overly impressed by mathematics.

~ I will never sacrifice reality for elegance without explaining why I have done so.

~ Nor will I give the people who use my model false comfort about its accuracy. Instead, I will make explicit its assumptions and oversights.

~ I understand that my work may have enormous effects on society and the economy, many of them beyond my comprehension.

Around the same time that Emanuel and Paul were signing their manifesto, in a spooky case of synchronicity, David was sitting at his desk drinking a cup of tea. But he was also writing, in his robust yet user-friendly way, that the main thing that makes banking unusual, for such an important profession, is "its failure to develop sound ethical standards. Doctors and engineers have ethical codes; bankers have dress codes."[17] For example, the code of the US National Society of Professional Engineers, which dates to 1964, begins: "Engineers, in the fulfillment of their professional duties, shall hold paramount the safety, health, and welfare of the public." By contrast, as economist Jason West observes, "The International Association of Financial Engineers does not consider ethics worthy of inclusion in their suggested core body of knowledge."[18] The same is true in economics.[19]

This omission is partly related to the fact that quants and economists do not directly and graphically experience the results of their mistakes – their actions might cause a factory to close, but its boiler doesn't blow up in their face.[20] But it is also related to the equivalence between models and markets, which is unique to the field: because, if finance is a quantitative science and the markets obey its laws, then it is purely objective and there is no room for individual choice or interpretation. We have outsourced ethical judgments to the invisible hand, or increasingly to algorithms – with the result that our own ability to make ethical decisions in economic matters has atrophied.

Even worse, it appears that the finance culture actually primes people to behave unethically. Experiments published in the journal

---

[17] *Economyths* was first published in 2010, but written in 2009 (Orrell, 2017).
[18] West (2012).
[19] Though at least Oxford University Press recently published *The Oxford Handbook of Professional Economic Ethics* which might help (DeMartino and McCloskey, 2016).
[20] Such an explosion in a Massachusetts shoe factory caused 58 deaths in 1905, and prompted the state to enact a legal code for the design of boilers and pressure vessels, a version of which has since been adopted in over a hundred countries.

Nature showed that thinking about their jobs makes bankers more likely to cheat. As the study's authors noted, "an oath, supported by ethics training, could prompt bank employees to consider the impact of their behaviour on society rather than focusing on their own short-term benefits."[21] In other words, it could prime them in the other direction.

So, another thing we would add to our wish list for the financial sector is a similar code for bankers. Maybe something about being careful with other people's money. A good starting point would be "First, do no harm." Or, as Hippocrates put it in the original:

~ I will utterly reject harm and mischief.

And that would rule out quite a few current practices, while leaving some room for the inevitable trade-offs involved in financial decisions. An elaborate swearing-in ceremony involving blood and maybe chickens would be a plus, but not necessary.

Of course, cynics will say that codes are just there for the sake of appearances. Which brings us to…

The Nuclear Option

As discussed in Chapter 2, quantitative finance shares part of its intellectual inheritance with the development of nuclear weapons. In July 1955, a few weeks before Einstein's death, Betrand Russell issued to a crowded press conference in London what became known as the Russell–Einstein manifesto. It laid out the options for nuclear survival in stark terms: "We appeal as human beings to human beings: Remember your humanity, and forget the rest. If you can do so, the way lies open to a new Paradise; if you cannot, there lies before you the risk of universal death." The manifesto inspired the establishment of the Pugwash Conferences on Science and World Affairs, and the Union of Concerned Scientists. It energized the peace and anti-nuclear movements, and paved the way for the Nuclear Non-Proliferation Treaty. It marked a moment when physicists accepted a degree of ethical responsibility for their quantum creations; when they realized they were *involved*, so even doing nothing was a political act.

---

[21] Cohn *et al.* (2014).

At a purely professional level, though, the manifesto appeared to be a failure, in the sense that it did nothing to counter the flood of scientists and engineers into weapons programs.[22] One reason, as computer scientist Phillip Rogaway notes, is the belief in progress which characterizes such fields: "Unbridled technological optimism undermines the basic need for social responsibility."[23] But another reason is that codes are no use unless they are enforced. Doctors have oaths, but they also have malpractice suits.

In finance, one approach would be to get more public oversight of banks, but again there is the problem of the mathematical defeat device. This won't work unless the public has access to expert witnesses who are willing to point out the flaws in models. How about making model abuse as serious an offence in finance as malpractice is in medicine?[24] As much as this pains us to say it, it might be time to get the lawyers involved, and not just the ones who work for banks.

But for deeper change to take place, we need not just laws but a shift in awareness – a truly cultural transformation. We need to change the story around the economy and the role of finance. This will require the participation of quants, regulators, economists, scientists, journalists, educators, policy makers, but above all the public – the ones whose jobs and businesses and futures are at stake. The anti-nuclear movement may not have prevented career-building experts from working on nuclear weapons, but it moved forward the broader debate about their development, and something similar is required today for finance. Those quant devices are not as lethal as the nuclear sort, but their abuse can harm people and societies in other ways. It may be time for a non-proliferation agreement for complex derivatives and trading strategies, and a concerted political and societal effort to roll back the power of the financial sector.

Nuclear non-proliferation ultimately depends on controlling and limiting the production of the fissile material used to make bombs.

---

[22]Orrell (2012, p. 133).

[23]Rogaway (2015). The similarly agnostic approach of cryptographers, he notes, has led to the modern surveillance state. The financial equivalent is a naive trust in the invisible hand and efficient markets.

[24]In 2007 a number of patients successfully sued Duke University for using faulty prognostic models as a basis for selecting cancer treatments – the case was brought to light by a whistleblower who later said "I discovered what I perceived to be problems in the predictor models that made it difficult for me to continue working in that environment" (Neff, 2015). See dig.abclocal.go.com/wtvd/duke%20lax%20lawsuit.pdf.

The financial version of weapons-grade plutonium is debt – it has the power to create enormous energy, or destroy countries. So, if simplicity is the aim, there is always the option of monetary reform. Make it so that banks can only lend money they actually have. An early proponent of full reserve banking, as it is known, was Nobel Laureate physicist Frederick Soddy, who was explicitly motivated by what he saw as the banking sector's threat to world peace.[25] Versions have also been proposed, for different reasons, by people including Irving Fisher, Milton Friedman, and Frank Knight. It has come back in favor following the crisis, with the Swiss currently planning a referendum to adopt it (though they do that kind of thing a lot), and Iceland also considering it (!).[26] It has its disadvantages – not least the total lack of support from banks – but would certainly make the system easier to control.

So, now that we have set the financial world straight, we'll end with some thoughts on what this all means for the average investor (and you thought we'd never get round to it!).

Paul and David Answer Your Personal Finance Questions!

Question: I'm an investor, and am wondering what commodity will continue to hold its price well into the future?

Answer: Stupid predictions about the future.

Question: As a small trader, can I ever really win on the stock market, or will I always be beaten by the "efficient market"?

Answer: You won't be beaten by the efficient market. You'll be beaten by a robot.

Question: I'm concerned about the huge and unprecedented global build-up in debt. How can I hedge against its collapse?

Answer: If you haven't already done so, take out a massive, obviously unpayable loan, and then default along with everyone else.

Question: I don't understand how people make money from cattle futures. Whenever I see a cow I always think, doesn't have much of a future, does it?

Answer: (Awkward silence.[27])

---

[25] Soddy (1926).
[26] Wolf (2014). See also Orrell and Chlupatý (2016) for a discussion.
[27] This joke was in David's 1996 play *Steppenpuppy*. People laughed then.

Question: I am moving to Vancouver, and am not sure whether to buy a house or rent. According to your book, a reasonable price/rent ratio is around 200–220, but here it can easily be three or four times that, implying that I should rent. However my spouse, who I love dearly, really wants a house and says that renting is just "throwing money away" and "paying the landlord's mortgage." Who is right?

Answer: Your spouse.

Question: You mentioned the quantum nature of money. How and when can I apply this in my everyday life?

Answer: The same way you apply quantum mechanics.

Question: I'm interested in predicting the market based on global macroeconomic and political trends. In particular, I'm thinking about the rise of China, issues around debt (e.g., Chinese holdings of US treasuries), flashpoints in the Middle East and in Eastern Europe, the risk of pandemics (the next Ebola), and so on. Any insightful suggestions?

Answer: Stop reading the news.

Question: I'm an economist at a leading university who blogs regularly and is an opinion-maker and thought-leader in the media. I have read parts of your book online while at work. I found it juvenile, inept, etc. and think you owe economists an apology. I am planning to obtain an actual copy (using my university account) for a ceremonial book burning at our diverse and inclusive, economics department. How do you respond?

Answer: Make sure you get the kindling version.[28]

Question: I'm finding the answers to these questions kind of glib and dismissive. It's exactly the know-all attitude that people find irritating about quants and mathematicians. Why don't you propose some actual solutions if you're so smart.

Answer: (No answer.)

Question: Well?
Answer: ¡Vaya mierda!

Question: Now you're just being offensive.

Answer: Well those "questions"? We made them up – and sold you the answers!

Question: You mean... this has all been fiction?

Answer: Only 34%.

---

[28]Inspired by a true story (Orrell, 2017).

Bibliography

Ackman, Dan. "Enron The Incredible." *Forbes*, January 15, 2002.

Adams, Douglas. *The Original Hitchhiker Radio Scripts*. Edited by Geoffrey Perkins. London: Pan Books, 1985.

Ahmad, Riaz and Paul Wilmott. "Which free lunch would you like today, Sir? Delta hedging, volatility arbitrage and optimal portfolios." *Wilmott magazine*, November 2005: 64–79.

Ahmad, Riaz and Paul Wilmott. "The market price of interest rate risk: Measuring and modelling fear and greed in the fixed-income markets." *Wilmott magazine*, January 2007.

Anonymous. "Dismal science, dismal sentence." *Economist*, September 9, 2006.

Anonymous. "Efficiency and beyond." *Economist*, July 16, 2009.

Aristotle. *Aristotle's Politics*. Translated by Benjamin Jowett. New York: Modern Library, 1943.

Arrow, Kenneth J. and Gérard Debreu. "Existence of a Competitive Equilibrium for a Competitive Economy." *Econometrica* 22 (1954): 65–90.

Baaquie, Belal E. "A Path Integral Approach to Option Pricing with Stochastic Volatility: Some Exact Results." *Journal de Physique I* 7 (1997): 1733–1753.

Bachelier, L. "Théorie de la spéculation." *Annales Scientifiques de l'École Normale Supérieure* 3, no. 17 (1900): 21–86.

Bailey, Tom. "Flash and burn: high frequency traders menace financial markets." *World Finance*, July 3, 2015.

Bank for International Settlements. "82nd Annual Report, 1 April 2011–31 March 2012." Basel, 2012.

Baram, Marcus. *Government Sachs: Goldman's Close Ties To Washington Arouse Envy, Raise Questions*. July 3, 2009. http://www.huffingtonpost.com/2009/06/02/government-sachs-goldmans_n_210561.html.

Bentham, Jeremy. *An Introduction to the Principles of Morals and Legislation*. Oxford: Clarendon Press, 1907.

Bernanke, Ben S. *Basel II: Its Promise and Its Challenges*. May 18, 2006. http://www.federalreserve.gov/newsevents/speech/bernanke20060518a.htm.

Bernstein, Peter L. *Against the Gods: The Remarkable Story of Risk*. Toronto: Wiley, 1998.

Bockman, Johanna. *Markets in the Name of Socialism: The Left-Wing Origins of Neoliberalism*. Palo Alto, CA: Stanford University Press, 2013.

Buchan, James. *Frozen Desire: The Meaning of Money*. New York: Farrar, Straus and Giroux, 1997.

Burn-Callander, Rebecca and James Quinn. "Profile: Rev. Paul Flowers." *The Telegraph*, November 17, 2013.

Burton, Jonathan. "Revisiting The Capital Asset Pricing Model." *Dow Jones Asset Manager*, May/June 1998: 20–28.

Burton, Katherine and Richard Teitelbaum. "Ex-Simons Employees Say Firm Pursued Illegal Trades." *Bloomberg.com*, July 30, 2007.

Carroll, Sean. *Purity of essence.* April 18, 2005. http://www.preposterousuniverse.com/blog/2005/04/18/purity-of-essence/.

Cassidy, John. "Interview with Eugene Fama." *New Yorker*, January 13, 2010.

Castelvecchi, Davide. "Quantum physics makes water different." *ScienceNews.org*, July 22, 2008.

Cecchetti, Stephen, M.S. Mohanty, and Fabrizio Zampolli. *The real effects of debt.* Working Paper No. 352, Bank for International Settlements, 2011.

CIA Office of Strategic Services. *Simple Sabotage Field Manual.* Washington, DC: OSS, 1944.

Clarke, Arthur C. "The Ultimate Machine." *Harper's*, August 1958.

Clement, Douglas. "Interview with Eugene Fama." *The Region*, December 1, 2007.

Cochrane, John H. *Eugene Fama: Efficient markets, risk premiums, and the Nobel Prize.* 2013. http://faculty.chicagobooth.edu/john.cochrane/research/papers/Fama_panel_nov_2013.pdf.

Cohn, Alain, Ernst Fehr, and Michel André Maréchal. "Business culture and dishonesty in the banking industry." *Nature* 516, no. 7529 (2014): 86–89.

Committee on Financial Services, U.S. House Of Representatives. *Monetary Policy And The State Of The Economy.* July 20, 2006. https://www.gpo.gov/fdsys/pkg/CHRG-109hhrg31539/html/CHRG-109hhrg31539.htm.

Confessore, Nicholas, Sarah Cohen, and Karen Yourish. "The Families Funding the 2016 Presidential Election." *New York Times*, October 10, 2015.

Cookson, Clive, Gillian Tett, and Chris Cook. "Organic mechanics." *Financial Times*, November 26, 2009.

Cootner, Paul H. *The Random Character of Stock Market Prices.* Cambridge, MA: MIT Press, 1964.

Cournède, Boris, Oliver Denk, and Peter Hoeller. *Finance and Inclusive Growth.* OECD Economic Policy Paper, Paris: OECD, 2015.

Cowles, Alfred. "Can stock market forecasters forecast?" *Econometrica* 12 (1933): 206–214.

Das, Rajarshi, James E. Hanson, Jeffrey O. Kephart, and Gerald Tesauro. "Agent-Human Interactions in the Continuous Double Auction." *Proceedings of the 17th International Joint Conference on Artificial Intelligence.* Seattle, WA, 2001, 1169–1176.

Delevingne, Lawrence. "Have Mercer! The money man who helped the GOP win." *CNBC.com*, November 8, 2014.

DeMartino, George F. *The Economist's Oath: On the Need for and Content of Professional Economic Ethics.* Oxford: Oxford University Press, 2010.

DeMartino, George F. and Deirdre McCloskey, eds. *The Oxford Handbook of Professional Economic Ethics.* Oxford: Oxford University Press, 2016.

Edgeworth, Francis Ysidro. *Mathematical Psychics: An essay on the application of mathematics to the moral sciences.* London: C.K. Paul, 1881.

Editors. "The blame game: will maths apologize to finance? Well, maybe no." *ParisTech Review*, June 7, 2010.

Eichengreen, Barry. "The Last Temptation of Risk." *The National Interest,* May/June 2009.

Eisinger, Jesse. "Why Only One Top Banker Went to Jail for the Financial Crisis." *New York Times Magazine,* April 30, 2014.

European Finance Association. *Keynote Address: Prof. Myron S. Scholes.* August 28, 2008. http://www.efa-online.org/efa2008/speakers.html.

Fama, Eugene F. *Random Walks in Stock-market Prices.* Chicago: Graduate School of Business, University of Chicago, 1965.

Farmer, J. Doyne and John Geanakoplos. "The virtues and vices of equilibrium and the future of financial economics." *Complexity* 14, no. 3 (2009): 11–38.

Farrell, Greg. "Sealed HSBC Report Shows U.S. Managers Battling Cleanup Squad." *Bloomberg.com,* July 7, 2015.

Farrell, Sean. "Bankers still overpaid, says top German banker." *The Guardian,* November 24, 2015.

Financial Conduct Authority. *Hedge Fund Survey.* June 2015. https://www.fca.org.uk/publication/data/hedge-fund-survey.pdf.

Finch, Gavin and Liam Vaughan. "Rain Man Hayes With Superhero Duvet Loses Last Libor Gamble." *Bloomberg.com,* August 4, 2015.

Fleischacker, Samuel. "Adam Smith's Reception among the American Founders, 1776–1790." *The William and Mary Quarterly,* October 2002.

Flood, Alison. "Authors' incomes collapse to 'abject' levels." *The Guardian,* July 8, 2014.

Flynn, John T. *Men of Wealth: The Story Of Twelve Significant Fortunes From The Renaissance To The Present Day.* New York: Simon and Schuster, 1941.

Galbraith, John Kenneth. *Money: Whence It Came, Where It Went.* New York: Houghton Mifflin, 1995.

Galton, Francis. *Natural Inheritance.* London: Macmillan, 1889.

Gandel, Stephen. "By every measure, the big banks are bigger." *Fortune,* September 13, 2013.

Gisiger, Christoph. "The business of central banks is like pornography." *Finanz und Wirtschaft,* May 18, 2016.

Gitlin, Todd. "Where are the Occupy protesters now?" *The Guardian,* June 17, 2014.

Gleick, James. *Chaos.* London: Viking, 1987.

Gopikrishnan, Parameswaran, Martin Meyer, Luis A. Nunes Amaral, and H. Eugene Stanley. "Inverse cubic law for the distribution of stock price variations." *European Physical Journal B* 3 (1998): 139–140.

Grantham, Jeremy. "Obama and the Teflon Men, and Other Short Stories. Part 1." *GMO Quarterly Letter,* January 2009.

Greco, Albert N., Jim Milliot, and Robert M. Wharton. *The Book Publishing Industry.* 3rd ed. New York: Routledge, 2014.

Greene, John. C. *Darwin and the Modern World View.* Baton Rouge: Louisiana State University Press, 1961.

Greenspan, Alan. *The Age of Turbulence: Adventures in a New World.* New York: Penguin, 2007.

Greenspan, Alan. "Testimony of Dr Alan Greenspan." *House Committee of Government Oversight and Reform.* Washington, DC, October 23, 2008.

Greenspan, Alan. *The Map and the Territory: Risk, Human Nature, and the Future of Forecasting.* New York: Penguin, 2013.

Haldane, Andrew G. "Rethinking the Financial Network." Speech delivered at the Financial Student Association, Amsterdam, April 2009.

Haldane, Andrew. "The Revolution In Economics." In *Economics, Education and Unlearning: Economics Education at the University of Manchester,* 3–6. Manchester: Post-Crash Economics Society, 2014.

Hamilton, Dane. "Renaissance hedge fund: Only scientists need apply." *Reuters,* May 22, 2007.

Hamilton, Sir William. *The Collected Works of Dugald Stewart, Esq. F.R.SS.* London: Thomas Constable and Company, 1858.

Harding, Sy. "Stock Market Becomes Short Attention Span Theater Of Trading." *Forbes,* January 21, 2011.

Haug, Espen Gaarder and Nassim Nicholas Taleb. *Why We Have Never Used the Black–Scholes–Merton Option Pricing Formula (fifth version).* 2009. http://ssrn.com/abstract=1012075.

Hedlund, Stefan. *Invisible Hands, Russian Experience, and Social Science: Approaches to Understanding Systemic Failure.* New York: Cambridge University Press, 2011.

Hendershott, Terrence, Charles M. Jones, and Albert J. Menkveldf. "Does Algorithmic Trading Improve Liquidity?" *Journal of Finance* 66, no. 1 (2011): 1–33.

Henderson, Hazel. "The "Nobel" Prize That Wasn't." *Le Monde Diplomatique,* December 2004.

Hill Strategies Research Inc. "A Statistical Profile of Artists and Cultural Workers in Canada." 2014.

International Monetary Fund. "Global Financial Stability Report: Market Developments and Issues." Washington, DC, 2006.

Jevons, William Stanley. *The Theory of Political Economy.* 5th ed. New York: Kelley and Millman, 1957.

Jopson, Barney and Ben McLannahan. "Bank living wills reveal Wall St victims." *Financial Times,* July 6, 2015.

Kahneman, Daniel. *Thinking, Fast and Slow.* New York: Farrar, Straus and Giroux, 2011.

Kahneman, Daniel and Amos Tversky. "Prospect Theory: An analysis of decision under risk." *Econometrica* 47 (1979): 263–291.

Keepin, Bill and Brian Wynne. "Technical analysis of IIASA energy scenarios." *Nature* 312 (1984): 691–695.

Kelton, Stephanie. *Money is No Object.* Presentation to FPC, 2012.

Kendall, Maurice G. and Austin Bradford Hill. "The Analysis of Economic Time-Series-Part I: Prices." *Journal of the Royal Statistical Society, Series A* 116, no. 1 (1953): 11–34.

Kennedy, Gavin. *Adam Smith's Lost Legacy.* New York: Palgrave Macmillan, 2005.

Kennedy, Paul. *It's The Economists, Stupid.* CBC. January 5, 2016. http://www.cbc.ca/radio/ideas/it-s-the-economists-stupid-1.3219471.

Keynes, John Maynard. *Newton, the Man.* 1946. http://www-groups.dcs.st-and.ac.uk/history/Extras/Keynes_Newton.html.

Keynes, John Maynard. *The General Theory of Employment, Interest and Money.* New York: Harcourt, Brace, 1936.

Kiatpongsan, Sorapop and Michael I. Norton. "How much (more) should CEOs make? A universal desire for more equal pay." *Perspectives on Psychological Science* 9, no. 6 (2014): 587–593.

Kiladze, Tim. "Nobel laureate is attacking age-old economic rules (he's also Mr. Janet Yellen)." *The Globe and Mail*, October 30, 2015.

Knutson, Brian. *Expected Value (and beyond)*. 2012. http://edge.org/response-detail/11558.

Krugman, Paul. "How Did Economists Get It So Wrong?" *New York Times*, September 2, 2009.

Krupa, Gregg. "Detroit aims at predatory home lending." *Detroit News*, November 26, 2002.

Leonhardt, David. "Buy vs. Rent: An Update." *New York Times*, December 22, 2010.

Levine, Matt. "Senate Literary Critics Don't Like Fictional Derivatives." *Bloomberg.com*, July 22, 2014.

Levine, Matt. "Algorithms Had Themselves a Treasury Flash Crash." *Bloomberg.com*, July 13, 2015.

Levy, Adam. "Mapping the trader's brain." *Bloomberg Markets*, February 1, 2006: 34–45.

Lichtblau, Eric. "'Super PACs' Spent Millions Before Candidates Announced, Filings Show." *New York Times*, July 31, 2015.

Linskey, Annie. "The Man Who Out-Koched the Kochs." *Bloomberg.com*, October 23, 2014.

Lucas, Robert. "In defence of the dismal science." *The Economist*, August 6, 2009.

Lux, Hal. "The Secret World of Jim Simons." *Institutional Investor* 34, no. 11 (November 2000).

Luyendijk, Joris. "How the banks ignored the lessons of the crash." *The Guardian*, September 30, 2015.

Mackenzie, Donald. *An Engine, Not a Camera: How Financial Models Shape Markets*. Cambridge, MA: MIT Press, 2006.

MacKenzie, Donald and Taylor Spears. "'The Formula That Killed Wall Street?' The Gaussian Copula and Modelling Practices in Investment Banking." *Social Studies of Science* 44 (2014): 393–417.

Malkiel, Burton. *A Random Walk Down Wall Street*. New York: Norton, 1999.

Mamudi, Sam, John Detrixhe, and Ben Bain. "Flash Boys Welcome: World Exchanges Woo High-Frequency Firms." *Bloomberg.com*, July 13, 2015.

Martin, Timothy W. and Andrew Grossman. "How the Justice Department, S&P Came to Terms." *Wall Street Journal*, February 2, 2015.

Massad, Timothy. *Remarks of Chairman Timothy Massad before the Conference on the Evolving Structure of the U.S. Treasury Market*. October 21, 2015. http://www.cftc.gov/PressRoom/SpeechesTestimony/opamassad-30.

May, Robert M., Simon A. Levin, and George Sugihara. "Ecology for bankers." *Nature* 451 (2008): 891–893.

McCain, John. *Opening Statement by Senator John McCain At PSI Hearing On Basket Options*. July 22, 2014. http://www.mccain.senate.gov/public/index.cfm/2014/7/opening-statement-by-senator-john-mccain-at-psi-hearing-on-basket-options.

McGee, Suzanne. "Can Wall Street be fixed? Ex-banker's memoir examines a broken system." *The Guardian*, July 15, 2016.

McGrayne, Sharon Bertsch. *The Theory That Would Not Die: How Bayes' Rule Cracked the Enigma Code, Hunted Down Russian Submarines, and Emerged Triumphant from Two Centuries of Controversy.* New Haven, CT: Yale University Press, 2011.

McKinsey Global Institute. "Debt and (not much) deleveraging." 2015.

Minder, Raphael. "A Not-So-Quixotic Search for Cervantes." *New York Times,* March 10, 2014.

Minsky, Hyman P. "Financial instability revisited: the economics of disaster." In *Reappraisal of the Federal Reserve Discount Mechanism,* 95–136. Washington, DC: Board of Governors of the Federal Reserve System, 1972.

Moffatt, Mike. "Can't beat the market? There's a theory for that." *Globe and Mail,* October 29, 2012.

Morris, Regan. "Is Hollywood screenwriting success easier to find online?" *BBC News,* June 17, 2014.

Muir, Hazel. "Einstein and Newton showed signs of autism." *New Scientist,* April 2003.

Neff, Joseph. "Duke University settles suit with cancer patients over clinical trials." *The News & Observer,* May 2, 2015.

Newton, Isaac. "Fragments from a Treatise on Revelation." In *The Religion of Isaac Newton,* by Frank E. Manuel, 120. Oxford: Clarendon Press, 1974.

Newton, Isaac and N.W. Chittenden. *Newton's Principia: The mathematical principles of natural philosophy.* Translated by Andrew Motte. New York: Daniel Adee, 1846.

Ormerod, Paul. *Butterfly Economics: A New General Theory Of Social And Economic Behavior.* New York: Basic Books, 2000.

Orrell, David. "Role of the metric in forecast error growth: how chaotic is the weather?" *Tellus* 54A (2002): 350–362.

Orrell, David. *Apollo's Arrow: The Science of Prediction and the Future of Everything.* Toronto: HarperCollins, 2007.

Orrell, David. *The Other Side of the Coin: The Emerging Vision of Economics and Our Place in the World.* Toronto: Key Porter, 2008.

Orrell, David. *Truth or Beauty: Science and the Quest for Order.* New Haven, CT: Yale University Press, 2012.

Orrell, David. "Book burning economists." *World Finance,* July 1, 2015.

Orrell, David. "A quantum theory of money and value." *Economic Thought* 5, no. 2 (2016a): 19–36.

Orrell, David. "Are corporate banks stretching themselves thin?" *World Finance,* July 2016b.

Orrell, David. *Economyths: 11 Ways That Economics Gets it Wrong.* London: Icon, 2017.

Orrell, David and Roman Chlupatý. *The Evolution of Money.* New York: Columbia University Press, 2016.

Orrell, David, Leonard A. Smith, Jan Barkmeijer, and Tim Palmer. "Model error in weather forecasting." *Nonlinear Proc. Geoph.* 9 (2001): 357–371.

Özler, Şule. "Adam Smith and Dependency." *Psychoanalytic Review* 99, no. 3 (June 2012): 333–358.

Para, Terence P. "Yes, You Can Beat The Market." *Fortune,* April 3, 1995.

Patterson, Scott. *The Quants: How a New Breed of Math Whizzes Conquered Wall Street and Nearly Destroyed It.* New York: Crown, 2009.

Patterson, Scott. *Dark Pools: High-Speed Traders, AI Bandits, and the Threat to the Global Financial System.* New York: Crown Business, 2012.

Patterson, Scott and Jenny Strasburg. "Pioneering Fund Stages Second Act." *Wall Street Journal,* March 16, 2010.

Piketty, Thomas. *Capital in the Twenty-First Century.* Cambridge, MA: Belknap Press, 2014.

Quetelet, Adolphe. *A treatise on man and the development of his faculties.* Edinburgh: W. and R. Chambers, 1842.

Ray, Paul H. and Sherry R. Anderson. *The Cultural Creatives: How 50 Million People Are Changing the World.* New York: Harmony Books, 2000.

Rich, Ben R. *Clarence Leonard (Kelly) Johnson 1910–1990: A Biographical Memoir.* Vol. 67, in *Biographical Memoirs,* 221–241. National Academies Press, 1995.

Rogaway, Phillip. *The Moral Character of Cryptographic Work.* December 6, 2015. http://web.cs.ucdavis.edu/~rogaway/papers/moral-fn.pdf.

Ross, Alice K, Will Fitzgibbon, and Nick Mathiason. *Britain opposes MEPs seeking ban on high frequency trading comments.* September 16, 2012. https://www.thebureauinvestigates.com/2012/09/16/britain-opposes-meps-seeking-ban-on-high-frequency-trading/.

Rowling, J.K. *By popular request, 2 of @RGalbrath's rejection letters! (For inspiration, not revenge, so I've removed signatures.) [Tweet].* March 25, 2016. https://twitter.com/jk_rowling/status/713298761288708096/photo/1.

Rubin, Richard and Margaret Collins. "How an Exclusive Hedge Fund Turbocharged Retirement Plan." *Bloomberg.com,* June 16, 2015.

Rubinstein, Mark. "Implied Binomial Trees." *Journal of Finance* 49, no. 3 (1994): 771–818.

Salmon, Felix. "Recipe For Disaster: The Formula That Killed Wall Street." *Wired,* February 23, 2009.

Samuelson, Paul A. *Economics.* 9th ed. New York: McGraw-Hill, 1973.

Saul, John Ralston. *Voltaire's Bastards: The Dictatorship of Reason in the West.* New York: Vintage, 1993.

Schachermayer, Walter and Josef Teichmann. "How Close are the Option Pricing Formulas of Bachelier and Black-Merton-Scholes?" *Mathematical Finance* 18, no. 1 (2008): 155–170.

Schrage, Michael. "Daniel Kahneman: The Thought Leader Interview." *Strategy+Business,* 2003.

Schwartz, John. "Science Museums Urged to Cut Ties With Kochs." *New York Times,* March 24, 2015.

Sedghi, Ami. "Global debt has grown by $57 trillion in seven years following the financial crisis." *The Guardian,* February 5, 2015.

Sedláček, Tomáš. *Economics of Good and Evil: The Quest for Economic Meaning from Gilgamesh to Wall Street.* New York: Oxford University Press, 2011.

Simons, Jim, interview by Chris Anderson. *A rare interview with the mathematician who cracked Wall Street* TED2015, (March 23, 2015).

Skypala, Pauline. "Ditch the hokum on asset diversification." *Financial Times,* September 1, 2014.

Smith, Adam. *An Inquiry into the Nature and Causes of the Wealth of Nations.* London: W. Strahan & T. Cadell, 1776.

Smolin, Lee. *The Trouble with Physics: The Rise of String Theory, the Fall of a Science, and What Comes Next.* New York: Houghton Mifflin, 2006.

Soddy, Frederick. *Wealth, Virtual Wealth and Debt. The solution of the economic paradox.* New York: Dutton, 1926.

Sorensen, Alan T. *Bestseller Lists and Product Variety: The Case of Book Sales.* Palo Alto, CA: Stanford University, 2004.

Soros, George. *The New Paradigm for Financial Markets: The Credit Crisis of 2008 and What It Means.* New York: PublicAffairs, 2008.

Spreeuw, Jaap and Xu. Wang. *Modelling the Short-term Dependence between Two Remaining Lifetimes of a Couple.* London: Cass Business School, 2008.

Stevenson, Alexandra. "Hedge Fund Chief Testifies at Senate Tax-Avoidance Hearing." *New York Times,* July 22, 2014.

Stewart, Heather. "Boris Johnson accused over hedge funds' election donations." *The Guardian,* October 11, 2009.

Taylor, Mark C. *Confidence Games: Money and Markets in a World Without Redemption.* Chicago: University of Chicago Press, 2004.

Teitelbaum, Richard. "Simons at Renaissance Cracks Code, Doubling Assets." *Bloomberg.com,* November 27, 2007.

Tett, Gillian. "Could 'Tobin tax' reshape financial sector DNA?" *Financial Times,* August 27, 2009.

The Midas Formula. Directed by Malcolm Clark. Produced by BBC. 1999.

Thorp, Edward. "What I Knew and When I Knew It – Part I." *Wilmott magazine,* December 2002.

Thorp, Edward. "What I Knew and When I Knew It – Part III." *Wilmott magazine,* January 2003.

Treanor, Jill. "HBOS's former bosses wait to learn their fate." *The Guardian,* November 19, 2015.

Tudball, Dan. "In for the Count." *Wilmott magazine,* January 2003.

Turner, Adair. "Printing money to fund deficit is the fastest way to raise rates." *Financial Times,* November 10, 2014.

UCSD Department of Mathematics. *Biography: James B. Ax.* http://euclid.ucsd.edu/library/biography.html (accessed September 19, 2016).

Unger, Roberto Mangabeira and Lee Smolin. *The Singular Universe and the Reality of Time: A Proposal in Natural Philosophy.* New York: Cambridge University Press, 2015.

University of Oxford. *Mathematics and Statistics.* February 25, 2016. https://www.ox.ac.uk/admissions/undergraduate/courses-listing/mathematics-and-statistics?wssl=1.

US Department of Justice. *Acting Associate Attorney General Tony West Speaks at the Press Conference Announcing Lawsuit Against S&P, Washington, DC.* February 5, 2013. https://www.justice.gov/opa/speech/acting-associate-attorney-general-tony-west-speaks-press-conference-announcing-lawsuit.

US House of Representatives, Committee on Banking and Financial Services. *Conduct of Monetary Policy.* July 25, 2000. http://commdocs.house.gov/committees/bank/hba65973.000/hba65973_0f.htm.

Vigen, Tyler. *Spurious Correlations.* New York: Hachette Books, 2015.

Wasik, John. "John Maynard Keynes as an Investor: Timeless Lessons and Principles." *AAII Journal*, March 2014.

Watson, Tom. "Journalists vs. high-frequency traders." *Canadian Business*, September 27, 2011.

West, Jason. *Ethics and Quantitative Finance*. Discussion Paper No. 2012-04, Griffith Business School, 2012.

White, William R. "Is Monetary Policy A Science? The Interaction Of Theory And Practice Over The Last 50 Years." In *50 Years of Money and Finance – Lessons and Challenges*, edited by Morten Balling and Ernest Gnan. Vienna: SUERF, 2013.

Wigglesworth, Robin. "Hedge funds poach computer scientists from Silicon Valley." *Financial Times*, November 22, 2015a.

Wigglesworth, Robin. "Renaissance Technologies winds down $1bn investment fund." *Financial Times*, October 14, 2015b.

Wilmott, Paul and Philipp Schönbucher. "The feedback effect of hedging in illiquid markets." *SIAM J. Appl. Math.* 61(1) (2000): 232–272.

Wilmott, Paul, Alan L. Lewis, and Daniel J. Duffy. "Modeling Volatility and Valuing Derivatives Under Anchoring." *Wilmott magazine*, September 2014.

Witten, Edward. "Reflections on the Fate of Spacetime." *Physics Today* 49, no. 4 (April 1996): 24–30.

Woit, Peter. *Not Even Wrong: The Failure of String Theory and the Search for Unity in Physical Law*. London: Vintage, 2006.

Wolf, Martin. "Strip private banks of their power to create money." *Financial Times*, April 24, 2014.

Wolfram, S. *A New Kind of Science*. Champaign, IL: Wolfram Media, 2002.

Writers' Union of Canada. "Devaluing Creators, Endangering Creativity." 2015.

Zandi, Mark, Celia Chen, Cristian deRitis, and Andres Carbacho-Burgos. *Housing in Crisis: When Will Metro Markets Recover?* February 2009.

Zweig, Jason, *et al.* "The Best (and Worst) Investments They Ever Made." *Wall Street Journal*, December 26, 2014.

Index